MR. LINCOLN'S ADMIRALS

MR. LINCOLN'S ADMIRALS

by

CLARENCE EDWARD MACARTNEY

WITH A FOREWORD BY

George Fielding Eliot

NEW YORK

Funk & Wagnalls Company

1956

2

FOREWORD

IT IS DOUBTLESS INHERENT in the nature of sea power that many of its greatest achievements are unspectacular. An unhappy consequence of this fact is that many of the men responsible for those accomplishments remain relatively unknown to a public whose gratitude and remembrance they have richly earned.

Battles, of course, are remembered. There is hardly any incident of war more exciting and colorful than a sea fight. Frigate duels of the War of 1812, with no more than incidental effect on the outcome of that conflict, retain a measure of renown to this day. The tremendous and far more significant accomplishment of blockading the southern coastline from 1861 to 1865 remains in the backwater of public understanding. Specific naval incidents of the Civil War—such as the ironclad duel between the *Monitor* and the *Merrimac*, or Farragut's bold dash into Mobile Bay—are perhaps better recalled, but rarely in their relation to the progress of the war as a whole. This is in part because, as Mahan remarks, "naval historians have troubled themselves little about the connection between general history and their own particular topic, limiting themselves generally to the duty of simple chroniclers of naval occurrences."

In the current revival of interest in the Civil War and the men and women who took part in it, the Navy has had little share. Grant, Sherman, Sheridan and Thomas, Lee, Stonewall Jackson, and "Jeb" Stuart seem almost contemporary, and certainly are thoroughly well-known personalities by reason of able biographers and painstaking chroniclers. The portrait of any one of these, hung in an art gallery or the window of a print shop anywhere in the United States, would be readily recognized by many who saw it. Just possibly, a portrait of Admiral Farragut might also be recognized by a reasonable number of Americans. But who would recall the square-hewn Puritan features of Andrew Hull Foote, the dashing black-bearded Porter, the magnificent whiskers of Du Pont, or the ascetic Viking face of Dahlgren in its frame of blond sideburns?

Herein, as I see it, lies the peculiar and timely value of Dr. Macartney's book. He has revived the forgotten men of the Civil War—the naval leaders, the men who commanded the blockading squadrons in fair weather and foul, who played a mighty part in the opening of the Mississippi, who gave invaluable if not always well-remembered support to the Union armies wherever, as Lincoln remarked, "the ground was a little damp." He has made the five great admirals once more into living figures, understandable as military commanders and as human beings: and to these five— Farragut, Foote, Du Pont, Dahlgren, and Porter—he has added four officers of lesser rank whose achievements and diverse personalities, taken together, are exemplary of the professional naval officer of the war.

Dr. Macartney does not keep his subjects on their quarter-decks. He takes them ashore now and then, lets us see how they worked in double harness with the generals, and in so doing begins to put the naval contribution to the war into perspective for the reader who is familiar only with the land operations. Never since the invention of gunpowder had there been a war in which naval and land operations were so constantly and persistently interconnected as the War between the States. Even the great blockade included constant small-scale, occasional large-scale, amphibious operations; the far-flung river war in the west and the lesser river wars in Virginia and the Carolinas were scenes of the closest kind of army-navy interdependence. As in all our wars, some admirals and generals could work together and others could not. Farragut, by all odds the greatest naval figure of the Civil War, seems to have done only indifferently well when it came to cooperating with the Army. Porter was much better at it, but only with generals he respected—Grant, Sherman, Terry; he was scornfully

intolerant of *lumpen-militar* such as Butler and McClernand. Dahlgren seems to have been born thorny: certainly his relations with
General Gillmore were not happy. Du Pont was unfortunate in
his military colleagues—the slow-witted, over-cautious T. W.
Sherman, the incompetent Hunter. Foote could not abide Halleck,
but loyally made the best of the association; with Grant he worked
in effective harmony.

The Civil War was our first machine-age conflict: a fact
which bore on the Navy with revolutionary emphasis. The war
came along when the Navy was shifting from sail to steam, from
wooden ships to iron, from smooth-bore guns and solid shot to
rifled cannon and explosive shells. It saw the first effective use in
naval warfare of revolving turrets, of mines, of submarines, of
graduated gun sights. The controversies within the naval service
as to these innovations were vigorous, at times bitter. The era
of specialization was just beginning: engineers were still a separate
corps, not entitled to executive command, and some of the old
salt-horse skippers were said to be far more anxious about their
own boilers than they were about the enemy. Of the five admirals,
Farragut, Du Pont, and Foote were blue-water sailors, happier
under a cloud of canvas than a cloud of smoke, though all three
used steam warships effectively. Dahlgren was a gunnery expert
first and a seaman afterward. Porter was the one true steamboat
man of the lot. It is a matter for regret that limitations of space
have necessarily excluded an appraisal of the engineer-in-chief of
the Navy throughout the war, Benjamin Franklin Isherwood,
whose contribution to victory was probably not less than that of
any sea-going naval officer.

Dr. Macartney's portraits are well-chosen: the cross-grained,
ill-starred Winslow whose great opportunity was slow in coming;
the explosive Napoleon Collins; steady, clear-headed Worden; and
finally young Lieutenant Cushing, hero of more daring exploits
than any other naval officer of the war, the youth who must ever
be "seeking the bubble reputation in the cannon's mouth." Again,
one might wish that space had allowed the expansion of the list

to include John Rodgers, ill-starred like Winslow, but probably the best captain of the war; at least one prime example (other than Farragut) of a southern officer who remained loyal to the Union, such as Percival Drayton or Charles Steedman; and at least one example of the many versatile and capable volunteer officers who made up the bulk of the naval officer corps—such as Budd, Conroy, Breck, or Hooker.

An account of Mr. Lincoln's admirals would have been incomplete, indeed, without the opening chapter on Gideon Welles and Gustavus Vasa Fox, respectively Secretary and Assistant Secretary of the Navy throughout the whole course of the great conflict. History records few happier or more fruitful personal associations than this Welles-Fox team which directed the course and the emphasis of Lincoln's naval policy. The contrast in consistency, firmness, and steadiness between the Navy Department's high direction and that of the War Department is perhaps the true measure of the difference between Welles on the one hand and Cameron and Stanton on the other. However, in justice to the latter, it must be kept in mind that Welles had, in Fox, a professional adviser of the highest quality, possessing the confidence of the officers of the Navy and capable of choosing the men who could be trusted to carry out the designs of the department. The Navy had no political admirals, no amateurs in high command. No volunteer officer rose above the rank of lieutenant commander, or commanded a squadron or a ship of the first rate, or, except on the western rivers, an ironclad. From first to last, from Hatteras Inlet to Fort Fisher, the conduct of the naval war was professional; and after a few superannuated old gentlemen, employed *faute de mieux* at the beginning, were quietly set aside (Mervine, McKean, Pendergrast), changes in important commands were surprisingly few. There was no painful, bloodstained search for admirals; the good men were known, were chosen, and in most cases were unswervingly supported. The one notable exception was the case of Du Pont, as to whose abilities and opportunities there is ample room for critical discussion and argument. One of the few instances in which the Welles-Fox team failed to maintain a balanced viewpoint was in their unbounded confidence that the wonderful monitors could do everything; whereas, as the inventor Ericsson himself pointed out, they were built for a single purpose: to engage Confederate casemated rams in smooth water. Although they were uniformly successful at that, they were of small value for fighting forts because of their slow rate of fire, and quite useless for high-sea operations. Unhappily, the department became publicly committed to the naval omnipotence of the monitors; Du Pont thought otherwise. Du Pont was right and the department was wrong, as Dahlgren, Du Pont's successor, proved and officially stated. However, it was Du Pont who had to haul down his flag and retire to Delaware with a broken heart.

This, however, was an exceptional instance. For the most part, the Welles-Fox high direction of the war was admirably managed; indeed, there are few examples of naval administration in war which can compare with the record of these two New Englanders. Mr. Lincoln was fortunate both in his admirals and his admiralty.

GEORGE FIELDING ELIOT

New York
February 12, 1956

PREFACE

IN 1884, Commander Alfred T. Mahan was at Callao, Peru, in command of the U.S.S. *Wachusett*. This was the steam sloop with which Commander Napoleon Collins rammed and captured the Confederate cruiser and commerce destroyer *Florida* at Bahia, Brazil in 1864. It was at Callao, too, that Collins, court martialed out of the navy for his action at Bahia, and then restored, died in 1875, a rear admiral held in high respect. While on duty at Callao, Mahan received an invitation from Commodore Stephen Luce to deliver a course of lectures at the newly established Naval War College at Newport, Rhode Island. Of the two subjects proposed by Luce, naval tactics or naval history, Mahan chose the latter. In preparation for his lectures he began his studies on the *Wachusett* by reading Mommsen's *History of Rome*. As he read Mommsen's pages relating the history of the Second Punic War and Hannibal's invasion of Italy, he suddenly realized "how different things might have been could Hannibal have invaded Italy by sea instead of the long land route, or could he after arrival have been in free communication with Carthage by water." Thus was born Mahan's most famous book, *The Influence of Sea Power on History, 1660-1783*.

It is to be regretted that Admiral Mahan did not pursue his theme into the 19th century and write a treatise on the influence of sea power in the American Civil War (his *The Gulf and Inland Waters* is strictly a narrative of a portion of the war), for that war is one of the most striking illustrations of his favorite thesis. If the South had possessed a strong navy or the means and the time to create one and had been able to keep its ports open to the commerce of the world, the subjugation of the Confederacy would have been either impossible or it would have been achieved at a far heavier cost in blood and treasure.

In contrast to the numberless books on the campaigns of the Union armies, the Union navy and its contribution to the downfall of the Confederacy have received scant notice. This is due in part to the fact that the navy's major task was to blockade the ports of the South. All-important as the blockade was, it is not a stirring subject compared with the marches and collisions of great armies. To those who served on the blockading ships, all the way from Chesapeake Bay to the Rio Grande, in winter storm and summer hurricane and on all manner of vessels from frigates and sloops-of-war to reinforced Hudson River ferryboats, blockade duty, save for the occasional chase of a blockade runner, was deadly monotony. George Perkins, one of Farragut's most dashing officers, described it as a "living death." Yet it was the blockade, at first loose but growing more and more effective each month of the war, which spelled the doom of the Confederacy.

Aside from the blockade, the naval warfare in the great struggle may be described as a war of ships against forts, for the major naval engagements were against the forts on the Tennessee, the Mississippi, at Mobile Bay, Port Royal, Charleston, and Fort Fisher. Many of these engagements were desperate encounters which thrilled the nation when they were fought; ninety-four years after Admiral Du Pont won the first naval victory at Port Royal, the story of these encounters still stirs the mind and quickens the pulse.

In addition to the battles against the forts, there were occasional sea duels the record of which is a part of our naval heritage: the fight between the *Monitor* and the *Merrimac* at Hampton Roads; the fight between Farragut's fleet and the Confederate ram *Tennessee* at Mobile Bay; and, most spectacular of all, the duel between the *Kearsarge* and the *Alabama* off the harbor of Cherbourg, France. In these pages I have endeavored to portray the character and personality of the different commanders as we see them in action and to tell the story of their battles.

There were no admirals in the United States Navy prior to the Civil War, the highest rank being that of captain.[1] But of the nine officers sketched in this book, five—Farragut, Du Pont, Foote, Dahlgren, and Porter—were commissioned admirals during the war; three others—Winslow, Worden, and Collins—were so promoted after the war. The only one of the nine who did not become an admiral was Cushing, just twenty when he sank the Confederate ram *Albermarle* and only thirty-one when he was made a commander, the youngest officer to hold that rank. Had it not been for his untimely death in 1875, he too would undoubtedly have attained the rank of admiral. Of the five who became admirals during the war, two—Farragut and Porter—became Admirals of the Navy, a rank created for Farragut and, after the death of Porter in 1891, held by no officer until Dewey won his victory at Manila Bay in 1898.

These, then, are the men who dared the fire of the forts and the armored rams in their tall wooden ships and "tin-clad" gunboats. These are the men, with the religious and personal backgrounds behind their exploits, whose contribution to the victory achieved by Lincoln and the Union far outweighed their numbers and their strength.

[1] Until 1862 when Congress created the rank and legal title, "commodore" was merely a courtesy title for a captain who commanded a squadron.

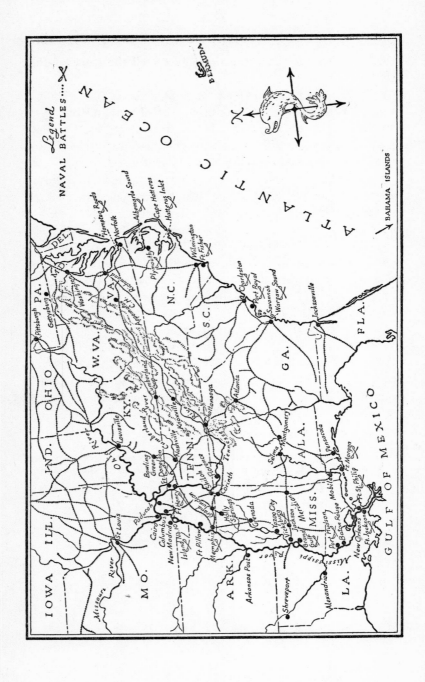

CONTENTS

Illustrations

Illustrations courtesy National Archives, Washington, D. C.

MR. LINCOLN'S ADMIRALS

It is hard to say that anything has been more bravely, and well done, than at Antietam, Murfreesboro, Gettysburg, and on many a field of lesser note. Nor must Uncle Sam's web-feet be forgotten. At all the watery margins they have been present. Not only on the deep sea, the broad bay, and the rapid river, but also up the narrow muddy bayou, and wherever the ground was a little damp. Thanks to all. For the great republic —for the principle it lives by, and keeps alive— for man's vast future—thanks to all.

ABRAHAM LINCOLN

I

WELLES AND FOX

As FREQUENT REFERENCE will be made to them in the pages of this book, it will be in order to sketch briefly the two New Englanders who were at the head of the Navy Department during the Civil War, Gideon Welles and Gustavus Vasa Fox. Both men deserve to stand side by side with the famous naval commanders in the war, for the two Secretaries gave the commanders the means with which to achieve their victories. Speaking for the high officers of the navy, David D. Porter, then Admiral of the United States Navy and the second to hold that rank, said: "The naval officers who obtained success in the war of the rebellion ought not to forget, amidst the honors and rewards they won, how much they were indebted to the herculean efforts of those in the Navy Department, for the support they received under the most trying circumstances—how after the first surprise of being forced into a great war, and the slow process of realizing the situation had been passed, ships and guns were furnished as if by magic."

Gideon Welles was born July 1, 1802, at Glastonbury, Connecticut. One of his ancestors, Thomas Welles, a governor of Connecticut, had settled at Hartford as early as 1636. At the age of seventeen Welles was a student in the Episcopal Academy at Cheshire, Connecticut, where one of his schoolmates was Andrew Hull Foote, destined to win fame in the Civil War as commander of the Mississippi squadron. He attended also the American Literary, Scientific, and Military Academy at Norwich, Vermont, now Norwich University. For a time he studied law, but soon gave it up for journalism. He early evinced marked ability as a writer, and at the age of twenty-four was editor and part-owner of the Hartford *Times,* an organ for the advocacy of the policies and administrations of Andrew Jackson. For seven years, from 1827 to 1835, being the youngest member when he took his seat, he served in the state legislature. As a member of the legislature Welles, although a deeply religious man and a consistent church member, led a fight against a Connecticut statute which barred from the courts any witness who was a disbeliever in a state of future rewards and punishments. This proscription he succeeded in reducing to a disbelief in God. In 1836 Jackson appointed Welles postmaster at Hartford, a post he occupied until removed by President Harrison in 1841. In 1846 President Polk appointed him Chief of the Bureau of Provisions and Clothing in the Navy Department. In this capacity he served during the Mexican War, acquiring experience which was later to prove useful. It was when he was serving in this bureau that he had his first contact with the future admiral, David Glasgow Farragut. He heard Farragut, then a commander in the navy, present to the Navy Department a plan for a naval attack on the castle of San Juan de Ulloa at Vera Cruz. He was much impressed with Farragut's ability and character, and sixteen years later, when looking for an officer to lead the expedition against New Orleans, he remembered Farragut's appearance at the Navy Department in the Mexican War.

Deeply stirred by the moral principle involved in the slavery question, Welles left the Democratic Party when the Democrats in Congress helped to pass the Kansas-Nebraska bill which, in effect, revoked the Missouri Compromise and opened new territory to slavery. He said he abandoned the Democracy when it became a "shamocracy." Henceforth he was active in the organization of the Republican Party, and was its unsuccessful candidate for governor of Connecticut in 1856. As chairman of the Republican delegation from Connecticut he attended the Republican National Convention at Chicago in 1860. In the convention he worked against William H. Seward and advocated the nomination of Salmon P. Chase. After Lincoln's nomination he was a member of the committee which waited upon him at Springfield to notify him of his election.

Because of New England's maritime interests and history, many of the Secretaries of the Navy have been New England men. In following that tradition, Lincoln's first choice for Secretary of the Navy was Nathaniel P. Banks, who had risen from millboy to the governorship of Massachusetts and to the speakership of the House of Representatives. But in January, 1861, at the expiration of his term as governor, Banks became president of the Illinois Central Railroad, succeeding George B. McClellan in that post, and removed to Chicago. This ruled him out for the Navy Department, and Welles, who had been suggested by the Vice-President-elect, Hannibal Hamlin, was appointed. Lincoln made this appointment in spite of strenuous objection by William H. Seward, whom he had chosen for Secretary of State. Seward regarded Welles as one of the chief architects of his overthrow at the Chicago convention.

Lincoln's first meeting with Welles occurred when, after his famous speech at the Cooper Union at New York on February 27th, 1860, he went on to Cambridge to visit his son Robert, then a student at Harvard. On the way he delivered speeches at New Haven, Hartford, and other New England cities. On March 5th he spoke in the city hall at Hartford, where Gideon Welles was one of his hearers. The next day Lincoln visited Welles in the office of the Hartford *Evening Press*, a paper he helped found after he left the Democratic Party, and had a long conversation with him. In the *Evening Press* the following day Welles wrote this appraisal of the Illinois lawyer: "This orator and lawyer has been caricatured. He is not Apollo, but he is not Caliban. He was made where the material for strong men is plenty; and his loose, tall frame is loosely thrown together. He is in every way large— brain included, but his countenance shows intellect, generosity, great good nature and keen discrimination. . . . He is an effective speaker, because he is earnest, strong, honest, simple in style and clear as crystal as a speaker." Thus at their first meeting Welles saw what many of Lincoln's contemporaries failed to see, that he was no ordinary man.

When he entered upon his duties as Secretary of the Navy, Welles was confronted by a problem such as none of his predecessors and none of his successors had to face. The few ships the navy possessed were widely scattered; the one which was to become most famous of them all, the *Hartford*, Farragut's flagship, was on the China station. Every day officers of the navy were resigning and joining the Confederacy. The work of the navy was obvious: to establish a blockade of Southern coasts and ports all the way from Cape Henry to the Rio Grande; to get possession of the Mississippi and its tributary streams and thus cut the Confederacy in two, separating Texas, Louisiana and Arkansas from the seceded states east of the Mississippi; to procure fast cruisers to run down blockade runners and commerce destroyers; and to attack forts defending such cities as Wilmington, North Carolina, Charleston, Savannah, Mobile, New Orleans, and Vicksburg. For this gigantic undertaking the navy at the beginning of the war was pitifully inadequate. The following tables reveal the situation which Welles had to face, also what he accomplished in the four years of war:

	1861	*1865*
Ships	90	670
Officers	1,300	6,700
Seamen	7,500	51,500
Budget	$12,000,000	$123,000,000

The total length of the Atlantic blockade was 3,549 miles; one hundred and eighty-nine harbors were blockaded. On the Mississippi and its tributaries, gunboats patrolled 3,615 miles of river; on the sounds, bayous, and rivers of the Atlantic and the Gulf coast the navy patrolled 2,000 miles of water. Thus the total length of patrol and blockade was 9,164 miles. Never before in the history of war did a navy undertake such a stupendous task. Yet with the leadership, patience, and wisdom of Secretary Welles the task was accomplished. He was not infrequently the target of abuse because things were not done more rapidly.[1] Today the considered judgment is that the building, assembling, arming, and manning of so vast a fleet was done with remarkable dispatch.

The task of raising, equipping and training the great armies was also a formidable one; but the army and the Secretaries of War, first Simon Cameron and then Edwin M. Stanton, had no such innovations in land warfare to deal with as did the navy. One of the signal accomplishments of Welles was the adoption and the development of the monitor type of warship. At the outbreak of the war the United States, in contrast with England and France, had no armored vessels. As early as 1842, however, Congress had entered into a contract with Edward Stevens, of the noted Stevens engineering family of Hoboken, New Jersey, for the building of an armored ship which was to be "shot and shell proof." Robert Stevens, the leader in the enterprise, died in 1852 when the vessel, known as the "Stevens Battery," was still unfinished. In June, 1861 Congress directed the Secretary of the Navy to appoint a board to examine the Stevens Battery and report as to the time it would take to complete it and the expediency thereof. The report of the five members of the board, among them Joseph Henry of the Smithsonian Institute, was adverse.

In July, 1861, at a special session of Congress Secretary Welles called attention to the experiments France and England had made with armored ships, and asked authority to construct such vessels if plans for them were approved by a competent

---

[1] Characteristic of the attempts to discredit Welles is a stanza which appeared in *Frank Leslie's Illustrated Newspaper* for June 5, 1862:

> Retire, O Gideon, to an onion farm,
> Ply any trade that's innocent and slow.
> Do anything, where you can do no harm.
> Go anywhere you fancy—only go.

board. Within a few weeks Congress directed the Secretary to appoint a board to investigate plans and specifications for "iron or steel-clad ships and steam batteries." In the event of a favorable report, the Secretary was authorized to build one or more ironclads. For this purpose Congress appropriated one million, five hundred thousand dollars. Welles appointed to this board Commodore Joseph Smith, Commodore Hiram Paulding, and Commander Charles H. Davis. Of the twenty-one plans submitted, the Board recommended three: that of C. S. Bushnell & Co., New Haven; that submitted by Merrick & Sons of Philadelphia; and that of John Ericsson. Thus three ironclads were built for the navy. Bushnell & Co. built the *Galena*, a gunboat; Merrick & Sons built the *New Ironsides*, the most powerful battleship then afloat, which served as Du Pont's flagship in the attack on Charleston in April of 1863; Ericsson built the soon-to-be-famous *Monitor*, one of the five best-known vessels of the United States Navy. The others were John Paul Jones' *Bon Homme Richard;* the *Constitution* ("Old Ironsides"); the *Hartford*, Farragut's flagship; and Dewey's flagship, the *Olympia*. The contract with Ericsson and his sureties specified a speed of eight knots. In case the vessel did not develop the stipulated speed or fell short in other stated requirements, the contractors were to refund to the government the full amount of money received.

The builder of the *Galena*, C. S. Bushnell, merits some of the credit for the *Monitor*. Ericsson had showed him a dust-covered model of a turret ship which he had submitted to the French naval authorities in 1854. Bushnell showed it to Welles, then on vacation in Connecticut. At once impressed, Welles told Bushnell to present the model to the naval board in Washington. At Washington he had an interview with Lincoln, always ready to hear of or examine a new device. The President, too, was taken with the design, and the next day went with Bushnell to the Navy Department. There the model was examined by Fox, the Assistant Secretary, and several naval officers. The following day the design was submitted to the naval board at its regular session.

The members of the board appeared to be skeptical or indifferent. Somewhat discouraged, Bushnell returned to New York to
ask Ericsson to go before the board in person. Because he had
been unjustly blamed for the explosion of a gun on the *Princeton* some years before, Ericsson had vowed he would never appear in Washington again. But Welles finally persuaded him to
go and in his own way explain the advantages of his vessel. At
this meeting of the board Welles, who had returned from Connecticut, was present. After Ericsson had given them a glowing
account of the capacities of the proposed ship, Welles asked each
member of the board if he approved making a contract with
Ericsson. The verdict was unanimously in favor of doing so.
Without waiting for a formal contract to be signed, Ericsson returned to New York, and in a few days the plates for the *Monitor* were passing through the rolling mill.

Much of the credit for this happy issue belongs to Secretary
Welles who, aware that Ericsson was sensitive over the supposed
affront by the Navy Department in connection with the explosion on the *Princeton*, had made it a point to speak with the
chairman of the board, Commodore Joseph Smith, and request
him to see that the impulsive and explosive inventor was "treated
tenderly, and opportunity given him for a full and deliberate
hearing." When, in December, 1862, Welles learned of the foun-
dering of the *Monitor* in a storm off Cape Hatteras, he could
write this: "The fate of this vessel affects me in other respects.
She is a primary representative of a class identified with my
administration of the Navy. Her construction and qualities I
adopted, and she was built amid obloquy and ridicule. Such a
change in the character of a fighting vessel few naval men, or
any Secretary under their influence, would have taken the responsibility of adopting— Her success with the *Merrimac* directly
after she went into commission relieved me of odium and anxiety, and men who were preparing to ridicule were left to ad-
mire."

Regardless of ridicule, caricature, and the almost invincible prejudice against monitors of some of the older and most distinguished officers of the navy, such as Du Pont, Welles patiently persevered in building ironclads and monitors, faster and more powerful every year. The result was that toward the end of the war the United States, which at the beginning of the conflict had only a skeleton navy of a type soon to be outmoded, possessed a fleet which could bid defiance to England and France, which "in consequence, let us alone to work out our destiny." There can be little doubt that the monitors and other ironclads produced by Welles and the Navy Department had more effect in restraining England and France from intervening in the struggle and from continuing to give hospitality to Confederate commerce destroyers than all the expostulations of the State Department delivered through our ambassadors, Adams and Dayton.

Welles was singularly fortunate in his selection of officers. Although he had the advice of his able assistant, Fox, and of others, the final decision was his. Rarely did the men he selected disappoint him or the country. There was no department of the government so free from political influence. Welles was altogether fearless and independent in his administration. The Vice President, Hannibal Hamlin, was largely responsible for his appointment as Secretary of the Navy, yet Welles did not shrink from refusing to give a contract to certain contractors in Maine, Hamlin's home state, whom the Vice President had commended. It cost him the friendship of Hamlin, who never spoke to him again; but he retained the consolation of a good conscience. Preble was one of the great names in the history of the United States Navy; nevertheless, when Welles was convinced that Commander George Preble, nephew of the famous Commodore Edward Preble of the *Constitution,* had been remiss in permitting the Confederate raider *Florida* to run through the blockade into Mobile Bay, he summarily dismissed him from the navy. It was too severe a punishment; yet it illustrates Welles' independence. When Captain Charles Wilkes, already greatly distinguished as an Antarctic explorer and naval scientist, seized the Confederate commissioners, James Mason and John Slidell on the British steamer *Trent,* Welles was one of the great number who congratulated him on his exploit. But later, when Wilkes, who for a time was one of the heroes of the war, displayed insubordination in command of a squadron in the West Indies operating against Confederate raiders, and also equivocated regarding his age, thus securing a permanent commission as commodore, Welles recalled him and cancelled his promotion. Then when Wilkes violated the regulations of the Department by giving to the press a letter he had addressed to the Navy Department, Welles brought him before a court martial, with the result that he was found guilty of insubordination and conduct unbecoming an officer, and suspended for three years.

Welles was heavily bearded and wore a wig, and thus had an air of patriarchal benignity. It was this which led Governor Andrew of Massachusetts, who had come to see him on business in Washington, to inquire, "Where can I find that old Mormon deacon, the Secretary of the Navy?" His appearance also prompted a bitter remark by Thurlow Weed, when, as Seward's spokesman, he was vigorously protesting to Lincoln against the appointment of Welles as Secretary of the Navy. He observed that, if Lincoln would "stop long enough in New York, Philadelphia or Baltimore to select an attractive figurehead, to be adorned with an elaborate wig and luxuriant whiskers and transfer it from the prow of a ship to the entrance of the Navy Department, it would in my opinion, be quite as serviceable as his Secretary and less expensive." To this Lincoln rejoined, "Oh, wooden midshipmen answer very well in novels, but we must have a live Secretary of the Navy." There can be no doubt that Welles was in every respect a "live" Secretary of the Navy.

Welles left behind him a *Diary* which entitles him to rank among the great chroniclers of history. Certainly this journal, dealing with the events and personalities of the Civil War, is the most notable in the history of our country, outranking that of his great contemporary, Salmon P. Chase, Secretary of the Treasury under Lincoln. It is a mine of information for the student of the Civil War. Here we see just what Welles thought of men and measures. Some of his characterizations are very severe and mordant, occasionally unjust, but always sincere; most of his verdicts have stood that hardest of all trials, the test of time.

On the dreadful night of April 14th, 1865, Welles hurried first to the home of the Secretary of State, where Seward and his son Frederick lay wounded by the assassin's knife, and then to the bedside of Lincoln in the house on 10th Street. Of the events of that tragic night and the passing of Lincoln, the account Welles gives in his *Diary* is perhaps the most moving and most reliable of the many narratives which have been written. As he watched the "giant sufferer" lying diagonally across the bed which was too short for him and listened to his heavy breathing, he thought the President's features were "calm and striking. I had never seen them appear to better advantage than for the first hour, perhaps, that I was there." He remained standing in the room until six in the morning, when he took a chair which had been vacated at the foot of the bed. "I occupied it for nearly two hours, listening to the heavy groans, and witnessing the wasting life of the good and great man who was expiring before me."

Welles continued in the office of Secretary of the Navy until the end of President Johnson's term. Although he had been shocked at Johnson's inebriated behavior when he addressed Congress in the Senate chamber at the time of his inauguration as Vice President, he stood loyally by Johnson during the stormy years of his administration when the Radicals sought to remove him from office. His favorable opinion of President Johnson was prophetic of the reversal of judgment concerning Lincoln's successor which has come about in the eighty-seven years which have passed since Thaddeus Stevens and John A. Bingham appeared at the bar of the Senate and, in the name of the House of Representatives and the people of the United States, impeached the President of high crimes and misdemeanors. On the March day in 1869, after Welles bade Johnson farewell, he made this entry in his *Diary:* "In the evening I parted with ex-President Johnson and his family who leave in the morning for Tennessee. No better persons have occupied the Executive Mansion, and I part from them, socially and personally, with sincere regret. Of the President, politically and officially, I need not here speak further than to say he has been faithful to the Constitution, although his administrative capabilities and management may not equal some of his predecessors. Of measures he was a good judge, but not always of men."

On August 1st, 1861, Gustavus Vasa Fox was named Assistant Secretary of the Navy. This was one of the most important appointments made during the war. The post was created for Fox, for up to that time there had been no Assistant Secretary. From then on, Welles had by his side a trained seaman who counselled him in a way not possible for a civilian. Fox was to Welles as a chief of staff is to a commanding general. Fox, the son of a physician, was born June 13th, 1821, at Saugus, Massachusetts. After two years at Phillips Academy, Andover, he received an appointment as midshipman in 1838. After the usual instruction afloat he was commissioned. In the Mexican War he saw service transporting troops to Vera Cruz. Made a lieutenant in 1852, he left the navy in 1856, and took a position with the Bay State Mills at Lawrence, Massachusetts.

Fox had married Virginia Woodbury, the daughter of a New Hampshire judge. Another daughter of the judge had married Montgomery Blair, of the powerful Missouri Blair family, who became Postmaster General in Lincoln's Cabinet. It was this connection by marriage between Fox and Blair which opened a door of great opportunity and service for Fox in the Civil War. Montgomery Blair, above all other members of Lincoln's Cabinet, advocated holding Fort Sumter; even if reinforcing it brought on war, he believed it was the only wise and honorable course for the government to take. In February, 1861, before he took office, Blair advised Lieutenant General Winfield Scott to consult Fox as how best to provision and reinforce Sumter. In response to Scott's request, Fox submitted to President Buchanan a plan for the relief of Fort Sumter. The vacillating Buchanan rejected the plan; however, when Lincoln became President he sent Fox down to Charleston to report on the real situation at Sumter. At the beleaguered fort Fox had an interview with the commanding officer, Major Robert Anderson. On his return Fox reported to Lincoln that the garrison were all for resistance, but that their commander had little zeal for a fight. Anderson had informed Fox that it was too late for an army to land on Morris Island, that entrance to the fort by sea was impossible, and that his provisions would be exhausted by April 15th. In spite of this discouraging report and the strong objection of Seward, his Secretary of State, Lincoln ordered Welles and Cameron, the Secretary of War, to prepare a joint expedition by the army and navy under the command of Fox to provision Fort Sumter. In one respect it was a strange arrangement, for Fox was now a civilian with no commission in either the army or the navy. The story of this ill-fated expedition, and how Lincoln gave the same ship, the *Powhatan*, to both Fox and to Porter for simultaneous but different expeditions, one to relieve Sumter, the other to reinforce Fort Pickens at Pensacola, Florida, is related in our chapter on Admiral Porter. The one redeeming feature about the Sumter expedition was that it was at least an attempt to relieve the fort and put an end to vacillation and hesitation on the part of the government. It is, however, doubtful if Fox's plan of getting into Sumter with three hundred sailors, several launches, and three tugs could have succeeded, even if the *Powhatan*, on which he put such reliance, had not been taken from him and given to Porter for the Pickens expedition. Nor was it strange that when Fox, a civilian, requested Commander Rowan of the *Pawnee* to stand in toward the Charleston bar, Rowan refused to do so, saying that his instructions were to lie ten miles off the light and await the arrival of the more powerful

Powhatan, the ship on which Porter was then steaming toward Pensacola, and that he would not go into Charleston harbor to inaugurate a civil war. However, when Rowan heard the thunder of the guns firing on Sumter he changed his mind and asked for a pilot, declaring that he would share the fate of his brethren in the army. He was standing in toward Sumter when he met Fox coming out on the steamer *Baltic,* who told him that the government did not expect such a sacrifice. Fox could now do no more than take the surrendered garrison of Sumter on the *Baltic* and return to New York.

After the humiliating fiasco of the Sumter relief expedition, Fox served for a time as chief clerk of the Navy Department, and then on August 1st became Assistant Secretary. One of his first suggestions, adopted for a time by Welles, was to block the entrance to Southern ports with barges and hulks filled with rocks. Thirty of these stone-filled hulks were sunk at the entrance to Charleston harbor. These attempts to seal off Southern harbors were, as many had predicted, futile; they did, however, occasion great anger in the South. The Richmond *Enquirer* declared that "the rivers and the ocean cannot be parted from each other. The currents and the waves will force for themselves new channels. Lincoln, as Satan's agent, will fail." Abroad, particularly in England, there was great outcry over this proposal to block the harbors of the South. The *Times* of London thundered: "Even the tribes of the desert would not destroy the well which gave life to an enemy. Yet here was a Christian Government ruthlessly destroying the principal harbor on a dangerous and stormy coast— No belligerent has the right to destroy the features of nature and deprive the mariner, for ages to come, of refuge from perils of the sea."

When first shown the model of the *Monitor,* Fox was indifferent, if not actually hostile, toward this new kind of warship; in the end, however, he became the most enthusiastic of all in his advocacy of monitors. As soon as the tidings of the havoc wrought by the *Merrimac* on the Union fleet at Hampton Roads was flashed to Washington, Fox started for the scene of hostilities, arriving in time to witness the fight between the *Merrimac* and the *Monitor* on March 9th. Observing how the *Monitor*'s shots were glancing harmlessly off the sloping sides of the Confederate ironclad and likewise how the shots of the *Merrimac* did no damage to her small foe, Fox was struck with the thought that if the *Monitor* had had larger guns and could have fired heavier shots, the *Merrimac* would have been quickly disposed of. At the same moment his eye happened to fall on a huge 15-inch gun lying near him on the dock. On making inquiry, he discovered that it was a piece of ordnance with which the army had once experimented, but of which the Navy Department knew nothing. From that time on Fox was an earnest advocate of more monitors with heavier guns.

It was a sore disappointment to Fox, who had done all in his power to provide him with the best of ships and the best of officers, when Du Pont's South Atlantic Blockading Squadron met with complete repulse in the attack on Sumter and Charleston on April 7th, 1863. Up to that time Fox had been Du Pont's warm friend and backer. However, after the Sumter repulse the relationship between the two men was strained; so much so, that in a letter to Captain Charles H. Davis a few weeks after the battle, Du Pont said: "I have been forty-seven years in the Navy. My name is identified now with my country— I hope I can say this much—while where will Fox be in twenty-two months? Such a man is an ephemera. So I am doing nothing, lest I might disappoint my country and my friends, while avoiding the puncture of an insect which lives but a day."

Fox had such confidence in the capacities and seaworthiness of the new monitors that he said he would be willing to cross the ocean in one of them, and he actually did so. In 1866 he was sent to St. Petersburg to convey the congratulation of the United States to the Emperor Alexander II on his escape from assassination. He sailed for Russia in the *Miantonomah,* the first time a monitor had crossed the ocean. Welles was not altogether pleased

Gideon Welles
1802—1878

Gustavus Vasa Fox
1821—1883

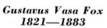

David Glasgow Farragut
1801—1870

with this trip, for some, the President among others, said to him that it was for "self-glorification and a design to steal fame" at Welles' expense. Welles, however, refused to attribute any such intent to Fox, and thought that his impelling motive was to "obtain useful celebrity" so that he might become the agent of foreign states in building turreted vessels.

If the *Diary* of Secretary Welles is a source of information about the Civil War, and especially the navy's part in it, which can never be improved upon, such also is the confidential correspondence of Fox. These letters from naval officers to Fox, and from Fox to the officers, are all the more valuable since they are not official letters or orders from the Navy Department, nor official reports to the Department from the lieutenants, commanders, captains, and admirals, but friendly personal letters, often bringing up matters which it would be difficult to mention in official correspondence. The navy men knew that Fox, out of his own experience, understood their difficulties, trials, and problems, and they unburdened themselves to him freely. In the midst of all his arduous labors in the Department, Fox took time to write letters of friendly counsel, sympathy, and encouragement. Two volumes of these letters were published in 1920 by the Naval Historical Society; the whole collection is in the Library of the New York Historical Society. Perhaps the most interesting letters are those between Fox and Porter. Fox had the highest opinion of Porter and admired his fighting spirit. Porter wrote to Fox with little restraint, sometimes with considerable humor. The letters reveal Fox's deep love for his country. Perhaps the best illustration of his ardent desire for the preservation of the Union is found in the conclusion of a letter Fox wrote to Du Pont just after Du Pont's important victory at Port Royal, South Carolina on November 7th, 1861: "That you may continue to gather laurels amongst those misguided people, laurels, which if necessary, should be steeped in the heart's blood of every inhabitant, rather than the Union perish, is the prayer and hope of your friend, G. V. Fox."

There were occasions when Welles thought Fox presumptuous and assuming, as when he signed Welles' name to certain orders without permission. Farragut made a similar complaint, and thought that Fox should be rebuked. Some have sought to praise and elevate Fox to the disparagement of Welles, and show that Fox was the real power in the Navy Department. Such an opinion is altogether without foundation. Welles was always the commanding officer; Fox the chief of staff. Each was great in his sphere.

When, in January, 1866, Fox first spoke with Welles about resigning his post and taking the presidency of a steamship line, Welles thus records his opinion of his colleague through the stirring years of the war: "I regret to lose him from the Department, where, notwithstanding some peculiarities which have caused dissatisfaction with a few, he is of a most invaluable service. He has a combination of nautical intelligence and common sense such as can hardly be found in another, and we have worked together with entire harmony, never in a single instance having had a misunderstanding."

When Fox finally left the department where he had served with such honor and distinction, he bade Welles farewell, not at the department, lest it should be too much for him, but at Welles' home. That night Welles wrote in his *Diary:* "He was very much affected, said words were wanting to express his high respect and admiration for me and the qualities which I possessed for the position which I filled. Spoke of over five years' intercourse during which there had not been one unpleasant word, nor, as he was aware, an unpleasant thought between us. He has been useful to the country and to me, relieving me of many labors and defending me, I believe, always. His manner and ways have sometimes given offense to others, but he is patriotic and true."

President Lincoln declared a blockade of the Southern coastline with the exception of Virginia and North Carolina, which had not yet seceded, on April 19th, 1861. Eight days later those two States were included in the blockade. At that time in the whole navy there were only twenty-nine steam vessels of war. On the day Lincoln was inaugurated only three warships, steam or sail, were in Northern ports, ready for use. Yet, despite such a shortage of ships for blockade duty, so quickly and in such large numbers were ships built or purchased that in a remarkably short time the South began to feel the constricting coils of the blockade.

To the leaders of the South "cotton was king." To them it seemed an incredible thing that war could be waged against cotton. How profound was this illusion that the withholding of cotton from world markets would bring the North to terms is illustrated by a speech made in the United States Senate two years before the war by Senator James H. Hammond of South Carolina: "Would any sane nation make war on cotton? Without firing a gun, without drawing a sword, should they make war on us, we could bring the whole world to our feet. . . . What would happen if no cotton were furnished for three years? I will not stop to depict what everyone can imagine; but this is certain: England would topple headlong, and carry the whole civilized world with her, save the South. No; you dare not make war on cotton."

Yet, if "cotton was king," it was soon to be shown that it was a discrowned and dis-sceptered monarch. When the blockade was proclaimed the Federal Government, as we have seen, had few ships to enforce it. Yet, such was the energy and efficiency of the Navy Department that, for the fiscal year 1861-62, the total export of cotton from the South was only thirteen thousand bales. The year before it had been two million bales. Of course, this vast cut in cotton exports was partly a result of Jefferson Davis' self-imposed embargo on shipments abroad.

The procuring of ships necessary for battle and the even greater number necessary for blockade duty; the maintenance of these ships after they had been bought or built, keeping the engines in running order, the guns ready for action, and their crews in health and discipline, was a gigantic enterprise. Altogether, two hundred and eight vessels of war were built and an additional four hundred and eighteen ships were bought and converted to purposes of war. The Navy Department's special agent for the purchase of merchant ships was George D. Morgan. Secretary Welles was attacked because Morgan was given a commission which rewarded him richly for such vessels as he purchased; but he challenged his critics to name any man who could have done this service better, or to show a single instance where any department of the Government had done as well. He pointed out, too, that the commissions paid by the War Department to its agents for the purchase of vessels were never less than those paid by the Navy, and that the prices paid by the War Department were from twenty-five to fifty percent higher than those paid by the sea service. Ships of every description were bought and placed in service before the end of 1861: screw steamers, side-wheelers, stern-wheelers, schooners, and barges. All over the nation, wherever there were machine shops, factories, or shipyards, wheels were turning, anvils were ringing, forges were glowing, clouds of smoke were ascending skyward from thousands of stacks, and the streets echoed with the tramp of a great army of artisans and laborers without whose help the victories on land and on sea could not have been won.

Throughout the war Welles and Fox labored under the hostility of Senator John P. Hale, chairman of the Senate committee on naval affairs. Yet Welles patiently endured Hale's misrepresentations and obstructions and maintained courteous official relations with him; but privately in the secret meditations of his diary, he dismissed Hale as "a mass of corruption." In 1863 Hale was brought before the Senate judiciary committee on the charge that he had accepted a bribe from a man convicted of fraud against the Government and had appeared on his behalf before the Secretary of War. On the ground that it was a fee, and not a bribe, the committee exonerated him of illegal dealing,

yet simultaneously censured him by incorporating in its report a
bill which outlawed such practice in the future. Hale had been a
valiant leader in the anti-slavery crusade and in the organization
of the Republican Party. It was in view of this and also, as
Lincoln put it, "to break his fall" after he had been defeated for
renomination to the Senate by a New Hampshire Republican
caucus that the President appointed Hale minister to Spain in
March, 1865. There his career was anything but a credit to
himself or the nation.

It must have been with no little satisfaction that, in his
Report for 1865 (submitted in December of that year, only eight
months after the Confederate surrender), Welles could write:
"There were in the several blockading squadrons in January
last, exclusive of other duty, 471 vessels and 2245 guns. There
are now but 29 vessels remaining on the coast, carrying 210
guns, exclusive of howitzers." On dune and headland, on river
and bayou, the ships of the vast armada which under Welles'
hand had been created for the preservation of the Union had
melted away. Hundreds of the ships had been sold and the money
returned to the national treasury; the thousands of officers and
seamen were engaged once more in the creative and bloodless
arts of peace.

A keen observer of men during the Civil War, Charles A.
Dana, the War Department's special observer at Grant's headquarters in the West, wrote of Welles that he was "a curious-
looking man: he wore a wig which was parted in the middle, the
hair falling down on each side; and it was from his peculiar
appearance, I have always thought, the idea that he was an old
fogy originated. I remember Governor Andrew, of Massachusetts,
coming into my office at the War Department one day and asking where he could find that old Mormon Deacon, the Secretary of the Navy. In spite of his peculiarities, I think Mr. Welles
was a very wise, strong man. There was nothing decorative
about him; there was no noise in the street when he went along;
but he understood his duty, and did it efficiently, continually,

and unvaryingly. There was a good deal of opposition to him, for we had no navy when the war began, and he had to create one without much deliberation; but he was patient, laborious, and intelligent at his task."

One evening Welles was entertaining in his home Senator James R. Doolittle of Wisconsin and Montgomery Blair, the Postmaster General. The subject of the many attacks which were being made on Welles and the Navy Department came up and Blair said to Welles that he was fortunate above most men in his enemies, for they were making him great. He quoted an aphorism of Senator Thomas Hart Benton to the effect that "a man is made great by his enemies, and not by his friends." There is no doubt that Welles' opponents contributed greatly to his becoming one of the great figures of the Civil War.

II

FARRAGUT

IN THE ILLUSTRIOUS CAREER of Farragut, our first admiral, and the most famous of our naval commanders, there was one keen disappointment. All his battles were waged against forts; he never fought a battle on the open sea against other ships. He did, indeed, participate in one desperate and sanguinary sea fight, but that was when he was a boy of thirteen with Commodore David Porter on the *Essex* in the battle with the British ships *Cherub* and *Phoebe* off the harbor of Valparaiso in the War of 1812. The nearest he came to a duel with another ship was the encounter with the Confederate ram *Tennessee* in Mobile Bay, where that one ship fought the entire Union fleet.

When Farragut heard of the *Kearsarge*'s victory over the long-hunted *Alabama* off the harbor of Cherbourg in June of 1864, he sent his personal card to Mrs. Winslow, the wife of the commander of the *Kearsarge*, with these words written on the back: "I would rather have fought that fight with the *Alabama* than all I have done in the war." This was more than a generous congratulation for the victor in that battle. It was also an expression of regret that he had never had an opportunity like that of Winslow; in his journal for July 20th, 1864, he repeated the sentiment. "The victory of the *Kearsarge* over the *Alabama* raised me up. I would sooner have fought that fight than any ever fought on the ocean." The guns which achieved his victories at New Orleans and Mobile Bay echoed around the world; but he always regretted that he had never had a chance to lead the fleet to battle on the open sea against a hostile squadron, or lay the *Hartford*, his flagship, alongside another ship in the manner of the sea duels of the War of 1812. With his always careful preparation for battle, his flaming spirit, and his magnificent courage, he would have made a splendid commander after the style of Nelson or Rodney, leading a squadron into combat with another fleet. But since the Confederacy had no real navy to oppose, that opportunity was denied him.

New Orleans was the queen among the cities of the South. In population it was the sixth city of the United States; its population was larger than that of any four cities of the South combined; and in its export trade it ranked almost first in the nation. Situated a hundred miles from the mouth of the Mississippi, it was the natural point of export for cotton and sugar. Its capture would not only bring depression to the South and corresponding exultation to the North, but would have immense strategic importance. The possession of the lower Mississippi would cut the Confederacy in two, leaving Texas, Arkansas, and Louisiana, a chief source of supply for the Confederate armies, separated from the seceded states east of the Mississippi. The capture of New Orleans would also be of international importance, for it would put a damper on the enthusiasm of Napoleon III to intervene, and also make sympathizers with the Confederacy in the English government act with caution.

The importance of taking New Orleans as a chief military objective was early recognized by the Federal government. The then general in chief of the armies, the venerable hero of the War of 1812 and the Mexican War, Lieutenant General Winfield Scott, at the very beginning of the war outlined a plan for sending an army of 85,000 well-drilled troops down the Mississippi by river and land to New Orleans. He advised, however, that such a campaign be postponed until November, when the autumnal frosts had killed the virus of malignant fevers in the swamps and river bottoms. But the impatient public of the North could not tolerate the thought of waiting until November be-

fore marching into the seceded states, and heaped derision upon
Scott's soldierly plans. Cartoons appeared in the newspapers and
magazines showing a monster serpent, with General Scott's head
on it, coiled around the cotton states, and called it "Scott's
Anaconda." But the course of events vindicated Scott's judgment
and foresight; the ports of the South had to be blockaded and a
far larger army than Scott had proposed had to fight its way
down the Mississippi before the "Father of waters flowed unvexed
to the sea."

The chief defenses of New Orleans were the two forts, Jackson and St. Philip, seventy-five miles down the Mississippi, Jackson on the right, or west, bank of the river and St. Philip on the
left, or east, bank, and a little above Jackson. The two garri-
sons, under the command of General Johnson K. Duncan, to-
talled one thousand men. The forts stood at one of the great bends
of the Mississippi, where a hostile vessel ascending the river
would have to come under close fire of one or the other. In spite
of Du Pont's success in attacking the forts at Port Royal in the
first important naval engagement of the war, and Foote's more
recent successes at Fort Henry on the Tennessee River and at
Island No. 10 on the Mississippi, the opinion prevailed at New
Orleans that no fleet could safely pass forts Jackson and St.
Philip. It was likewise believed that heavy warships could not
cross the bar outside the passes of the Mississippi. Furthermore,
the real attack was expected to come down the river from the
north, and not up the river from the Gulf. Hence many of the
troops of New Orleans and Louisiana had been sent north to
strengthen the army under Generals Beauregard and Albert Sidney Johnston.

Much of the credit for initiating the campaign against New
Orleans belongs to David D. Porter, then a junior officer.
He had spent weary months on blockade duty off the passes of
the Mississippi, where he talked with fishermen and pilots and
learned much about the defenses of the city. He was quite fa-

miliar with the river, for before the war he had ascended it to New Orleans on some thirty occasions in command of a merchant vessel plying between that city and Cuba. When he came north on the *Powhatan* at the end of 1861, after a futile chase of the Confederate commerce raider *Sumter*, commanded by Raphael Semmes, he went at once to Washington to lay before the Secretary of the Navy a plan for the capture of New Orleans. But when he called at the Department Welles refused to see him, and Fox, the Assistant Secretary, was "not communicative." Porter thought the Secretary's refusal to see him was based on the part he had taken in Lincoln's and Seward's expedition to strengthen the garrison of Fort Pickens at Pensacola, Florida, an expedition of which the Navy Department knew nothing until it was under way.[1] Fortunately, before he left the offices of the Navy Department, he encountered Senator John P. Hale of New Hampshire, chairman of the Senate Committee on Naval Affairs, and Senator James Wilson Grimes of Iowa. When Porter told them what he had in mind, they at once manifested interest and took him in to see Welles who, to Porter's surprise, greeted him kindly. When Welles had listened to the proposal, he suggested that they all go over to the White House and talk with the President, whom they found "pacing the floor, calm and thoughtful."

After he heard Porter's plan, Lincoln responded with one of his frontier anecdotes about a man who sat up all night with his gun for a polecat which had been raiding the chicken house, but in the morning brought in two rabbits, pets of his wife, instead. Then, turning to Welles, Lincoln said, "Now, Mr. Secretary, the Navy has been hunting pet rabbits long enough. Now suppose you send them after the polecats." His point was that so far the Navy had gone after small game and should take on a more powerful adversary. There was some truth in this, for, although Du Pont's expedition against Port Royal on the North Carolina coast had been a resounding success, it was but a small affair

[1] See Chapter on Porter.

compared with the proposed attack upon the great commercial capital of the South and the Mississippi forts which protected it. Lincoln then continued, "It seems to me that what the lieutenant proposes is feasible. The Mississippi is the backbone of the rebellion, it is the key to the whole situation. While the Confederates hold it, they can obtain supplies of all kinds, and it is a barrier against our forces. Come, let us go and see General McClellan." Just at that moment Secretary of State Seward came in, and all of them went off with the President to see McClellan.

Porter, an old acquaintance of McClellan's, was greeted warmly by the young commander of the armies. Noting this, Lincoln remarked, "Why, do you fellows know each other? So much the better." When Porter had stated his proposal, Mc-Clellan said that he could spare as many as 20,000 troops to co-operate with the Navy in the attack against New Orleans. With his wonted foresight, the President saw the importance of taking not only New Orleans, but Vicksburg, four hundred miles up the Mississippi from New Orleans. He stated his belief that, after taking New Orleans, the victorious force ought to proceed at once against Vicksburg, "which is the key to all that country watered by the Mississippi and its tributaries. If the Confederates once fortify the neighboring hills, they will be able to hold that point for an indefinite time, and it will require a large force to dislodge them." [2] Here the President spoke truly, for, except for two half-hearted attacks, Vicksburg was left unmolested until it became one of the strongest bastions of the Confederacy, and its eventual capture took thousands of lives and a vast store of treasure.

As the President was leaving McClellan's headquarters, he said to the two officers, "We will leave this matter in the hands of you two gentlemen. Make your plans, and I will come over here at eight o'clock this evening to see what conclusion you

[2] Porter gives two accounts of this meeting with the President and General McClellan. There are minor differences, but substantially they are the same. *Incidents and Anecdotes of the Civil War,* 64-66; *Battles and Leaders of the Civil War,* II, 23-26.

have arrived at." Left to themselves, Porter and McClellan worked out their plans, and when the President came that night at the appointed hour they submitted them to him. Lincoln at once ratified them and directed the Secretary of the Navy to prepare the necessary ships. This task Welles delegated to his efficient assistant, Fox. Porter's plans included not only warships, but a fleet of mortar boats to bombard the forts both before and at the actual time the ships attacked the forts. He was appointed commander of the mortar fleet and given authority to prepare it. This he did with great dispatch and enthusiasm. The mortar barrels and shells were cast in the arsenal at Pittsburgh, and the carriages for them at New York; before Farragut's ships arrived, Porter had his twenty mortar schooners in the Mississippi.[3]

After the President and the Secretary of the Navy authorized the expedition against New Orleans, the next move was to secure the right commander for it. Fox thought Porter well-qualified for the post; but he was only a commander,[4] and the department thought it unwise to give the command to a man of that rank. A man of smaller caliber might have sulked in his cabin when, having suggested the expedition and secured its authorization, he was denied the command. On the contrary, Porter's enthusiasm for the attack on the forts was not in the least abated.

One of the first to commend Farragut for some important post was Captain Hiram Paulding, son of the John Paulding who was one of the captors of Major André, the British spy. Paulding was one of those officers who, because of age and ability, were kept in administrative work and had no oppor-

---

[3] Secretary Welles did not give Porter credit for the part which he claims for himself in preparing the expedition against New Orleans, and says that an attack on the city had long been considered by the Navy Department; but adds that the views of the Department were "speculative and uncertain." Welles, *Galaxy*, November and December, 1871, p. 683.
[4] Porter was promoted to commander August 22nd, 1861.

tunity to distinguish themselves in battle. At the beginning of
the war he was head of the bureau charged with the responsibility of selecting officers for wartime service. After that he was
assigned the unhappy task of evacuating and destroying the
Norfolk Navy Yard. In the fall of 1861 he became head of the
New York Navy Yard, and in this post gave encouragement and
support to Ericsson in the construction of the *Monitor*. In a
letter to Gustavus V. Fox, Assistant Secretary of the Navy,
Paulding spoke of the advisability of dividing the Gulf as well as
the Atlantic Blockade Squadron: "We have great and important
work to be done there [in the Gulf] I hope at no distant time.
Don't be unmindful of Farragut. He is a valuable officer whenever you can use him."

During the Mexican War Welles, then Chief of the Bureau
of Provisions and Clothing for the Navy, had formed a favorable
opinion of Farragut. The additional fact that, when so many
high officers in the navy were resigning their commissions and
joining the Confederacy, Farragut stood by the flag enhanced
his good standing with the Secretary of the Navy. Nevertheless, there was a natural reluctance at that early stage in the
war to give important posts to officers of Southern birth and
associations. Farragut was a native of Tennessee and his first and
second wives were both from Norfolk.

Farragut was near the middle of the list of captains of the
Navy, regarded by all as an able officer of good sense and good
habits. But few, if any, thought of him in the same class as
Du Pont or two of the officers who had "gone South," Tattnall
and Buchanan. The Assistant Secretary named several officers
whom he regarded as well-fitted for the New Orleans command,
but Porter spoke against them all and urged the appointment of
Farragut. There was a close family relationship between Porter
and Farragut, for Farragut was his adopted brother, and Porter's
oldest brother, William, who was to destroy the Confederate
ram *Arkansas* on the Mississippi, had married a sister of Farragut's second wife. Yet there is no evidence of nepotism on Por-

ter's part in pushing Farragut for the command. The officers whom Welles consulted on the matter were not of a united opinion. "Most of them, I think, while speaking well of Farragut, doubted if he was equal to the position—certainly not so well appointed a man as others,—but yet no one would name the man for a great and active campaign against Mobile or some other point. They knew not of New Orleans." After Welles had finally decided on Farragut, not a few members of Congress thought he had made a mistake. Senator Hale, Chairman of the Senate committee on naval affairs, asked Welles if he was certain of his man, "Southern born, a Southern resident, with a Southern wife, etc." The chief credit for the selection of Farragut to command the expedition against New Orleans must go to David D. Porter, just as the chief credit for initiating the campaign against New Orleans must be allotted to him.

When it seemed to Welles and Fox that Farragut was likely to be chosen, Porter was sent to New York to sound him out, not particularly as to New Orleans, but on his general attitude toward the war, the part the Navy ought to play in it, and his willingness to take an important command. "I found him," said Porter, "as I had expected, loyal to the utmost extent; and although at that time he did not know the nature of the expedition he authorized me to accept for him the Secretary's offer, and I telegraphed the Department: 'Farragut accepts the command, as I was sure he would.'" After this word from Porter, Welles ordered Farragut to report to him at Washington. There he had a conference, first with Fox at the home of Postmaster General Montgomery Blair, whose wife was a sister of Mrs. Fox, and then with Welles. In the interview with Welles Farragut said he "expected to pass the forts and restore New Orleans to the Government or never return. He might not come back, but the city would be ours." That was the kind of speech Welles liked to hear. In seeking the right commander for the New Orleans expedition before Farragut's name was mentioned Welles had laid down the following qualifications: "courage, audacity,

tact, and fearless energy, with great self-reliance, decisive judgment, and ability to discriminate and act under trying and extraordinary circumstances." When the choice fell on Farragut,
Welles had found the man he thus described.

Let us look now at the record and personality of this officer
to whom destiny gave the opportunity which made him one of
the most famous of our naval heroes. The four best-known
names in our naval history are John Paul Jones, David D. Porter,
Farragut, and George Dewey of Manila Bay. It is an interesting
fact that, in a certain sense, the United States owes a debt to
Spain for two of these four, Farragut and Dewey; for Dewey indirectly, because it was in the war with Spain that he won his
fame; for Farragut directly, because on his father's side he was of
pure Spanish blood.

George Farragut, the father of the admiral, was born at Ciudadela, the chief town of Minorca, one of the Balearic Islands
off the eastern coast of Spain. He was of distinguished lineage,
being a descendant of a Don Pedro who had taken a prominent
part in the expulsion of the Moors from Minorca and from Spain.
At the age of ten George went to sea. For a brief period he
served in the Russian Navy in the war with Turkey. In 1776 he
came to Charleston, South Carolina, where he volunteered for
service with the colonies in their revolt against Great Britain.
He became a first lieutenant in the South Carolina Navy, and
took part in land battles, fighting as a volunteer under the
"Swamp Fox," General Marion; also at Cowpens, and in the campaign against Cornwallis as a cavalry officer. In 1807 President
Jefferson appointed him a sailing master in the Navy. This soldier
of fortune who had fought in so many battles on land and sea
finished his military career fighting against the British under
Andrew Jackson at New Orleans. In 1795, while serving as a major
in the Tennessee militia, he married Elizabeth Shine, of Scotch-
Irish ancestry, and took up his residence at Campbell's Station,
not far from Knoxville. It was there that the future admiral
was born on July 5th, 1801.

If beauty and splendor of early environment play any part in the molding of character, Farragut was fortunate, indeed. The wilderness cabin in which he was born, as plain and rude as that in which Lincoln was born, stood on a point of land jutting out into the great Tennessee River. Looking eastward and northward where the Tennessee makes one of its grand sweeps and bends, one sees a mountain crag of grey limestone, the foot of which is washed by the river and the summit of which is crowned by noble pine trees. Looking westward and southward, one sees the broad river rushing on its journey of six hundred and fifty-two miles before, having traversed eastern Tennessee and northern Alabama and again crossed Tennessee, it empties its flood into the Ohio at Paducah, Kentucky.

The first six years of the future admiral's life were spent in the cabin on the Tennessee. On the river, and on the nearby highway where Campbell's Station was a stopping place for the stages, he saw the rolling or floating procession of pioneers pass his cabin home to possess the fertile lands to the south and the west. Farragut's most vivid recollection of his childhood was the day hostile Indians made their appearance, and his courageous mother, having put the children in the loft of the barn, stood at the door with an uplifted axe in her hand.

An act of Christian kindness opened the door to fame for Farragut. When his family was living at New Orleans early in the century, the father of Commodore Porter was taken ill. Farragut's father brought him to his house, where he was tenderly cared for until his death. When Commodore Porter learned of this kindness, he proposed to George Farragut that he adopt the second son, David Glasgow. As the family was in straitened circumstances and the mother now dead, the father gave his consent. "I mention this kind act on the part of my parents," wrote Farragut long after in his journal, "because it is to this circumstance that I am indebted for my present rank in the Navy of the United States."

Commodore Porter obtained for Farragut, at the now incredible age of nine years, an appointment as midshipman in the navy. In the War of 1812 he served with his adopted father on the *Essex*, the first naval vessel to display the American colors in the Pacific. He was only thirteen when the *Essex*, driven by a storm into the harbor of Valparaiso, was blockaded by two British ships, the *Cherub* and the *Phoebe*. Attempting to run the blockade, the *Essex* was attacked by the British ships in neutral waters. The engagement which ensued was the longest and most sanguinary of all the battles in which Farragut participated. Before the *Essex* struck her flag she had lost 155 of her crew of 225. In the midst of the bloody engagement it was reported to Commodore Porter that a gunner had deserted his post. Addressing the thirteen-year-old Farragut, Porter said, "Do your duty, sir." Farragut at once seized a pistol and went in search of the gunner with the purpose of shooting him, but failed to find him.

Farragut never forgot the "horrid impression" made on him by the sight of the first man he had ever seen killed in battle, a terribly mutilated boatswain's mate. At first he was staggered and sickened, but as others began to fall around him he recovered his composure. It was in this battle, too, that he received his first and only wound in all his years in the navy. A gunner was struck in the face by an eighteen-pound shot and hurled backward on Farragut, both of them tumbling down an open hatch. Farragut struck his head when the two-hundred-pound gunner fell on top of him, but fortunately was not seriously injured.

Like all the midshipmen of that day, Farragut served his apprenticeship as an officer in cruises in the Mediterranean, where he made the acquaintance of the noted captains and commodores of that day. One of the favorite stopping places for those fine old frigates was the harbor of Mahon, at the Island of Minorca where Farragut's father was born. A popular Spanish rhyme had it that "June, July, August, and Port Mahon are the best harbors of the Mediterranean." At that time Farragut seems to have had no interest in the fact that his father had come from Minorca; but after the Civil War, when the European squadron which he commanded stopped there, he paid a visit to Ciudadela, his father's birthplace, and received a hero's welcome. On one of these early Mediterranean cruises Farragut, to his lasting gratitude, came under the influence of his chief schoolmaster, Chaplain Charles Folsom, who was not only his teacher, but inculcated in him the highest principles of morality. When Folsom was appointed American consul to Tunis, he invited Farragut to accompany him. He spent the better part of a year with Folsom at Tunis, and in that brief period learned to speak Italian, French, Spanish, and Arabic.

At the outbreak of the Mexican War Farragut, well-qualified because of service in the Gulf and his knowledge of Spanish, sought active duty. He outlined to the Navy Department a plan for taking the castle San Juan de Ulloa at Vera Cruz, and in February, 1847 was given command of the sloop-of-war *Saratoga;* but before he reached Vera Cruz the castle had surrendered to the army under Scott. Assigned to blockade duty, he had no chance to distinguish himself or reveal his talents.

In 1854 he established the Mare Island Navy Yard near San Francisco. The momentous winter of 1860-61 found him at Norfolk awaiting orders. Closely associated with Norfolk through his first and second wives, he hoped that he would not be compelled to draw his sword against the South. But when Virginia seceded from the Union on April 17th, he declared openly that President Lincoln was justified in taking military measures to recover the national forts which had been seized by the seceding states. When informed that a man who entertained such sentiments would find it difficult to live in Norfolk, Farragut replied, "Well, then, I can live elsewhere." He left Norfolk at once and took his family north, where he established them in a cottage in New York at Hastings-on-Hudson. Even there, his experience was somewhat trying, for there were rumors that he was one of a group of Southern sympathizers who were planning to wreck the Croton Dam Aqueduct, then New York City's source of water supply.

Among Southern-born navy officers who went with the Confederacy, already distinguished when the war came or to achieve distinction in the war, were Franklin Buchanan, Commandant at the Washington Navy Yard, organizer and first superintendent of the Naval Academy, and in the war commander of the *Merrimac* and the *Tennessee;* Samuel Barron, son of the commodore of that name who killed Decatur in a duel; Matthew F. Maury, the great oceanographer; Josiah Tattnall, a Georgian who had held high posts in the navy; he led the Confederate Squadron at Port Royal and in March, 1862 succeeded Buchanan as commander of the *Merrimac;* John M. Brooke, inventor of the Brooke gun; and Raphael Semmes of *Alabama* fame. Buchanan and Tattnall were top officers in the navy, and their defection to the Confederacy was a shock to many of their former comrades. Neither Tattnall, however, nor Buchanan, were ardent secessionists. Buchanan, supposing that his native state would secede, had resigned his commission; but when Maryland stayed in the Union he asked permission to withdraw his resignation. The Navy Department refused his request. As for Tattnall, at the opening of the battle at Port Royal in October, 1861, he paid a singular tribute to Du Pont and his association with the old navy.[5]

Since navy officers were often absent from the country on long cruises, and therefore aloof from politics and inclined to regard their ship as their home, it might be supposed that the percentage of naval officers who stood by the flag would have been higher than that of army officers. Such, however, was not the case. As of January 1st, 1860, there were in the United States Army 1,083 commissioned officers, of whom 282 joined the Confederacy, or 26 percent.[6] As of January 1st, 1861, there were 856 commissioned officers in the United States Navy; of

[5] See Chapter IV on Du Pont.
[6] F. B. Heitman, *Army Register*, II, 180-184.

these 322 resigned their commissions and served with the Confederate Navy, or 37 percent.[7] It will thus be seen that the percentage of naval officers who joined the Confederacy was considerably higher than it was in the Army. However, it is interesting to note that youth was more loyal to the flag than maturity. As of January 1st, 1861, 267 midshipmen were enrolled in the Naval Academy at Annapolis; of these only 11, or less than 5 percent, joined the Confederacy.

Almost a year of the war had passed, and the only duty to which Farragut, midway in rank among the captains of the navy, had been assigned was membership on a naval board sitting at the New York Navy Yard to select officers for retirement. But now the great opportunity for which he had waited all through his long years in the navy had come. On January 9th, 1862, he was appointed to the command of the West Gulf Blockading Squadron, and on January 20th received orders to go up the Mississippi, "reduce" the forts defending New Orleans, take possession of the city, and "hoist the American flag thereon." Realizing that destiny was knocking at his door, Farragut wrote to his wife: "I have now obtained what I have been looking for all my life—a flag—and having obtained it, all that is necessary to complete the scene is victory. If I die in the attempt, it will be only what every officer has to expect. He who dies in doing his duty to his country, and at peace with God, has played out the drama of his life to the best advantage."

The vessel assigned to Farragut as his flagship was the steam sloop *Hartford*, a 1900-ton vessel capable of eleven knots and armed with twenty-two powerful guns, most of them Dahlgrens of the latest design. Three other ships in Farragut's squadron were of similar design and tonnage: the *Brooklyn*, the *Pensacola*, and the *Richmond*. The *Hartford* was on the China station when the war broke out and was at once recalled. She was fitted for battle at the Philadelphia Navy Yard, and then

[7] Office of the Chief of Naval Operations; letter to the author, 1955.

dropped down the Delaware to New Castle, where she took on stores and ammunition. It was there, on January 25th, that Farragut first boarded the ship which was to be his home for almost three years and the scene of his glorious achievements.

One of the best sketches we have of Farragut as he began his Civil War career, and also one of the best accounts we have of the battles in which he won fame on the *Hartford*, comes from the pen of a seventeen-year-old gunner, Bartholomew Diggins, who served with Farragut in all his engagements. He gives us this picture of Farragut as he saw him for the first time that January day at New Castle: "Square build, about 160 pounds; hair medium, between light and dark; clear hazel eyes, heavy eyebrows; very bald, which he tried to cover by combing the side hair across the top of his head. The expression of his face earnest and agreeable. He was very plain and unassuming in his manner; very quick and active in his movements. He wore a dress uniform of a captain, and his coat buttoned by a single button at the throat." When Farragut came out of his cabin after greeting the officers on the ship, he saw young Diggins, who was having a "good look" at the Flag-officer, standing nearby, and sent him to bring a hammer. "When the hammer was brought, Farragut fastened the picture of a lady on the wall."

The first difficulty Farragut encountered in his campaign against New Orleans was that of getting his heavy ships over the bar at Pass à L'Outre, the northeast mouth of the Mississippi. According to Admiral Porter, some of the Southern leaders in Congress had planned for just such an obstacle when they voted for new ships. "Jeff Davis," said Porter, "who got it into his head that I was some sort of a secessioner, made a remark in my presence one day that he would have voted against all appropriations for small vessels had not Mr. Mallory[8] taken precautions that they should draw too much water for Southern

---

[8] Stephen R. Mallory was then a Senator and Chairman of the Senate Naval Affairs Committee. Afterwards he became Jefferson Davis' Secretary of the Navy.

ports." However that may have been, Farragut was forced to remove the guns from many of his ships, for a vessel drawing more than eighteen feet could not cross the bar without being lightened. Even so, his most powerful ship, the *Colorado*, could not be gotten over, and her guns were distributed among the other ships of the squadron. Farragut handed this problem over to Porter, who was familiar with the river and its channels. He went to work with his usual energy and enthusiasm; by the middle of April the seventeen warships and Porter's twenty mortar schooners were up the river, the fleet three miles below the forts and the mortar schooners half a mile below Fort Jackson. The latter were around a bend near the west bank, and save for the tips of their masts, were invisible from the fort.

At the time of Farragut's assault on the forts a deep quiet had fallen upon New Orleans. Warehouses which once burst with stores of cotton and sugar and grain were shut and bolted. The sleek, low-cut blockade runners no longer came stealthily up the river to the foot of the city streets. Real money had disappeared. There was a current joke that one could pass a bottle of olive oil for money "because it was greasy, smelt bad, and bore an autograph." Where once ships from all parts of the world filled their holds with cargoes of rice, sugar, and cotton, now only an occasional ship could be seen, lying idly at the wharves, while the restless river ate at the levee and threatened to inundate the city.

The only stir of life was on the streets where soldiers were drilling. New Orleans had sent many of her sons to the front where, in Shiloh's woods and rolling fields, they wrote a record of high valor; but when the hour of trial came they were not at hand to defend the once opulent and still proud and defiant city. Those who remained in the city could not conceive that New Orleans might fall. The two rams, the *Manassas* and the almost-finished *Louisiana;* the swamps and bayous; the powerful forts, Jackson and St. Philip, with impassable morasses around them; the boom of logs and hulks; the fire rafts and the rushing current of the Mississippi—were not all these a wall of defense about the city? And thus it was that not until noon on that eventful 25th of April, when the church bells rang out the warning and the tall masts of Farragut's frigates came slowly around Slaughter House Bend, that the city realized that its doom was at hand.

At ten o'clock on the morning of the 18th of April the signal was given, and the first of 15,800 mortar shells hurled at Fort Jackson traced its fiery course across the sky and fell upon the stronghold. The discharge of these huge pieces was like a geyser of flame bursting skyward from the mouths of the mortars. For five days and nights the bombardment was maintained, each mortar ship firing once every ten minutes. This constant firing was a severe strain on the mortar crews, for before every discharge the crew went aft and stood on tiptoe with mouths wide open to lessen the shock of the concussion. At the end of the first day Fort Jackson was in flames and all its woodwork had been consumed; yet the batteries themselves were little damaged. The men defending them suffered almost no loss, for they took shelter in the casemates against the shells raining down on the fort. Had the ground been dry, the damage would have been greater. The river, however, was at flood, all the ground in and about the forts was soft and miry, and the shells buried themselves in the mud with a minimum of destruction.

At the end of five days the store of mortar ammunition was almost exhausted; the crews were worn out by their day-and-night labors, and the mortar schooners, although only one was sunk by the fire from the fort, were shaken and strained by the ceaseless concussion. When Porter reported this state of affairs to Farragut, he decided that the time had come for the warships to attack. At a conference of the commanders of the different vessels on the flagship, some of the captains advocated the assault, some considered it too hazardous, and others opposed an attack by night. But Farragut had summoned his captains, not so much to get their opinion as to announce to them his decision to run by the forts. Immediately after the conference he issued a general order in which he said, "When in the opinion of the flag-officer the propitious time has arrived, the signal will be made to weigh and advance to the conflict . . . and abide by the result—conquer or be conquered."

Some distance below Fort Jackson the Confederates had thrown across the river a formidable barrier consisting of hulks of ships and rafts of huge cypress logs held together by chain cables. On the night of the 20th of April, Captain H. H. Bell and two officers in a daring and dangerous adventure had cut the boom and made an opening sufficiently large to let the ships through. A few hours before the attack on the forts, an inspection of the boom revealed that the break made a few nights before was unmended. That was all Farragut needed to know; soon the signal to weigh anchor was passed to the fleet.

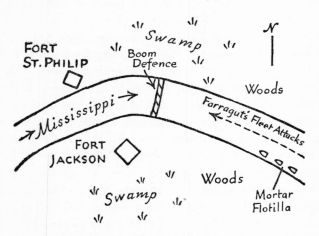

As always, Farragut prepared his ships for the battle with the utmost care. Cables were fastened to the sides of the ships opposite the engines, and sandbags, ashes, and coal were placed to protect the boilers. The sides of the vessels were plastered with mud to make them less visible to the gunners at the forts,

and on some ships the decks were whitewashed to give some light
to the crew in the forthcoming night action. Grappling irons
were laid in boats on the decks to lay hold of the fire rafts and
fire ships which were expected and which appeared soon enough.
Jacob's ladders were hung over the sides of the ships so that the
carpenters could descend quickly and make repairs in case a shot
penetrated the hull of the ship. Tubs of water were distributed
over the decks for use if fire broke out; every ship had a well-
trained fire brigade. These preparations, as we shall see, paid a
rich dividend in the battle. On the afternoon before the ships
started, Farragut visited every vessel to make sure that its commander understood his instructions.

Before the guns begin to speak let us look at some of the
captains and other officers of the fleet whose courage and ability
made Farragut's victory possible. The names of many corps, division, and even brigade commanders of the armies, such as Hancock, Sedgwick, Sickles, "Baldy" Smith, Doubleday, and Logan,
are well-known today; but this is not true of the naval commanders. The names of Farragut, Porter, Foote, Du Pont, and
Winslow are familiar, but not those of the officers who served
under them. Richard Wainwright was the captain of the *Hartford*, Farragut's flagship, and played a distinguished part in her
battles. His untimely death soon after the second attack on Vicksburg deprived the squadron of one of its ablest and most popular
commanders. He was succeeded by James S. Palmer, a man of
imposing appearance but no favorite with the crew, some of
whom he drove from the deck on one occasion when the *Hartford* was crowded with refugees. The seamen called him "Lady"
Palmer because he wore kid gloves in action. There was considerable discontent on the *Hartford* after he succeeded Wainwright,
who had been idolized by the men, and a number of desertions
followed. The executive officer on the *Hartford* was J. S. Thornton, of whose splendid service we shall hear again when we come
to the duel between the *Kearsarge* and the *Alabama*.

The captain of the old sidewheeler *Mississippi*, one of the heavyweights, was Melancthon Smith. Smith's eyesight was poor and, because the battle was to be fought at night, he charged his twenty-four-year-old executive officer, George Dewey: "I cannot see in the night. I am going to leave that to you. You have younger eyes." In the engagement Smith took charge of one of the batteries and left the handling of the ship to Dewey. Dewey described Smith as "absolutely fearless, deeply religious—a strong advocate of temperance, and a chain smoker, lighting one cigar after another with the shells bursting about him."

The fleet captain and chief of staff to Farragut was Henry Haywood Bell, one of that notable group of Southern-born officers who stood by the flag. Shortly before the battle he was detached from the *Hartford* to take command of the third division of the fleet. His departure cast a cloud of gloom over the ship, for the crew were warmly attached to him. They knew him as the "Fighting Captain," for he had fought a number of duels and was reputed to be the best swordsman in the Navy. That in itself would have commended him to Farragut, who was an expert swordsman and considered it disgraceful for an officer to wear a sword and not know how to use it. "Six feet high, straight and wiry; heavy white mustache," is the portrait one of the gunners on the *Hartford* left of him.

Theodorus Bailey, second in command, was in poor health at the time of the battle. However, despite the report of a medical board which examined him and warned him that it would be dangerous to participate in the battle, he said to Farragut, "I'll lead your fleet up the river if I burst my boiler!" He had commanded the *Colorado*, too heavy to be brought over the bar, and so was transferred to the smaller *Oneida*. This was not pleasing to S. P. Lee, who commanded the *Oneida*, and Bailey magnanimously transferred his flag to the little *Cayuga*. Samuel Phillips Lee belonged to a branch of the Lee family of Virginia, being the son of Francis Lightfoot Lee. He received a midship-

man's appointment at the age of seven and passed through
the usual training and cruises of the midshipmen of that day.
The war's beginning found Lee at the Cape of Good Hope in
command of the *Vandalia*. Although descended from one of Virginia's first families, he did not hesitate for a moment in choosing
his side in the conflict. Without waiting for orders, he returned
at once, took part in the early blockade of Charleston, and then
was given command of the *Oneida* at New Orleans.

Thomas T. Craven commanded the *Brooklyn*. Charles Stuart
Boggs was captain of the *Varuna*, the only Union ship lost in the
battle. His wife was a sister of Captain James Lawrence who,
when being carried below after receiving his mortal wound on
the *Chesapeake* in the battle with the British ship *Shannon*,
uttered the famous sentence, "Don't give up the ship!" Boggs'
record on the *Varuna* in his fight with the Confederate fleet
after he had passed the forts showed that he was of the same
mettle as his illustrious brother-in-law. James Alden, sixth in a
direct line from the *Mayflower* Pilgrims, had the *Richmond*, and
later the *Brooklyn* at Mobile Bay, where his stopping and backing almost brought disaster to the Union fleet.

At 2 A.M. on the morning of April 24th, after Farragut
received the signal that the passage through the boom was still
open, two red lanterns appeared at the mizzen of the *Hartford*,
and the great action was underway. Farragut's first plan was to
lead the attack with the flagship, closely followed by the heavyweights of the fleet, *Brooklyn, Richmond, Pensacola,* and *Mississippi*. This undoubtedly would have been the better plan, for
the heavy ships, following one after the other in close order,
would have poured a devastating fire on the two forts. The senior
captains, however, persuaded him that the flag officer should not
court the risk of leading the attack, and Captain Bailey was given
the honor of leading the fleet into action with the little *Cayuga*,
followed by the *Pensacola,* the *Mississippi,* and five other vessels.

The second division was made up of the *Hartford, Brooklyn,* and *Richmond.* The third division of six small vessels, under command of the fleet captain, H. H. Bell, brought up the rear.

What were the feelings of the men behind the guns as they watched cots being rigged to lower the wounded down the main hatch, and saw here and there on the deck buckets of sand to be scattered over the decks when they became slippery with blood? Whose blood would it be? Gunner Diggins has recorded his feelings for us: "This is the most depressing experience of a warrior's life, waiting to be engaged. One has nothing to do to occupy the mind. The mind runs on the great uncertainty about to take place, until it is a relief when the battle opens." And what were the thoughts of their leader, who had little intercourse with his men, as he sat on the poop deck of the *Hartford* conversing with his officers? These we know; in a letter written to his son on the second anniversary of the battle, when the *Hartford* was off Mobile Bay and he paused to reflect on that great night at New Orleans, Farragut wrote: "My son: This night two years ago was the anxious night of my life, when I felt as if the fate of my country, and my own life and reputation were all on the wheel of fortune, to be turned by the finger of the All-Wise; when 'Dixi'—'I said it.' It was only left to do or die. God was my leader, and we passed through the fiery furnace where none but He could have carried us."

Because this was a night battle, waged simultaneously against two forts on opposite sides of the river and a motley collection of Confederate ships above the forts, it was impossible for either attackers or defenders to see much of what was taking place. For our knowledge of what occurred we must depend upon the narratives of officers and men on the different ships, relating what happened within their view.

Like vast somber shadows the ships of the fleet, almost noiselessly, save for the sound of the paddlewheels on the *Mississippi,* began to move slowly up the broad and dark current of the river. All reports agree on the awesome splendor and majesty

of the night battle: the big mortars of Porter's fleet pouring out
fire and their exploding shells raining down like meteors on
the forts; the blasts of flame from the batteries of Forts Jackson
and St. Philip; the thunder of the broadsides from the *Hartford*
and the other ships as they came abreast of the forts; the flaming
firerafts drifting down with the current and at times turning
night into day. An officer on General Ben Butler's staff who
witnessed the battle from the latter's headquarters boat thus
described the scene: "Imagine all the earthquakes in the world,
and all the thunder and lightnings together in a space of two
miles, all going off at once; that would be like it."

The leading division under Bailey on the little *Cayuga*
passed the forts quickly with little loss, and at once engaged the
Confederate fleet above the forts. The most dramatic incident
in this phase of the battle was the running fight between the
Varuna, commanded by Charles S. Boggs, and the Confederate
ship *Governor Moore*, commanded by Captain Beverly Kennon.
For some reason, picket boats had not been sent down the river
to warn of the approach of Farragut's fleet, with the result that
the Union ships were almost abreast of the forts before either the
forts or the Confederate ships, which lay at the turn of the river
just above the forts, were aware of their presence. The *Governor Moore* lay near St. Philip on the east side of the river. At
3:30 A.M. Kennon heard distinctly the paddlewheels of the
Mississippi and, although he could see nothing, opened fire. Almost at the same moment the two forts let go with their batteries.
In three minutes the *Governor Moore* had steam up and went
out to meet the ships of Bailey's leading division. When hailed
by the *Oneida*, Kennon identified himself as the *Mississippi*, hoping thus to deceive the *Oneida*, for, like the *Mississippi*, the
Governor Moore was a sidewheeler. Not deceived by the ruse,
the *Oneida* opened fire.

In the midst of the engagement, Kennon saw a vessel, which
proved to be the *Varuna*, "rushing up stream like a race horse,"
and at once pursued her. Because of the way the smoke was

drifting, Kennon could see the *Varuna*, but those on the *Varuna* could not see the *Governor Moore*. This permitted the Southern gunboat to get within a hundred yards of the *Varuna* without being observed. Almost before the *Varuna* knew that a hostile ship was near, the *Governor Moore* rammed her, then backed off and rammed her a second time on the starboard side. The *Varuna*, badly hurt, was beached, and in that condition was rammed a third time by the *Stonewall Jackson*. Meanwhile the *Cayuga* and the *Oneida* made their appearance on the smoky scene. Kennon was starting down the river to ram one of them if possible, but his wounded first lieutenant, who was at the compass conning the ship, exclaimed to him, "Why do this? We've no men left. I'll be damned if I'll stand here to be murdered!" With that he pushed the helm hard to starboard and beached the ship just above the *Varuna*. Kennon then fired his ship with his own hands, pouring oil on the ladders leading down to the magazine and the shell room. Out of a crew of 93, 57 were dead, and 17 wounded, four of whom later died in the hospital. If the other Confederate ships had fought as courageously as the *Governor Moore*, the Union fleet would have suffered much heavier losses. Captain Kennon was taken on board the *Oneida* where he was treated kindly by Lee, who had known him since he was a child. He was afterward transferred to the *Hartford*, where Lieutenant Thornton gave him his cabin.

Let us turn now to the other two divisions of Farragut's fleet. The *Hartford*, leading the second division, was soon in trouble. Farragut's nearest approach to disaster occurred when the *Hartford* grounded almost immediately in front of Fort St. Philip, so near that her bowsprit extended out over a part of the fort. The gunners, seeing the bowsprit looming up over them and expecting a landing party, for a time deserted their guns. While the *Hartford* lay against the bank of the river, one of the fire rafts which had been set loose by the Confederates came against her port side. These rafts were huge river barges filled with cotton, pine knots, and other combustibles. The raft was pushed against the *Hartford* by a five-ton tug. Lieutenant Dewey, who was on the *Mississippi* and saw the tug push the raft against the *Hartford*, said: "To the captain of the little tug belongs the credit of one of the most desperate strokes of hero- ism I have ever known." The captain of the tug and all his crew soon perished.

The moment the fire raft came alongside, the *Hartford* was in flames from the water line to the top of the rigging, the fire driving the men on that side of the ship from the guns. For a time there was great confusion on the flagship. As Farragut walked along the deck through the smoke he was heard to ex- claim, lifting up his hands, "My God! Is this to be the end!" The mingled roar of the guns of the fleet and the batteries of the forts; the rush of the great river, its dark waters lighted up from time to time by the drifting fire rafts; the flames leaping up the rigging of the *Hartford;* all combined to produce a scene which those who saw it could never forget. "My youthful imagi- nation of hell," wrote one of the *Hartford*'s crew, "did not equal the scene about us at this moment."

A gunner, seeing a master's mate grab a grating and start toward the forecastle, followed his example, intending to leap overboard when the ship became too hot. At that moment, how- ever, he heard the voice of Captain Wainwright, as he walked slowly along the deck speaking through his trumpet, order the men to their fire stations. The voice of their captain, fearless and self-possessed, calmed the men on the verge of panic and restored confidence to the crew. By the side of Wainwright walked Farragut and his executive officer, Thornton. Soon every man was at his post, inspired by the example of the officers. The gunner who, like the master's mate, had been carrying a grating to sustain him in the river when he leaped overboard, dropped it and laid hold of a fire hose instead.

Meanwhile, the *Hartford*'s powerful engines were straining to back the flagship off the bank. With the ship ablaze from the water line to the masthead and the crew engaged in a desperate battle with the flames, Captain Wainwright hailed the engine room, asking for the chief engineer. The answer came back that Mr. Purdy was in temporary charge. "Tell Mr. Purdy I want to see him." When Purdy reported, Wainwright said to him, "Mr. Purdy, are you doing all you can with the engines? You know we are in a bad way if she don't back off."

"The throttle," replied Purdy, "is wide open on the engines, sir."

"Is there anything you can do to increase her power?"

"By reducing her water, which would endanger the boilers."

"Well, try anything to get her afloat."

Purdy then returned to the fire room and reduced the water. In a few minutes the ship commenced "jumping"; the vibrations from the engines were so great that those on the deck could hardly keep their feet. As the *Hartford* at length came off, clearing the fire raft, a roar of spontaneous cheering rose from the crew. With the ship clear of the fire raft, the flames were soon extinguished. "We all felt," wrote Diggins, "that the safety of the ship was wholly due to Captain Wainwright. His powerful voice claimed the attention of the men; his tall form and commanding presence, and his cool, fearless manner inspired all who heard or saw him with his own courage, and made men feel that with such a leader there was nothing to fear. From this time until his death he was the idol of the crew."

It was inevitable that the ships, steaming in darkness in a swift current and a tortuous river, and constantly sheering to avoid the fire rafts, should get out of line. The *Brooklyn* lost sight of the *Hartford*, which she was supposed to follow, and struck one of the hulks which composed that part of the boom which remained. The blow swung the ship around with her bow grazing the left bank of the river close to Fort St. Philip, which poured a heavy fire on her before she broke free. At that moment a cry arose, "The ram! The ram!" It was the dreaded *Manassas*. Captain Craven called out, "Give her four bells! Put your helm hard-a-starboard!" Despite this maneuver, the ram

struck the *Brooklyn* amidships, but, because of the position of the
two vessels, inflicted only a glancing blow. As she passed up the
river, the *Brooklyn* fired a broadside into the other Confederate
ram, the unfinished *Louisiana,* which lay near Fort St. Philip.
When Craven saw the *Hartford* enveloped in flames after the
fire raft had been pushed against her, he slowed down with the
intention of going to the rescue of the flagship. Although this
brought him under the direct fire of the fort, he maintained his
position until he saw that the *Hartford* was clear of the fire raft
and on her way up the river. This brave deed was not mentioned
in any of the reports of the battle nor in any of the newspaper
accounts, for Craven allowed no correspondents on his ship. The
Brooklyn experienced more hard fighting in the passage of the
forts than any of the Union ships and sustained heavier casualties, nine killed and twenty-six wounded.

The thunders of the night battle died away with the dawning
of a beautiful April morning over the great river and the forests
and swamps which bordered it. It was the sudden stillness after
the uproar of battle which informed Farragut that he had passed
the forts in safety. "At length the fire slackened, the smoke
cleared off, and we saw to our surprise that we were above
the forts." When the victorious fleet anchored, the commanders
of the ships visited the flagship to congratulate the flag officer.
Hundreds of flags flew from every ship of the squadron to greet
the rising sun and salute the victory. After breakfast and a few
hours' rest, the fleet started up the river toward the proud city
which was its destination and objective. At Quarantine a whole
regiment of Confederate soldiers surrendered to Captain Bailey.
Most of them were Germans who had no heart for the battle and
had joined the Confederate forces with the thought that there
would be no fighting on the river below New Orleans.

At ten o'clock the next morning, April 25th, the squadron
reached the Confederate batteries at Chalmette, on the outskirts
of New Orleans, where forty-seven years previously Andrew
Jackson's army behind their cotton-bale barricade on the dry

canal had beaten the veterans of the Iberian Peninsula. On Jackson Square, in front of the St. Louis Cathedral and the Cabildo, the old headquarters of the French occupation, there stood and still stands the splendid equestrian statue of Andrew Jackson. On the base of the monument are cut Jackson's words, spoken thirty years before when South Carolina threatened secession, "The Union Must and Shall Be Preserved." Farragut himself had been with the squadron which Jackson had dispatched to Charleston in that crisis. The broadsides of the *Hartford*, the *Brooklyn*, the *Richmond*, the *Pensacola*, and the other warships as they silenced the Chalmette batteries gave thunderous echo to the words of Jackson.

As the fleet drew near to New Orleans, a pall of smoke hung over the city. The torch had been put to whatever stores of cotton, rice, sugar, or molasses were left in the long-silent warehouses, and scores of burning barges, steamboats, and ships of every description came floating and smoking down the river. A little after noon, the inhabitants of the city saw the towering masts of the *Hartford* and the other warships come slowly round Slaughter House Bend and cast anchor at the foot of the streets leading down to the waterfront. Then ensued a scene almost without a parallel in the history of war. Inhabitants of other conquered cities have greeted in sullen silence the entrance of the victors. But not so New Orleans. Thousands came swarming down to the levee, raging and screaming, alternately cursing the defenders of the city, whose retreating drums they could hear as they marched out, and the crews of the invading fleet. Waving pistols and daggers, the mob shouted imprecations at Farragut and his men.

Soon after the fleet came to anchor, Captain Bailey, whose ship had led the fleet up the river, accompanied by a young Lieutenant, George H. Perkins, landed and marched to the City Hall to demand the surrender of the city. George Washington Cable, the well-known Southern writer, then a youth of eighteen, was working in a store when the fleet came to anchor. He gives us a vivid picture of the march of Captain Bailey and his aide through the mob to the City Hall:

About one or two in the afternoon, I being in the store with but one door ajar, came a roar of shouting and imprecations, and crowding feet down Common Street. 'Hurrah for Jeff Davis!' 'Shoot them!' 'Kill them!' 'Hang them!' I locked the door on the outside and ran to the front of the mob, bawling with the rest, 'Hurrah for Jeff Davis!' About every third man had a weapon out. Two officers of the United States Navy were walking abreast, unguarded and alone, not looking to the right or left, never frowning, never flinching, while the mob screamed in their ears, brandished pistols in their faces, cursed, crowded, and gnashed upon them. So through the gates of death those two men walked to the City Hall to demand the town's surrender. It was one of the bravest deeds I ever saw done.

To describe these extraordinary scenes, the howls, the screams, the imprecations and curses, the pistols and daggers brandished in the faces of the two officers, the looting of the shops, the men smashing, the women scooping up the spoils, the burning ships and barges, and hanging over all the heavy cloud of smoke, nothing will suffice but the language of the Apocalypse where the fall of Babylon is described:

Alas, alas, that great city Babylon, that mighty city! for in one hour is thy judgment come. And the merchants of the earth shall weep and mourn over her; for no man buyeth their merchandise any more. Alas, alas, that great city, for in one hour so great riches is come to nought. And every shipmaster, and all the company in ships, and sailors, and as many as trade by the sea stood afar off, and cried when they saw the smoke of her burning, saying, What city is like unto this great city? And they cast dust on their heads and cried, weeping and wailing, saying, Alas, alas, that great city wherein were made rich all that had ships in the sea by reason of her costliness! for in one hour is she made desolate.

In the hour of victory Farragut was as patient and forbearing as he was fearless and determined in battle. Although the guns of the *Hartford* were trained on the city and in a single broadside could have swept the streets clear of the raging mobs, he calmly and without recrimination endured the insults of the mayor and the curses of the multitude. The forts passed and the city taken, Farragut ordered all the commanders to assemble their crews at eleven o'clock on Sunday, April 26th, and "return thanks to Almighty God for his great goodness and mercy for permitting us to pass through the events of the last two days with so little loss of life and blood. At that hour the Church pennant will be hoisted on every vessel of the fleet, and their crews assembled will, in humiliation and prayer, make their acknowledgments thereof to the Great Disposer of all human events."

While the ship's companies were assembled for Divine worship, a lookout on the *Pensacola* saw four men cut down the flag which Farragut had ordered hoisted over the Mint and make off with it. The howitzer in the maintop of the *Pensacola* was fired at the men, but without effect. The flag was delivered to the mob, which dragged it through the streets and tore it to shreds. Farragut took no steps to avenge the affront to the nation's emblem, but retribution soon came in the person of General Ben Butler, to whom Farragut turned over the rule of the turbulent city. William B. Mumford, head of a gambling ring, had led the men who tore the flag down from the Mint and desecrated it in the street. He went about wearing a piece of the flag in the buttonhole of his coat. When Butler entered the city and established his headquarters at the St. Charles Hotel, he had noted this man in the mob in front of the building. Learning who he was and what he had done, Butler vowed he would hang him if caught. In due time the man was apprehended, tried, convicted, and sentenced to be hanged.

Extraordinary influence was brought to bear on Butler. Threats poured in on the general, warning him that his life would be forfeit if Mumford were executed. Prominent citizens appeared to plead for Mumford, warning that his execution would let loose on the city a flood of mob fury. As a last resort, Mumford's weeping wife and children were sent to Butler's headquarters. But nothing could move him. Imitating the Spanish custom which places the scene of punishment as near as possible to the place of the crime, Butler had Mumford hung from a window of the Mint, from the roof of which he had pulled down the flag. A great throng assembled before the Mint at the time set for carrying out the sentence of death, loudly shouting that Butler would not dare to hang the man. Mumford, permitted to make an address to the throng, declared that in tearing down the flag he had been motivated by the highest patriotism. At the appointed hour he looked anxiously up and down the street for the hoped-for deliverance; but none came. The drop fell.

Lincoln and the Navy Department had their hearts set on taking Vicksburg as well as New Orleans. Farragut's instructions were to go up the river and capture Vicksburg as soon as he had taken New Orleans. When Captain Bailey arrived in Washington to report the victory at New Orleans, the first thing he was asked was how many ships Farragut had sent up the river to take Vicksburg. When he answered "None," the Assistant Secretary, Fox, exclaimed, "Impossible! The instructions were positive." But Farragut's ships needed overhauling before another battle, and it was three weeks before the fleet started for Vicksburg. When Commander S. P. Lee, who had been sent in advance, demanded the surrender of the city, the officer then in command answered that Mississippians did not know how to surrender, and if Farragut and Butler could teach them, "let them come and try it." The bluffs at Vicksburg, which rise to a great height, presented a problem for the guns on ships in the river far below. Farragut's first attempt was more of a reconnaissance than anything else. He himself was ill at the time and yielded to the opinion of his captains, only one of whom favored an assault. "I yielded to their advice," wrote Farragut, "which I think was good; but I doubt if I had taken it if I had been well."

There was great disappointment at Washington when the news came that Farragut had returned to New Orleans. Only five days after he had sent him a congratulatory message, hailing his "unparalleled achievements" at New Orleans and telling him that his "magnificent execution" there would render his name immortal, the Assistant Secretary of the Navy sent him a dispatch of singular severity for a flag officer who had just won one of the most important victories of the war, peremptorily ordering him to return to Vicksburg and carry out the instructions he had received when given command of the expedition against New Orleans.

Obedient to these orders, Farragut once more made the four-hundred-mile ascent to Vicksburg, taking with him this time some of Porter's mortar ships and several thousand troops under General Thomas Williams. The voyage up the treacherous river was one of great difficulty for the heavy ships. "Fighting is nothing to the evil of the river," Farragut wrote, "getting on shore, running afoul of one another, losing anchors, etc." Arrived before Vicksburg, he wrote his family, "Here we are once more in front of Vicksburg, by a peremptory order of the Department and the President of the United States, 'to clear the river through.' . . . If it is His pleasure to take me, may He protect my wife and boy from the rigors of a wicked world."

Farragut and most of his ships passed the Vicksburg batteries with little loss, and joined the river squadron under Flag Officer Davis which had come down from Memphis. But he knew that passing the batteries meant little or nothing unless such action were supported by a large army. He so reported to the Navy Department: "The Department will perceive from this report that the forts can be passed, and we have done it, and can do it again, as often as may be required of us. It will not, however, be an easy matter for us to do more than silence the batteries for a time, as long as the enemy has a large force behind the hills to prevent our landing and holding the place."

The most humiliating incident in Farragut's career occurred after he had passed the Vicksburg batteries and joined the fleet of Flag Officer Davis. Both fleets had received information that a formidable ram, the *Arkansas*, was almost completed at Yazoo City, up the Yazoo River. The two Union forces lay in the Mississippi, a few miles above Vicksburg and some distance below the mouth of the Yazoo. Farragut and Davis had been planning to go up the Yazoo and destroy the ram; but her commander, Lieutenant Isaac Brown, was the first to act. Early on the morning of the 15th of July, three Federal gunboats, the *Tyler*, the *Queen of the West*, and the ironclad *Carondelet*, already veterans of many battles, ascended the Yazoo on a reconnaissance. They had gone only a few miles when they encountered the *Arkansas* coming down the river. The smaller ships, *Tyler* and the *Queen of the West*, at once fled down the river; but the *Carondelet*, under Henry Walke (who when the war ended had been in more battles than any officer of the Navy), fought a running battle with the ram for several miles and then, badly hurt, ran ashore.

At seven in the morning the *Tyler* and the *Queen of the West* were seen coming out of the Yazoo with the *Arkansas* in pursuit. Only one of the ships in the combined Union fleets had steam up, and the *Hartford*'s engines were under repair. All the Northern ships could do was to fire on the ram as she passed through them to Vicksburg, where she took refuge under guns of the batteries amid great cheering from the soldiers and the citizens. It was, indeed, an exploit worth cheering. Farragut, aroused by the cannonade, appeared on the deck of the *Hartford* in his nightshirt; but there was nothing he or anyone else could do to stop the passage of the *Arkansas*. Diggins, the gunner who was on the *Hartford* in all her fights, said he saw Farragut angry only twice: once when the *Brooklyn* stopped ahead of him at Mobile Bay, and once when the *Arkansas* ran through his fleet. As Farragut went below, Diggins heard him murmur, "Damnable neglect, or worse, somewhere!" But if hearings had been held, as after the tragic surprise by the Japanese bombers at Pearl Harbor in 1941, Farragut undoubtedly would have been among those censured. In his report to the

Secretary of the Navy, he as much as confessed his carelessness, for he said, "It is with deep mortification that I announce to the Department that, notwithstanding my predictions to the contrary, the ironclad *Arkansas* has at length made her appearance and took us all by surprise." In a letter to Fox, the Assistant Secretary, Richard Wainwright, the able captain of the *Hartford,* had this to say of the *Arkansas* affair: "I have told the Flag Officer a good deal of what I am about to tell you, but he pooh poohed it. He pooh poohed the information he received from a deserter the night before, that the *Arkansas* would be down the next morning; but when the morning came it brought the ram with it, and caught him with his breeches down."

The Secretary of the Navy was exceedingly angry when he received word of the exploit of the *Arkansas.* "The most disreputable naval affair of the war," he wrote, "was the descent of the steam ram *Arkansas* through both squadrons, until she hauled into the batteries of Vicksburg, and there the two Flag-Officers abandoned the place and the ironclad ram, Farragut and his force going down to New Orleans, and Davis proceeding with his flotilla up the river."

It was not, however, quite so humiliating as the Secretary thought. The *Arkansas* had been badly hurt in her fight with the *Carondelet;* her smokestack was so perforated that she could hardly get up steam and her speed was reduced to one knot; it was only with the help of the river's current that she was able to get to Vicksburg. That very night the mortified Farragut went down to Vicksburg, determined to drag the *Arkansas* out from her hiding place and destroy her; in the darkness he was not able to find her and, passing the batteries, returned to New Orleans, leaving it to Flag Officer Davis to deal with the ram. This task Davis assigned to Commander William Porter, oldest brother of David D. Porter.

At the outbreak of the war William Porter was on duty in the Pacific. When his son joined the Confederacy, there had appeared in the newspapers what purported to be a letter from his father saying that he had made a mistake, but advising him, having taken the step, to stand by his decision and do his duty. When this was brought to the attention of the Secretary of the Navy he immediately ordered Porter to report at Washington. In great distress, Porter told Welles that his son for some time had been alienated from him and that the letter was a forgery; but when Welles mentioned the matter to David D. Porter, he said he was sure his brother had written the letter. In this opinion Welles concurred. "Untruthfulness," he wrote in his *Diary*, "was a failing of all the Porters." Nevertheless, he gave Porter another chance. In command of the *Essex*, named after his famous father's ship in the War of 1812, Porter proved himself worthy of all confidence in the battles on the western rivers. After Porter's death Welles learned that he had been mistaken, for Farragut and his wife (William Porter's sister-in-law) said they knew the letter to be a forgery.

William Porter made two attacks on the *Arkansas*, the first on the morning of July 22nd, when he tried to ram and sink her where she lay under the guns at Vicksburg. This attempt was not successful; but some time later he made a second attack when the *Arkansas* lay at Baton Rouge. The Confederate ironclad steamed out into the river and headed for the *Essex*, intending to ram her first; but a mechanical failure on the Confederate ironclad caused her to run ashore, where Porter poured shell after shell into the helpless vessel and set her on fire. At length, swinging free from the shore, the burning monster, abandoned now by her crew, drifted down the river like a huge flaming torch, her own guns saluting her as the flames reached them, until an explosion tore her asunder and she sank to the bottom of the Mississippi. It was with great joy and relief that Farragut learned of the end of the *Arkansas*. "It is one of the happiest moments of my life," he wrote the Secretary of the Navy, "that I am able to inform the Department of the destruction of the ram, *Arkansas*."

The last of the Confederate strongholds on the Mississippi to fall was Port Hudson. One hundred and thirty-five miles above New Orleans and fifty miles below the mouth of the Red River, Port Hudson stood on a bluff fifty feet high, at one of the great bends of the Mississippi, on the left, or east, side of the river. It commanded the mouth of the Red River, down which came cargoes of supplies from Louisiana, Texas, and Arkansas for the Confederate armies. Without specific direction from the Navy Department, Farragut on his own responsibility determined to assail this fortress.

At ten o'clock on the night of March 13th, 1863, the familiar red lantern signal appeared on the *Hartford*, but this time at her stern and not at the topmast. Here for the first time Farragut adopted the plan he followed successfully at Mobile Bay. Each of the heavy ships, except the *Mississippi*, which was a side-wheeler and therefore could not have a ship alongside, had lashed to its port side (the disengaged side) a smaller vessel. Lashed to the *Hartford* was the gunboat *Albatross*. As soon as the Confederates learned of the approach of Farragut's squadron, they set on fire huge piles of pine knots and branches on the bluffs to bring the attacking vessels into view. For a brief time the flames made the scene as light as day; but the night was heavy and close, and before long a pall of mist and smoke settled down on the river, making navigation difficult in the extreme. To overcome this disadvantage, Farragut had a speaking trumpet fixed on the mizzen top and leading to the man at the wheel. To this device Farragut said he owed the safe passage of his ship, for it permitted the ship to be directed from above the smoke of battle. Swung round by the seven-mile-an-hour current, the *Hartford* was heading straight for the shore and immediately under the batteries, but changed her course just in time and passed the fort in safety.

The other ships, however, were not so fortunate. The *Richmond* lost power because a shot carried away a boiler safety valve, and the *Monongahela's* engines failed; both dropped down the river. The *Mississippi*, thinking she had already passed a dangerous shoal point, struck heavily on the western bank under full steam. When every effort to get her off failed, Captain Smith instructed his executive officer, Lieutenant George Dewey, to destroy the engines and fire the ship. In a calm tone he said to Dewey: "It is not likely that we shall escape. We must make every preparation to insure the destruction of the ship." When the boats were sent off with the crew and the wounded, Dewey, in order to make sure that one of them would return, jumped aboard her. Remembering that an officer is supposed to be the last to leave a sinking ship, he was greatly troubled in mind. What if a shot should sink his boat, and he could not return to his ship? "This," wrote Dewey long after, "was the most anxious moment in my career."

When the boat reached the shore, Dewey sent four of his eight men ashore, and ordered the other four to return with him to the *Mississippi*; but all four, except the Negro cook, who said to him, "Sir, I am ready to go with you," scrambled quickly up the bank of the river. Calling out one by one the names of the fleeing men, Dewey shamed them, in the name of their race, for allowing a Negro to be the only one to return and save his shipmates. After he returned to the ship and examined her carefully to make sure that no one alive was left, he fired the ship with the mattress from his own cabin. Lightened by the removal of her crew and by the consuming fire, the *Mississippi* came off the shoal and like a huge torch went drifting down the river. The other ships scattered as her guns were fired one by one by the flames. Near Profit's Island, the squadron's anchorage, she struck on the shore and blew up with a roar which shook the earth for miles around.

In the opinion of Admiral Dewey the best account of the battle at Port Hudson is that written by the Reverend Thomas Scott Beacon. Beacon was Captain Alden's guest on the *Richmond* and also chaplain pro tempore of the squadron. He quotes Farragut as saying, "Give me wooden ships and iron hearts."

There is no question that at that time Farragut still preferred the *Hartford* to an ironclad. Of Melancthon Smith he reports, confirming what Dewey, his executive officer, said of him, that he was a deeply religious man, holding prayer meetings in his cabin and permitting only coffee to the men when going into action, saying, "I don't want any grog bravery on board my ship." According to Dr. Beacon, Farragut's plan of action against the forts was for the ships not to return the fire of the batteries, so as not to uncover their positions. But the *Hartford* herself was the first to open fire. Observing this, a midshipman remarked to Dr. Beacon, "There! just as I expected. I knew the old sea dog would bark. He couldn't help it!" Beacon was on the *Richmond*'s bridge when Commander Cummings was struck by a shell and lost his leg. When he was taken below and the surgeon was about to attend his wound, Cummings saw a fearfully mutilated sailor waiting his turn, and said to the surgeon, "No, he was here before me and must be attended to first."

Farragut and the *Hartford* passed out of range above the fort; but none of his ships, except the *Albatross* which had been lashed to the side of his vessel was with him. Anxiously he watched the flames of the burning *Mississippi* illuminate the night, and wondered what had happened to his ships. Rockets were fired in an effort to communicate with the other vessels. As soon as day dawned, the *Hartford* dropped down the river near the fort and fired guns to let the fleet below know that the fort had been passed. When no answer came, he floated bottles down the stream to let his captains know that the flagship and the *Albatross* were safe above the batteries. It was not until April 6th, almost three weeks after the battle, that he was able to open communications with his fleet. This was accomplished by sending his secretary down the river in a dugout camouflaged with the branches of a tree. Meanwhile, the Confederate authorities at Richmond had announced that Farragut and his flagship had been captured and the fleet dispersed. In his report to the Secretary of the Navy, Farragut said, "If, in

this effort to come up and cut off the enemy's supplies from
the Red River and recapture the *Indianola*,[9] misfortune has befallen some of our vessels, I can only plead my zeal to serve my
country, and the chances of war." The battle, however, was not
without good results, for two powerful ships, the *Hartford*
and the gunboat *Albatross*, were so placed that they were able
to cut off the flow of supplies down the Red River for the
Confederate armies. Not long after he passed the fort at Port
Hudson, Farragut took the *Hartford* up the river to Vicksburg, where he had an interview with Grant on one of Porter's
ships.[10]

In the battle at Port Hudson Farragut had with him on
the flagship his only son and future biographer, Loyall. Before
the engagement opened, the ship's surgeon suggested to the
admiral that he send his son below, out of danger's way. But
Farragut refused to do so, saying, "No, that will not do. It is
true our only child is on board by chance, and he is not in the
service; but, being here, he will act as one of my aides, to assist
in conveying my orders during the battle, and we will trust in
Providence, and *la fortune de la guerre*." After Port Hudson,
however, Farragut sent the young man home, telling his wife,
"I am too devoted a father to have my son with me in troubles
of this kind. The anxieties of a father should not be added to
those of a commander."

In the attack on Port Hudson there occurred an incident
which throws much light on Farragut's character, especially in
his dealings with the younger officers. The *Monongahela*, temporarily under the command of Lieutenant Winfield Scott
Schley, victor at Santiago in the war with Spain, had dropped
out of the fight after silencing one of the Port Hudson bat-

[9] The *Indianola*, a Union ironclad, had run the batteries at Vicksburg and
then gone downstream to the Red River. On her way back toward Vicksburg she was attacked by Confederate ships and captured after her crew had
scuttled her in shallow water. Her captors soon abandoned and destroyed
her.
[10] See Chapter X on Porter.

teries. In the midst of the action the quartermaster of the *Monongahela* reported to Schley that a signal was being made from the *Hartford*, but that he could not make it out because of the heavy pall of smoke which enveloped the ships. Since Schley had orders to destroy a battery which was still firing, he concluded that the signal could not refer to his ship, and continued firing at the battery until it was silenced, and then dropped down the river to the fleet's anchorage. Later, when the fleet was reunited, Schley went on the flagship to make the usual post-battle report. As he saluted the admiral on the quarter-deck, Farragut, in a very severe tone, said, "Captain, you begin early in your life to disobey orders. Did you not see the signal flying for near an hour to withdraw from action?"

Taken back at this reprimand, instead of the commendation he had expected, Schley started to explain that his ship could not see the signal clearly because of the smoke, but was cut short by Farragut, who said he "wanted none of this Nelson business in his squadron about not seeing signals." [11] Schley, however, mustered courage to continue his defense, telling the admiral that even if he had been able to read the signal, he would not have thought it applied to him, since his orders were to destroy the battery. Farragut then invited Schley to come with him to his cabin. "The moment the door was closed behind him there was an entire change in his tone and manner as he said smilingly, 'I have censured you, sir, on the quarter-deck for what appeared to be a disregard of my orders. I desire now to commend you and your officers and men for doing what you believed right under the circumstances. Do it again whenever in your judgment it is necessary to carry out your conception of duty.'"

After Farragut's battle at Port Hudson, the twenty-two

[11] At the Battle of Copenhagen, April 1st, 1801, when Nelson was attacking the Danish ships and forts, he received a signal from the commanding admiral, Sir Hyde Parker, to withdraw from action. When his attention was called to the signal, Nelson, putting the telescope to his blind eye, said he could not see it, and continued the action. It was one of his greatest victories.

big Dahlgren guns on the *Hartford* had a long rest. A year and five months passed before their thunders broke the silence on Mobile Bay on that memorable 5th of August, 1864. Next to New Orleans, Mobile, although a smaller city than Charleston, was the greatest cotton port of the South. The city was defended by two forts far down the bay: Fort Morgan at the end of Mobile Point, and Fort Gaines at the eastern end of Dauphin Island, three miles from Fort Morgan. Between these two forts piles had been driven and mines anchored. Between the eastern end of the mines (which in 1864 were called "torpedoes"), marked by a red buoy, and Fort Morgan, a narrow channel had been left open for the passage of blockade runners.

Besides the two forts, the principal defense of Mobile was the ironclad ram *Tennessee*. This vessel, the most formidable built by the Confederacy in the war, had been constructed at Selma, one hundred fifty miles up the Alabama River, and then towed down to Mobile. As she drew thirteen feet, she could not get over the Dog River bar into the bay. This difficulty was overcome by an engineering device. Wooden tanks, known as "camels," were filled with water and sunk at the sides of the ram. The water was then pumped out, and the rising tanks lifted the ram seven feet. Thus the *Tennessee* was carried over the bar. Her commanding officer, Franklin Buchanan, the first admiral of the Confederate Navy, had been a highly esteemed officer of the old navy, and at the outbreak of the war was the commandant of the Washington Navy Yard. He had commanded the *Merrimac* when she sank the *Cumberland* and destroyed the *Congress* at Hampton Roads in March of 1862. "Old Buck," as his comrades in both navies knew him, was a man of high ability, great courage, and extraordinary physical strength, reputed to have been the strongest man in the old navy.

Of the officers who had not hitherto accompanied Farragut to battle, the most distinguished was Percival Drayton. At Port Royal he had commanded a ship under Du Pont, and was now Farragut's fleet captain and also commander of the flagship. Drayton came of an old and aristocratic South Carolina family, but stood fast in his loyalty to the flag. At Port Royal he fought against his own brother, Thomas, who commanded the Confederate troops at the two forts. For his loyalty to the Union the legislature of South Carolina declared him "infamous." He had served with Farragut in the Bureau of Ordnance before the war, and there formed a warm friendship with the future admiral. At the beginning of the war, on duty at the Philadelphia Navy Yard, he immediately requested that in the Navy Register his name be entered as a citizen of Philadelphia. In action he was bold and courageous. "Drayton," Farragut said of him, "does not know fear, and would fight the devil himself; but he believes in acting as if the enemy can never be caught unprepared; whereas I believe in judging him by ourselves, and my motto is action [quoting the words of Danton, the French Revolutionary] 'L'audace, et encore de l'audace, et toujours de l'audace.'" Never wavering in his adherence to the flag, and in spite of the fact that his brother Thomas was a Confederate General, Drayton said that he would sacrifice every one of his relatives, however painful it might be, rather than interfere with the Union success. Regarding the action of the South Carolina legislature in declaring him "infamous," he said to a friend: "As for being an outlaw in my native state, I might as well go through with it. I am for crushing the rebellion if we come down to the original 3,000,000 of the first Revolution in doing so, and I am quite willing that I should not be one of the survivors." Drayton held the opinion that no man who could not say "No" could be called great; and added that on occasions Farragut said "Yes" when he should have said "No." Nevertheless, he regarded Farragut as a great man.

At 5:45 A.M. on August 5th, 1864, the attack signal went up on the *Hartford* and the fleet got under way. It had been Farragut's purpose to lead the squadron in the *Hartford*, but, as at New Orleans, his captains told him that he should not place the commander in chief in such jeopardy. He yielded to their importunity, and, instead of the *Hartford*, ordered the *Brooklyn* to lead the fleet in, partly because she carried at her bow a device for fishing up mines, and also because she carried four chase guns. After the *Brooklyn* came the *Hartford*. Each of the seven heavy ships had a smaller vessel lashed to the port side, the side away from Fort Morgan. The order of the battle line was as follows: *Brooklyn* and *Octorara*, *Hartford* and *Metacomet*, *Richmond* and *Port Royal*, *Lackawanna* and *Seminole*, *Monongahela* and *Kennebec*, *Ossipee* and *Itasca*, *Oneida* and *Galena*. The second named ship in each of these pairs was on the port or unengaged side. The four monitors, *Tecumseh*, *Manhattan*, *Winnebago*, and *Chickasaw* were a little in advance of the *Brooklyn*, somewhat to its starboard bow.

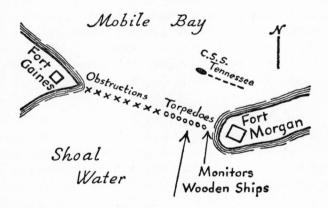

The early fog had disappeared when the fleet started and the summer morning was bright and clear. Army signal officers were on board the *Hartford* and other ships of the squadron so that, if necessary, the fleet could communicate with the land forces under General Gordon Granger. General Granger, one of the heroes of the battle of Chickamauga, had landed with a division of troops from General Edward Canby's army on the west end of Dauphin Island two days before the battle and was preparing to besiege Fort Gaines, the fort on the west side of the bay and a little to the north of Fort Morgan. Farragut thought more of possible death in this action than in his former battles, for a few days beforehand he wrote to his son, Loyall: "When it pleases God to take me hence, I shall feel that I have done my duty. I am not conscious of having wronged anyone, and have tried to do as much good as I can. Take care of your mother, if I should go, and may God bless and preserve you."

At six forty-seven the monitor *Tecumseh* let go with a fifteen-inch gun against Fort Morgan, and the great battle was on. Weather and sea conditions were favorable for the Union fleet; there was a flood tide and a light wind from the southwest blew the smoke of the Union guns away from the ships and toward the fort and the Confederate fleet. At the beginning of the engagement Farragut stood in the shrouds above the poop deck, holding his telescope in one hand and with the other holding to the rigging, to which he was secured by a "bridle" passed around his back and under his arms and fastened to the shrouds. This was done by quartermaster Knowles by order of Captain Drayton. Above Farragut stood Martin Freemantle, the able and trusted pilot, and below Farragut stood Captain Drayton on the poop deck. Freemantle communicated by a speaking tube with the deck, and by signals with his hands to the *Hartford*'s consort, the *Metacomet*, lashed to her side. In the chains stood the leadsmen calling out the depth of water as they sounded.

The army signal officers on board, much to their disappointment, had been ordered to the cockpit to assist the surgeons, but were told to be on call when the *Hartford* had passed the forts. Soon, however, the order was shouted down, "Send up an army signal officer; the *Brooklyn* is signaling." A signal officer then ran to the deck and translated the *Brooklyn*'s message: "The monitors are right ahead; we cannot go on without passing them." Farragut at once sent back the signal, "Order the monitors ahead, and go on." Because of the risk of running down one of the monitors, which were much slower than the wooden ships, the *Brooklyn* first halted, and then began to back. This involved great danger of collision, for the *Hartford* was following the *Brooklyn* closely and the other ships were directly behind the *Hartford*. Just at that moment, the *Tecumseh*, a short distance in front of the *Brooklyn*, suddenly reeled to one side and went down bow foremost, her screw revolving in the air. Her courageous commander, Tunis A. Craven, in his eagerness to get at the Confederate ram either forgot or disregarded Farragut's order to pass to the east of the easternmost buoy which marked the end of the field of moored mines and instead steered west of the buoy, where he struck one of the explosive canisters. Until the time of World War II, this was one of the worst disasters ever to befall a United States warship in action. Of the ship's company of 114, ninety-three perished and four were captured.[12]

It was in connection with the sinking of the *Tecumseh* that there occurred one of the finest and most stirring incidents in the history of the Navy. Just as the *Tecumseh* was going down, John Collins, the pilot, and Captain Craven met at the foot of the ladder leading to the top of the turret, the only avenue of escape. Perhaps troubled in spirit that his ship was going down and that most of her crew were about to perish because he had disobeyed an order and taken a wrong course, or perhaps out of the nobility of his character, Craven said, "After

[12] It will be noted that, contrary to most popular accounts of the battle, the *Brooklyn* was stopped, not because of the disaster which befell the *Tecumseh*, for that ship had not yet been sunk, but because she was in danger of running down one of the monitors ahead of her. The person who was in the best position to see what happened was the army signal officer, John C. Kinney, who received and translated for Farragut the message from the *Brooklyn* and sent back Farragut's signal, "Order the monitors ahead, and go on." There was nothing said at that moment about torpedoes. In his report to Farragut after the battle, the *Brooklyn*'s commanding officer, Captain James Alden, said his ship halted and then backed in order to clear "a row of suspicious-looking buoys directly under our bows. While we were in the act of backing to clear them, our gallant admiral passed us and took the lead." In his report to the Department Farragut said he did not know at the time why the *Brooklyn* had halted. "The *Brooklyn*, for some cause which I did not at the time clearly understand, arrested the advance of the whole fleet. A moment after I saw the *Tecumseh* struck by a torpedo and disappear almost instantaneously beneath the waves."

you, pilot." "But," said Collins, one of the twenty-one who escaped death, "there was nothing after me. When I reached the upmost round of the ladder, the vessel seemed to drop from under me." When the *Tecumseh* went down, the ships behind the *Brooklyn* at first thought that the *Tennessee* had been sunk, and waves of cheering rolled from ship to ship. The men were mistakenly cheering, not victory, but death to almost a hundred of their comrades.[13]

When the *Brooklyn* stopped and began to back, the whole column fell into great confusion, and it was at this time that the heaviest losses were sustained; the *Hartford* alone lost twenty-five killed. After the *Brooklyn* stopped, Farragut called to his pilot, standing above him, "What is the matter with the *Brooklyn?* She must have plenty of water." Freemantle called down, "Plenty, and to spare, Admiral; but her screw is moving." This created the impression that the *Brooklyn* was going ahead again; in reality, she was backing. When Farragut learned from his pilot that there was sufficient water for him to pass to the left of the *Brooklyn* he said, "I will take the lead," and ordered the *Hartford* ahead at full speed.[14] As the *Hartford* steamed past the halted *Brooklyn*, Diggins reports that sailors on the flagship

[13] After Farragut's death, his son and biographer, Loyall, found among his papers this memorandum in connection with the sinking of the *Tecumseh;* "General orders required the vessels to pass inside the buoys next to Fort Morgan. When the *Tecumseh* reached that point, it looked so close that poor Craven said to the pilot, 'The Admiral ordered me to go inside that buoy, but it must be a mistake.' He ran just his breadth of beam too far westward, struck a torpedo, and went down in two minutes. Alden saw the buoys ahead and stopped his ship. Allowing the *Brooklyn* to go ahead was a great error. It lost not only the *Tecumseh* but many valuable lives, by keeping us under the fire of the forts for thirty minutes; whereas, had I led, as I intended to do, I would have gone inside the buoys, and all would have followed me."
[14] I have been unable to find any confirmation of the alleged shout of Farragut as he was passing the *Brooklyn*, and was told that torpedoes were ahead, "Damn the torpedoes! Go ahead!" The story first appeared in Captain Foxhall Parker's "Battle of Mobile Bay." Lieutenant John C. Kinney, the army officer who passed Farragut's signals to the *Brooklyn*, comments that while the admiral may have said it, it is doubtful if he shouted it to the *Brooklyn*, for "there was never a moment when the din of battle would not have drowned any attempt at conversation between the two ships."

ran to the side of the ship, "hooting, groaning and howling, 'Coward! Take him out! He ran away at Vicksburg!'" These jeers were directed at Alden, the *Brooklyn*'s captain. The mention of Vicksburg referred to the fact that, when Farragut made his first attack on that stronghold, several of his ships did not follow the flagship past the Confederate batteries; among them was the *Richmond*, then commanded by Captain Alden.

It was with the *Brooklyn* halted and the *Tecumseh* sunk that Farragut made one of those quick and firm decisions which mark the great commander. Before Farragut was chosen to command the expedition against New Orleans, the Secretary of the Navy, searching for the man best qualified for the post, wrote in his diary that among other qualifications he must have "great self-reliance, decisive judgment, and ability to discriminate and act under trying and extraordinary circumstances." In those critical moments after the *Brooklyn* had stopped, Farragut proved that he possessed to a high degree the qualities which Welles considered indispensable.

In making his quick and momentous decision Farragut called for Divine aid. In after years he told his son that for a little he was at a loss whether to proceed or go back, and offered up a prayer, "O God, who created man and gave him reason, direct me what to do. Shall I go on?" and it seemed to him, he said, that he heard a voice commanding him, "Go on!"

During the brief period in which Farragut was delayed by the stopping and backing of the *Brooklyn* and the destruction of the *Tecumseh*, the flagship had drifted so far westward that it was not possible for Captain Drayton to follow Farragut's instructions before the battle and steer east of the easternmost buoy. He had no alternative but to drive the *Hartford* over the mine field in which the *Tecumseh* had met her death blow. As the flagship passed over, the crew could hear the bottom of the ship grating on the mines. Fortunately, none of them exploded. Farragut expected that some of his ships would be lost, perhaps even the flagship herself. But, like all great leaders, he was willing to take a risk and suffer loss for the sake of victory. The men on the ships following were also well aware of their peril; but only one, Farragut reported, exhibited cowardice. That one he covered with the magnanimous mantle of anonymity. "I dashed ahead," reported the Admiral, "with the *Hartford*, and the ships followed on, their officers believing that they were going to a noble death with their commander-in-chief."

After passing Fort Morgan, Farragut encountered the ram *Tennessee*, regarded by some as the most powerful ship afloat. With the *Tennessee* were three gunboats, the *Selma*, *Gaines*, and *Morgan*. In the first encounter the *Tennessee*, after failing to ram several of the Union ships, took refuge under the guns of Fort Morgan. The *Hartford* then anchored some three miles up the bay from the fort and the crew was sent to breakfast. This was at half past eight in the morning, three hours after the battle began. Captain Drayton came up to Farragut, who was standing on the poop deck, and said to him, "What we have done has been well done, sir; but it all counts for nothing so long as the *Tennessee* is there under the guns of Morgan." "I know it," said Farragut, "and as soon as the people have their breakfasts I am going for her." But there was no breakfast, for the *Tennessee* started first, steering straight for the *Hartford*.

In engaging with his one ship the whole Union fleet, the fire power of which surpassed that of the English, French, and Spanish ships combined at Trafalgar, Buchanan could have entertained little hope of final victory. But he did think he might sink the *Hartford,* and perhaps other Union ships before he was done for. Addressing his crew before the engagement, he said: "You shall not have it to say when you leave this vessel that you were not near enough to the enemy, for I will meet them, and then you can fight them alongside of their own ships; and if I fall, lay me on one side, and go on with the fight." When advised by some of his officers not to make the second attack on the *Hartford*, Buchanan answered, "No; I will be killed or taken prisoner; and now I am in the humor, I will have it out."

When Farragut saw the *Tennessee* coming out, he signaled the fleet to attack the ram, "not only with their guns, but bows on at full speed." It was a battle now of one ship against thirteen, ten wooden vessels and three monitors. The *Monongahela*, which had unsuccessfully rammed the *Tennessee* in the first engagement, now struck the ram at full speed amidships, but without injuring her. The *Lackawanna*, close behind the *Monongahela*, also struck the *Tennessee*, but with little effect. Buchanan drove the *Tennessee* straight on toward the *Hartford*. But just before the ships, bow on, made contact, the *Tennessee* changed her course slightly and the two vessels merely grazed each other. As they passed, the *Hartford* poured a broadside into the *Tennessee*, but the shots rebounded off the sides of the ram like rain.

As the *Hartford* was going about in order to have another try at the ram, she was struck on the side by the *Lackawanna*, also heading for the ram. The blow crushed a portion of the starboard side of the *Hartford*, and it was thought for a moment that she was going down. The cry went up, "Save the Admiral! Save the Admiral!" However, an examination showed that the blow was not mortal, and Farragut ordered the flagship again to attack the ram. But the *Lackawanna*, steering for the *Tennessee*, came up a second time on the *Hartford*'s starboard side, and for a moment a second collision seemed imminent. Out of patience, Farragut asked the signal officer who stood near him, "Can you say 'For God's sake' by signal?" When he answered that he could, Farragut ordered, "Then say to the *Lackawanna*, 'For God's sake, get out of the way and anchor!'" Farragut did not realize that, if there was any fault, it was equally divided, for the captain of the *Lackawanna* was doing what he could to obey the Admiral's orders to ram and sink the *Tennessee*. The signal officer[15] on the *Lackawanna* had made out only the first five words of the signal, "For God's sake get out—" when the

[15] The signal officer on the *Lackawanna* was Myron Adams, afterwards a well-known Congregational minister in Denver.

wind blew the flag in front of him and he missed the conclusion of the message. Thus the Captain of the *Lackawanna* escaped an unmerited rebuke.

The *Tennessee* had this one advantage in the battle: so many were the ships attacking her on all sides that she could fire in any direction and hit an enemy ship. The battle might have lasted much longer, for none of the shots of Farragut's ships had penetrated the iron-bound sides of the ram, had not the monitor *Chickasaw*, which had been hanging on the stern of the *Tennessee* for a good part of the fight, shot off her rudder chain so that she would no longer answer the helm. Buchanan, disabled by a splinter wound which broke his left leg at the knee, turned the ship over to Commander James G. Johnston. When Johnston reported that the *Tennessee* would no longer steer and that because of the loss of her smokestack steam could not be kept in the boilers, Buchanan told him to surrender, and the white flag went up.

In this singular engagement of one ram against thirteen Union ships, the losses on the *Tennessee* were only two killed and nine wounded. Some strange scenes were witnessed on the ships during the battle. On the deck of the *Galena* as she went into action stood a Negro with hands uplifted heavenward, singing a hymn. At the time the *Tennessee* and the *Hartford* were in close contact, each trying to ram the other, Captain Drayton saw the head and shoulders of Admiral Buchanan at an opening. Taking off the binoculars which were hanging from his neck, he hurled them at Buchanan, shouting as he did so, "You infernal traitor!" Thus did the aristocrat of South Carolina who fought for the North hail the aristocrat of Maryland who fought for the Confederacy. After passing the forts, Farragut made no effort to seize Mobile, for there was little to be gained by taking the city; when the forts surrendered soon after the battle and the blockade runners could no longer get up to the city, Mobile lost all importance.

When the white flag went up on the *Tennessee*, Farragut's

war career was ended. The Secretary of the Navy wanted him to take command of the North Atlantic Squadron in the contemplated attack on Fort Fisher at Wilmington, the last important port of call for the blockade runners; but Farragut asked to be excused from that duty. For two years and seven months the *Hartford* had been his home; the fierce battles he had fought and the weary months of blockade duty had taken their toll of his strength, rugged though his constitution was.

Six more years of life remained to him, and in these years he received the praise and plaudits of a grateful nation. On July 26, 1866, he was commissioned Admiral of the Navy. When he went abroad in command of the European Squadron, the nations of Europe vied with one another in bestowing honors upon him.

Farragut's relationship with some of his captains was far from happy. On the ground that whatever gallant deed an officer did in action, it was but his duty, Farragut was singularly sparing in praise in his reports to the Navy Department. In his report of the battle at New Orleans, he did the courageous Captain Theodorus Bailey, who led the fleet and played a hero's part in the fight, a grave injustice, saying that he himself had "led" the attack on the *Hartford*. After the battle, Farragut sent Bailey to Washington to give the Navy Department and the government an account of the victory. When Bailey appeared on the floor of the Senate, he was greeted with wild enthusiasm. But while the Senators were listening with rapt attention to Bailey's account of the battle, Welles, over at the Navy Department, was reading Farragut's report, which did not mention that Bailey on the *Cayuga* had led the fleet up the river. Immediately Welles dispatched a note to Senator Grimes, a member of the Senate Committee on Naval Affairs, asking him not to take any steps resulting from Captain Bailey's account of the passage of the fleet by the forts because there was a discrepancy between his report of the battle and that of Farragut which needed to be reconciled. In a few minutes Bailey would have received a vote of thanks and probably would have been the next rear admiral on the list. "Senator Grimes, in the kindness of his heart," writes Porter, "went to him and showed him Mr. Welles' letter, and told him that he had better go to the Department at once and set the matter right; that it was useless to remain in the Senate, that nothing further could be done, and Bailey went out crushed to the earth with mortification."

It was the letter of a noble, though deeply wounded, man that Captain Bailey wrote to Farragut in 1869. Speaking of Farragut's report, Bailey asked: "How could there have been a 'right' and left column practically, when I led my division to the attack and passage of the forts an hour before you lifted anchors on the *Hartford*, and your center division? What I did was done by your orders and inspiration, and to you the world has given the credit of the attack and its success, as fully as it gave Lord Nelson the credit of the battle of the Nile; but did it detract from his glory that the report of the battle described how it was fought, and the exact position of his own vessel, and those of his subordinates?"

The ill-feeling of some of the captains toward their commander was no doubt due to the corroding influence of jealousy at Farragut's success, first at New Orleans and then at Mobile Bay, and the praise heaped upon him. Writing to Fox, the Assistant Secretary, Farragut spoke of the tendency of some of his officers to adopt a defeatist attitude, how they "talk over the chances of the enemy's success, and they soon arrive at the conclusion that we must be captured. Poor Renshaw was a melancholy instance—I wrote him several letters to try and stimulate him to a sense of duty, but it only made him and his officers hate me." At the time of Farragut's humiliation, when the Confederate ram *Arkansas* ran through the two fleets above Vicksburg, Commander Renshaw wrote Captain David D. Porter: "Farragut is not fit to command, that's certain. He appears to be half crazy since last Tuesday [the day the *Arkansas* ran through the fleet]."

Captain James Alden of the *Brooklyn* was angry with Far-

ragut because, in a general order to the fleet after the Mobile
Bay battle calling upon all to give thanks, Farragut spoke of
"leading" the attack on the forts with the *Hartford*. When
he boarded the flagship and accosted the admiral, Alden asked,
"Is this so?," referring to Farragut's statement that he had led
the fleet in the battle. In an effort to conciliate the irate captain, Farragut asked him to step into his cabin with him. The
attempt to mollify Alden was not successful, for thereafter he
frequently spoke disparagingly of Farragut, and even went to
the amazing length of saying that Farragut had ordered the
Hartford to pass the *Brooklyn* on her port side, after that ship
had stopped, so as to use the *Brooklyn* as a shield of protection
from the fire of the batteries at Fort Morgan! Alden was still
more incensed when Farragut's official report was made public,
and at a gathering of officers refused to take Farragut's proffered
hand. Captain James E. Jouett, who commanded the *Metacomet*, which was lashed to the *Hartford*'s port side at Mobile
Bay, in his report spoke of the *Brooklyn* "backing down the line
of battle." Alden, who was very sensitive on this point and who
in his report wrote only of maneuvering his ship clear of the
torpedoes he supposed were in his path, demanded that Jouett
explain the meaning of his statement. Jouett replied that he had
stated "a well-known fact." Alden answered that his reply
was not satisfactory, and again demanded his meaning. Jouett
then referred him to a dictionary for a definition of his words.

Captain Thomas Craven, brother of the Tunis Craven who
went down with the *Tecumseh*, gave Captain Alden the same
kind of treatment that Alden had afforded Farragut. Craven
was one of a circle of officers when Alden appeared in their midst
and offered his hand to Craven, who stepped back with his hands
behind his back. Alden then bowed and begged pardon for offering his hand. Craven said, "Captain Alden, you have much more
than that to ask my pardon for." Craven had been brought before a court martial for declining a challenge of the Confederate
ram *Stonewall* off the coast of Spain in March of 1865, and was

found guilty of failing to do all he could to destroy that vessel. Craven felt that Alden's testimony at the trial had injured him.

Some of those who served under Farragut thought him lacking in feeling. One of his gunners said that after a battle he would walk along the deck seeming not to see, or paying no heed to, the dead and wounded, his whole attention fixed on the wounds of his flagship, ever dear to his heart. But another witness, Quartermaster Knowles, tells of Farragut weeping when he saw the dead laid out on the deck of the *Hartford* the morning after the battle.

Although Farragut always had the confidence of the seamen he led into battle, he never inspired the devotion of his officers as Du Pont did. He had much in common with Grant, who never won the affection of his soldiers as McClellan won the hearts of the soldiers of the Army of the Potomac. But like Grant, Farragut always went ahead, never backward; and, like Grant, he thought more of what he could do to damage the enemy than of what the enemy might do to injure him.

Farragut really belonged to the "wooden age" of warships. The victories he had won and the dangers he had survived on the deck of his beloved *Hartford* gave him high confidence in wooden ships. He held the opinion that, while a hostile shot might go clear through a wooden ship, it would inflict less damage than a shot which penetrated an ironclad. As late in the war as March, 1863, writing to Assistant Secretary Fox about the capture of the *Indianola* on her way back to Vicksburg after a raid up the Red River, Farragut said: "I confess that the capture of the *Indianola* by two common river boats, with no one killed, has astounded me. I never thought much of Iron Clads, but my opinion of them is declining daily. At any rate I am willing to do the little fighting left to me, as I told you before, in the wooden ships." The events of another year, however, modified somewhat Farragut's low estimate of ironclads, for we find him telling Fox that he wants some of them with his fleet when he goes into Mobile Bay.

Admiral George Dewey, who as a lieutenant was with Farragut at New Orleans and Port Hudson, said that to serve under him was an education and an inspiration. When Dewey spoke in 1900 at the unveiling of the memorial stone marking the birthplace of Farragut on the banks of the Tennessee River, he said:

I consider it a great honor and opportunity to pay my homage to the memory of Admiral Farragut, that great Naval Commander—in my opinion the greatest in the annals of our country. This opinion I have formed, not by reading of his gallant deeds, but from personal contacts with him. Having served in his squadron, under his immediate command, though I was but a young man, I am proud to say that Farragut was my friend. Many years ago I took him for my special example, and in all the important epochs of my life, particularly during the most recent years, I have always thought, before deciding upon a course of action when a crisis was pending, "What would Farragut have done under similar circumstances?"

Nelson took command of the British Mediterranean Fleet in July of 1803. It was two years lacking ten days before he set foot on shore again. In those two years he had vainly sought the French fleet in the Mediterranean, through the Atlantic to the West Indies and back again. One of his officers, writing to a friend about the hardships of those two years at sea, the monotony of the blockade off Toulon, the calms, the storms, concluded with these words, "But we had Nelson with us!" That was the way Farragut's sailors felt about him. The wearisome blockade duty in the hot waters of the Gulf; the tortuous voyages up the fever-haunted Mississippi to Vicksburg and back; the desperate night battles at New Orleans and Port Hudson; driving the *Hartford* through the mine-sown waters of Mobile Bay; the fight with the ram *Tennessee*—all this was of a nature to try the stoutest hearts; but all this the men on Farragut's ships willingly endured, for they had Farragut with them.

III

FOOTE

"HE PRAYS like a saint and fights like the devil." That was the comment of Admiral Francis Gregory on the character of Admiral Andrew Hull Foote. No one was ever more determined in battle than Foote. One look at that granite countenance reveals determination and indomitable courage. Among the chief personalities of the Army and Navy during the war, only the countenance of George Thomas, the "Rock of Chickamauga," shows a comparable iron will and strength of character. As for his saintliness, it would be no mistake to call Foote the "Stonewall" Jackson of the Navy.

The Navy has produced more saints and even more scientists than the Army. Among the scientists have been Matthew F. Maury, the great oceanographer, whose ocean charts still show the way to mariners; John M. Brooke, rebuilder of the *Merrimac* and inventor of the Brooke gun; and John A. Dahlgren who gave the Navy, and the Army too, the gun that bears his name and which spoke with authority on the deck of many a warship and on many a battlefield. As for the saints, although the armies had their O. O. Howard, the "Christian Soldier," their "Stonewall" Jackson, and their Robert E. Lee, the high officers of the Navy, in far greater proportion than in the Army, were men of devout faith and deep religious experience. In any sketch of Farragut or Du Pont (and, to a lesser degree, Porter), or such ship captains as Winslow, John Rodgers, and Percival Drayton, this fact must be taken into account. This tradition of godliness

78

among the naval officers appears at a later day in Admiral Alfred T. Mahan, for the man who wrote the famous work, *The Influence of Sea Power on History*, also wrote *The Harvest Within*, a book of meditations on the Christian life. In this respect, the leaders of the Navy in the Civil War illustrate the truth of what the Psalmist said: "They that go down to the sea in ships, they that do business in great waters, these see the works of the Lord and His wonders in the deep."

In nobility of character Admiral Foote stands at the head of all the officers who served in the Union Navy during the Civil War. His ability as a naval commander was equal to the strength of his character. When Admiral Du Pont was in command of the Philadelphia Navy Yard in January of 1861 and Foote was executive of the New York Navy Yard, Du Pont, troubled over the loss of the Navy Yard at Pensacola, Florida, wrote to Foote, who had taken measures to prevent any similar happening at the yard which he commanded: "I see you had no idea of being surprised by mobs. Oh, why was not someone like you at Pensacola?" And so one might have said when the Norfolk Navy Yard was abjectly abandoned, or when Fort Sumter was surrendered after little more than a "technical" resistance—"Oh, why was someone like Foote not there?" But Footes are rare; and they cannot serve everywhere.

Andrew Hull Foote was born at New Haven, Conneticut on September 12th, 1806. His father was a man of note in Connecticut, serving a term as Governor and as a United States Senator. He lives in history as the senator who introduced the "Foot[1] Resolution," in December of 1829. It was an apparently harmless resolution, asking that the Committee on Public Lands inquire into the expediency of selling certain lands, but was taken by some as unfavorable to the South and slavery interests, and to the advantage of the East. It led to the great debate between Webster and Robert Hayne of South Carolina. It was in one of his replies to Hayne that Webster delivered the now

[1] The admiral added an *e* to the family name.

famous sentence, "Liberty and Union, one and inseparable, now and forever." Senator Foot himself took no part in the debate which consumed the time of the Senate for several months; yet there was a certain fitness that the admiral who played so prominent a part in maintaining the Union in a war then twenty-one years in the future should have been the son of the senator whose resolution precipitated the debate in which Webster's undying phrase was heard for the first time.

When Foote was twelve years of age his family removed to the ancestral home in the village of Cheshire, thirteen miles from New Haven. There he was a student in the Episcopal Academy, and had for one of his schoolmates Gideon Welles, the future Secretary of the Navy. The friendship thus begun was destined to play an important part in Foote's career. Through the influence of his father he secured an appointment to West Point, where he spent part of a year. But his real love had always been for the sea, and in 1822 he was appointed acting midshipman in the navy. His age of 16 was somewhat greater than that of most midshipmen of that day, and in sharp contrast with that of Farragut, who received his appointment when only nine. His preference was due, in part, to the fact that as a lad he had seen the ships of his father, who for a time was in the shipping business with the West Indies, come and go at New Haven; but chiefly, no doubt, to the fact that his imagination and ambition, like that of many another youth, had been stirred by the exploits of the famous sea captains, Lawrence, Perry, Truxton, MacDonough, Bainbridge, Decatur, Hull, and the elder Porter, of whom all except the first three were still alive and in active service when Foote entered the Navy as a midshipman.

His first cruise was on the schooner *Grampus*, which served with Commodore Porter's fleet in hunting down pirates in the West Indies. When his father parted with him on the deck of the *Grampus* he charged him to be faithful to the training he had received in his home, and always to remember his duty to his country and to his God. Foote had the usual world-wide experiences of the young naval officers of that day, serving in the Pacific, the Mediterranean, and the Atlantic, and in 1839 sailed around the world in the sloop of war *John Adams*.

It was five years after he entered the Navy that Foote, then cruising in the West Indies, had a religious experience which changed the whole tenor of his life. In a letter to his mother he tells the story of the change that came over him, saying, "You may discharge your mind from anxiety about your wayward son." A lieutenant on his ship, the *Natchez*, spoke to him one day on religious subjects, but Foote "bluffed him off," saying that he aimed to be honorable and upright, and that was all the religion he needed. But some weeks later, when the *Natchez* was riding quietly at anchor on a beautiful Caribbean moonlight night, the same officer, who happened to be on duty with him, spoke to him again about religion, and with such wisdom and earnestness that his "knees for the first time bowed to his Maker." After many days of mental agitation, he found peace and satisfaction and made the firm resolve that "henceforth, under all circumstances, he would act for God."

The impression and conviction made upon Foote that night on the *Natchez* remained with him throughout his life. We hear the echo of it in his letters and journals which abound in prayers, confessions, resolutions, and vows, and in the sermons he occasionally preached on his ships. After he had been for some time in the navy, Foote's Christian convictions raised doubts in his mind as to whether he ought to continue in a service which might lead to war and the killing of his fellow men. He confided doubts to his father, who asked him if he did not think a navy necessary for the country. "Certainly," answered Foote, "the seas must be policed." "Then," replied his father, "should the navy be in the hands of good or bad men?" "Of good men," replied Foote. This effectively resolved his doubts.

Foote's religious life expressed itself in two very practical ways. One was his zeal for the suppression of the slave trade. In 1849 he was ordered to the West Africa station in command of the brig *Perry*. There he saw with his own eyes the horrors of "The Middle Passage" [2] and conceived a strong detestation of slavery and the slave trade, which he described as the "matured villainy of the world." A good portion of the slave trade was carried on in American-built vessels sold to slavers on the West African coast. The difficulties and problems which confronted Foote in the discharge of his duties and in dealing with slavers who took refuge under the American flag may be seen in the following incident. In June of 1850, the *Perry* was cruising off the African coast when a large ship was seen standing in for the land. The ship had the legend *Martha, New York* painted on her stern; and when the *Perry*, which had no colors flying, drew up, the *Martha* shortened sail and hoisted the American flag. Foote sent a lieutenant to board her; but as the boat was rounding the stern of the slaver, officers on her deck, seeing by the uniform of the lieutenant that his ship was an American cruiser, raised the Brazilian flag. When the boarding officer asked for the ship's papers, the captain of the *Martha* denied having any log or papers. At the same time, observers on the *Perry* saw a desk thrown overboard, and Foote sent a second boat to recover it. In the desk were papers which identified the captain as an American citizen and showed that three-fifths of the vessel was owned by another American living in Rio de Janeiro.

Although no slaves were on board, all the equipment for caring for and feeding them on an ocean passage was found: four hundred spoons, a slave deck, and a hundred and fifty barrels of farina. When seized by Foote, the captain of the slaver claimed that he could not be searched or seized when under the flag of Brazil. But when Foote told him that he could be seized as a pirate for sailing without papers, the captain confessed that his

[2] The term "Middle Passage" arose from the fact that many of the slavers came from English ports to West Africa, where they took aboard their human cargo, and then sailed for the West Indies or United States ports, where they landed the slaves and then returned to an English port. Thus the voyage in between, from Africa to America, came to be spoken of as "The Middle Passage."

ship was a slaver, and that on that very night he had expected to take on board eighteen hundred slaves! Foote put the crew in irons, and sent the *Martha* to New York under a prize crew, where she was condemned as a slaver. For this seizure Foote received the congratulations of the British slave trade commissioner at Loanda, who told him that the *Martha* was the largest slaver seen on that coast for many years, and that her capture and the sending of all her crew to the United States was one of the heaviest blows the slave traffic had received. In his book, *Africa and The American Flag,* Foote thus indicted the traffic in slaves: "If there is anything on earth which, for revolting, filthy atrocity, might make the devil wonder and hell recognize its own likeness, it was on one of the decks of the old slavers." Foote took great interest in the American Colonization Society, the object of which was to take the Negroes back to Africa. This movement was supported by many prominent men who were not Abolitionists, with Princeton as one of its chief centers. But He who rules the destinies of men and nations had decreed that the "offense of slavery" should be atoned for by a far greater price than that of transporting the slaves back to Africa.

The other way in which Foote's religious conviction expressed itself was in his advocacy of temperance. In 1843 he made a cruise of two years in the frigate *Cumberland,* commanded by his firm friend, Captain Joseph Smith. When the *Cumberland* was taking on stores at Boston for her long cruise, some of the sailors tapped a barrel of whiskey and became drunk, insulting and attacking one of the officers. This incident moved Foote to start a total abstinence society on the ship, commencing with the officers. In this he was encouraged by Captain Smith. Every seaman but one agreed to surrender his grog ration for its money equivalent. Thus the *Cumberland* became the first temperance ship in the Navy. In an address he made to the crew two years later, Foote said: "Look around, and we see ourselves in a ship where that great enemy of man—the enemy of hopes and happiness—ardent spirits, is abolished. Who would have believed a man thirty years ago, had he predicted that a ship, a frigate—flagship, too, of the squadron—would cruise a year without the grog tub, and that liberty in almost every port, and money every month, has been the case in this ship? But the credit of taking the lead in this reform, this matter which will prove so great a blessing to so many generations of seamen, will ever belong to the crew of the *Cumberland*." The reform which Foote instituted finally became the law of the Navy in 1862, when the grog ration was abolished.[3]

Like his friend Dahlgren, and Winslow, too, Foote suffered for a time from an attack of opthalmia, brought on by boat duty off Egypt and the glare of the Mediterranean. In a letter of encouragement to his old shipmate, Dahlgren wrote to Foote: "I regret to see the desponding tone of your letter. Five or six years passed with me in mental torture that no one can understand save a fellow sufferer; and yet my eyes now are so unexpectedly changed, that last summer I dispensed with glasses for the first time in ten years. They are still weak, and unequal to much exertion; but think how much better." About the same time bluff old Commodore Smith wrote him: "I trust the chastisement will be a lesson to you not to carry things to excess, as you, in your zeal to do good and work righteousness, are, or have been, prone to do. I may speak plainly now that you are on your pins again, and say I fear you have been a victim to your 'water cure.' Bless God for His unbounded mercies. You have a new lease of life, and have much more to see of this wicked world than you have seen, and more good to do than you have done."

Much to his disappointment, Foote failed to get into the Mexican War, being stationed throughout at the Charlestown Navy Yard at Boston; but in 1856, while on the China station he

---

[3] Fox, the Assistant Secretary of the Navy, was also a leader in the abolition of the grog ration. The officers' wine mess existed until 1914, when it was abolished by Josephus Daniels, Wilson's Secretary of the Navy.

saw more real action and fighting than he could possibly have experienced in the Mexican War. When England and China were at war, Commodore Armstrong sent Foote with the flagship *Portsmouth* and two other vessels to protect American property at Whampoa, some miles below Canton. In all his actions Foote was careful to observe a neutral attitude in the fighting between the Chinese and the English. When it was brought to his attention that an American flag had been carried with the Union Jack in an attack by the English on a Chinese position, he published a circular stating that the American flag was thus used without his sanction and that he strongly disapproved.

In order to avoid being drawn into the quarrel between the Chinese and the English, Commodore Armstrong in November, 1856 ordered Foote to withdraw his ships and men from the vicinity of Whampoa. While he was thus engaged, two of his boats were twice fired upon by one of the Chinese Barrier Forts, despite the fact that the American flag was clearly displayed. Foote was no appeaser; one can discern that by looking at his countenance. When no satisfaction or apology was forthcoming from the Chinese, Foote with a party of marines and seamen stormed the forts on three successive days and destroyed them. These forts were formidable works with granite walls seven feet thick and mounting 176 guns, some of which were served in the engagements by European-trained gunners.

If such a situation were to arise today, a naval officer would request permission of his government before taking similar measures. But it was the opinion of Foote's superior, Commodore Armstrong, and that of the Secretary of the Navy when he learned of the attack on the forts, that Foote's quick and courageous action had won respect for the American flag and had prevented much more serious fighting. In the attack Foote lost forty men; the Chinese lost several hundred. One of the officers under Foote's command at the attack on the Barrier Forts was Commander Henry H. Bell of the *San Jacinto*, who was to be Farragut's fleet captain in the attack on the New Orleans forts in 1862. A Navy chaplain took Foote to task for launching an unwarranted attack upon a friendly nation; the firing by the forts on the American flag, he said, was only what might have been expected in view of the hostilities then raging between the Chinese and the English and the indiscriminate hatred of the Chinese for all foreigners. To this letter Foote sent a blistering reply, pointing out that French ships and those of other nationalities had been passing the Barrier Forts unmolested, and informed the chaplain that his views, "where the honor of the country's flag was involved," were "as crude as they were perverse."

When the war began, Foote was acting commandant of the New York Navy Yard. The command of any navy yard at that critical hour was a post of great importance, and Foote took effective measures for the safety of the yard and the ships located there. He was promoted to captain in June of 1861; in August he was ordered to relieve Commander John Rodgers in command of naval operations on the western waters, and ordered to cooperate fully and freely with General John C. Frémont, then in command of the army in that area. The importance of the post to which Foote had now been named cannot be overestimated.

In the history of war there have been able organizers who failed as commanders in action; others who were distinguished in battle but poor in organization. It was the general opinion that Farragut was much greater as a fighter, a magnetic leader in battle, than as an organizer. Porter was another great commander in battle, but he was also a splendid organizer. Likewise Foote; he was courageous and determined in battle, and also able as an organizer. During the entire war no officer did a more important job of organization than Foote, the creator of the western flotilla. The significance of Foote's work as the organizer of the Mississippi squadron can be measured only by the part played by the gunboats in the western area of the war. The great rivers which traverse the western states, the Mississippi, the Tennes-

see, the Arkansas, and the Red were more important as lines of
operation for the armies than even the railroads; a railroad could
be cut or a bridge blown up by a small raiding party; but effectually to cut and block a river line of communications was well-
nigh impossible. Moreover, in wide areas there were no railroads,
and what roads existed were few and poor. Most of the food, war
material and other supplies for the armies had to be transported
by water. Therefore, the control of the rivers was the first condition of a successful campaign. Where the army would take a
day or more in marching to a desired position, the gunboats
could move the same distance in a few hours. It is no exaggeration to say that the gunboats, and the transports which they
convoyed, armed, clothed, and fed the armies of the west. A
single gunboat was regarded by naval and military authorities as
worth a whole brigade of troops. The Confederate naval historian, Scharf, has written that without the Union ironclads, "all
the armies of the Great West would not have been able to have
regained and held the navigation of the Mississippi River." We
shall see the truth of this demonstrated in this chapter. Even if
he had never fired a gun in action, Foote's creation of the river
flotilla would have ranked his name high in the roll of those who
on river, land, or sea led in the overthrow of the Confederacy
and the maintenance of the Union.

Soon after the fall of Fort Sumter, James B. Eads, ship and
bridge builder, was summoned to Washington, where he signed
a contract to build seven gunboats for the western rivers. The
vessels were 175 feet long, 51½ feet wide, drew 7 feet of water,
and had a speed of 9 miles an hour. They carried 13 heavy guns,
4 on either side, 3 on the bow, and 2 on the stern. The sides
of the vessels, which sloped at an angle of 35 degrees, were unar-
mored, save for a patch abreast the boilers. But there were 2½
inches of iron on the bow slope, backed by 24 inches of oak.
Their names were *St. Louis* (afterwards changed to *Baron de
Kalb*), *Cincinnati, Pittsburg, Mound City, Louisville, Cairo,*
and *Carondelet.* In addition, Eads converted two snagboats into

powerful armored vessels, similar to, but larger than, the City-class gunboats. They became the *Benton* and the *Essex*.

Within two weeks four thousand men in different parts of the country were engaged in building the gunboats and their parts. Neither the sacredness of the Sabbath nor the shadow of night was permitted to interrupt the work. The men were promised a generous bonus if they stayed on the job until the ships were completed. On October 12th, 1861, the first of the seven ships was launched at Carondelet, Missouri, just forty-five days after her keel was laid. The contract had stipulated that the gunboats were to be ready at Cairo, Illinois by October 10th, but they were not all delivered until the latter part of November. This was because of the Government's delay in paying for the work and the material used. Eads spent a large part of his own fortune, accumulated in the salvage business, and was aided by patriotic friends. The gunboats with which Foote took Fort Henry and attacked Fort Donelson were still the property of their builder at the time of these battles and when the *Carondelet* ran the batteries at Island No. 10 in April, 1862, she was still unpaid for. Without the skill and the splendid sacrificial zeal of Eads, the four different commanders of the Mississippi flotilla, Foote, Davis, Porter, and Lee, could not have won their victories.

When Foote arrived at St. Louis to take command in September, 1861, the river flotilla consisted of three wooden vessels which had been purchased and armed as gunboats by Foote's predecessor, Commander John Rodgers. Like all naval officers, Foote would have preferred a command at sea, but his high sense of duty led him to throw all his energies into the creation of the river fleet. Although Eads was the builder of the gunboats, the work of arming and equipping them and organizing their crews fell to Foote. His most difficult task was to man the ships with trained and efficient crews. We find him reduced to the straits of hoping (in vain) that, if Halleck gave permission, Grant would let him have "thirty or forty men of intemper-

ate habits from the army." The men's pay was almost always far
in arrears, and on occasions Foote out of his own pocket loaned
money to the officers for travel expenses.

At this stage of the war the river flotilla was under the
general direction of the army. It was galling to Foote to be
told that he must vacate a certain dockyard, or to have a colonel
order one of his gunboats on a mission. When Halleck took command in the Mississippi area it did not take Foote long to discover that he was a "military imbecile," and he did not hesitate
to tell the Secretary of the Navy that "little progress could be
made towards taking Vicksburg, opening the Mississippi and
subduing the insurrection while Halleck was in active command
of the Western Department." In a confidential letter to Fox,
Foote wrote: "I only wish that you could have spent one day
here for the last six weeks, as no imagination can fancy what it
is to collect materials and fit out western gunboats with western men without a navy yard, in the west, where no stores are
to be had." When at length the squadron had been built,
manned, and armed, and had done its valiant work at Forts Henry
and Donelson, Foote wrote to Fox: "I would not therefore
again pass through the mental agony and weary labor of the
months of preparation, and going into the first and second
fight half-manned, and shifting crews from disabled to sound
vessels, for all the applause which this world can give; but thanks
be to God who giveth us the victory, it is now all over, with
the addition of ten years added to my age of constitution."

In command of the Confederate forces in Kentucky and
Tennessee was Albert Sidney Johnston, at that time considered
the ablest general of the South. When he fell in the battle at
Shiloh, Tennessee, on April 6th, 1862, in what seemed the moment of great victory, Jefferson Davis said, "The fortunes of a
country hung by a single thread of the life that was yielded
on the field of Shiloh." However, Johnston's management of his
troops did not measure up to the high estimate in which he was
held. The Confederate line of defense stretched from Colum-

bus, Kentucky, on the Mississippi, to Bowling Green, in the same State, where Johnston had his headquarters. Two great rivers, both tributaries of the Ohio, form natural avenues of invasion into the territory occupied by the Confederate forces. One of these is the Tennessee, which rises in eastern Tennessee, a few miles above Knoxville, traverses northern Alabama, bites off the corner of Mississippi, returns to Tennessee, and finishes its six-hundred-and-fifty mile journey at Paducah, Kentucky, where it joins the Ohio. On the banks of this stream the three important battles at Fort Henry, Shiloh, and Chattanooga were fought and won by the Union forces. The other avenue of invasion is the Cumberland River, which rises in eastern Kentucky and by a long and devious course of almost seven hundred miles flows into the Ohio at Smithland, a few miles above Paducah.

Both Union and Confederate leaders recognized the importance of these waterways in the struggle for dominion in that part of the west. The Confederates early erected Fort Henry on the Tennessee. It was poorly located, on low-lying ground, and subject to flood at high water. Another, and a much more formidable work, Fort Donelson, was erected on the Cumberland River, a few miles below the sleepy county seat of Dover. Both forts were just south of the Kentucky border and about seventy miles northwest of Nashville, the capital of Tennessee. Early in January Brigadier General Ulysses S. Grant at Cairo, Illinois, sent his best officer, C. F. Smith, up the Tennessee to make a reconnaissance in the vicinity of Fort Henry. Smith returned with the report that the capture of Fort Henry was quite practicable. Thereupon Grant wrote to General Halleck in St. Louis, asking for an interview in which he could present his plan of campaign to drive the Confederates not only out of Fort Henry but out of the entire State of Kentucky. This opportunity was granted him, "but not graciously," Grant wrote in his *Memoirs*. It was an unhappy and disappointing occasion. "I was received," he said, "with so little cordiality that I perhaps stated the object of my visit with less clearness than I might have done, and I had not uttered many sentences before I was cut short as if my plan was preposterous. I returned to Cairo very much crestfallen." This was only one of many slights and affronts which Grant was to experience at the hands of Halleck.

Although "crestfallen" by his shabby treatment, Grant was not discouraged as to the great enterprise he had in mind. He conferred with Foote and, finding that Foote concurred in his own opinion that Fort Henry could and should be seized, he telegraphed Halleck on January 28th, 1862, "With permission, I will take Fort Henry, on the Tennessee and establish and hold a large camp there." At the same time Foote sent a similar dispatch. Whether it was Grant's importunity, or the opinion and request of Foote which finally persuaded Halleck, is not clear; but on the 1st of February Grant received instructions to move against Fort Henry. The next day the expedition was on its way.

With seventeen thousand troops on the transports, and Foote's gunboats leading the way, the expedition moved slowly up the flooded Tennessee. So strong was the current that Henry Walke's *Carondelet*, the ship which saw more fighting in the war than almost any other, was swept a mile down the swollen river, although both her anchors were down and she had a full head of steam on. Yet the flood, though it made it difficult for the ships of the fleet to maintain their position, also conferred a favor on them by acting as a minesweeper, carrying away the mines which the Confederates had planted in the river.

Fort Henry stood at a bend in the Tennessee which gave the batteries a direct line of fire downstream at any craft coming up the river. There were some three thousand troops at the fort under the command of General Lloyd Tilghman, and more held in reserve outside the fortifications in case of need. In order to get his troops as near as possible to the fort without coming under the fire of its guns, Grant boarded the *Essex*, commanded by William D. Porter, oldest brother of David Porter, and asked him to approach the fort and draw its fire. He wished to land his troops, if possible, south of a stream emptying into the Tennessee. The *Essex* had gone a short distance beyond the mouth of the stream when one of the batteries opened fire, the shot falling far short of the ship. Grant had decided that he could safely bring the troops up that far, and the *Essex* was just turning to go back when the fort opened fire again, this time sending a shot which barely missed Grant and Porter where they were standing together on the deck. The *Essex* immediately put on steam to get out of range, and the troops were landed, not south of the stream, as Grant had hoped, but north of it.

Grant had asked that the gunboats open fire on the fort at 11:30 on the morning of the 6th of February; the troops were scheduled to attack at the same time. But roads which the rains had turned into quagmires and little brooks which had become raging torrents delayed the army's march. Foote waited until 12:30, an hour after the appointed time, and then, with the *Cincinnati* for his flagship, went into action by himself, opening fire at a distance of four hundred yards. The big, well-aimed guns wrought havoc in the fort, dismounting the guns in the batteries, and in short order the white flag went up. The river flotilla had won a notable victory without assistance from the army. When General Tilghman surrendered, however, Foote took less than a hundred prisoners, for before the engagement opened the Southern commander had sent nearly all his troops across country to Fort Donelson on the Cumberland, eleven miles to the east.

In this brief but decisive engagement the only serious loss was on the *Essex*, which had forty-eight killed and wounded. In the midst of the bombardment a shot from the fort pierced and exploded the boilers of the *Essex*. At the time of the explosion Porter, who was standing in front of the boilers, was badly burned. He rushed at once for a nearby porthole, intending to throw himself into the rushing river. This would have meant as speedy, though less agonizing, a death as that from the scalding steam of the ruptured boilers. He managed to get through the porthole, and was standing on a narrow ledge near the water line when a seaman, seeing his commander's peril, caught him around the waist and, assisted by another seaman, carried him to a place of safety. Meanwhile, the *Essex* had drifted far down the river. When the Second Master of the ship reported that the white flag was waving over the fort, Porter, despite his agony, raised himself on his elbow and called for three cheers.

The fall of Fort Henry (which the Union army renamed Fort Foote) necessitated the abandonment of Bowling Green, the eastern anchor of the Confederate line of defense.[4] General Johnston then made a strategic blunder which soon brought disaster. He announced to the Confederate authorities that he was going to "fight for Nashville at Fort Donelson." Even had he sent his whole force to Donelson, its defense against Grant's rapidly growing army, with Foote's gunboats controlling the Tennessee and the northern part of the Cumberland River, would have been most difficult. But, instead of sending his main force to Donelson, or withdrawing the troops from there and falling back on Nashville, he divided his army, sending half of it to Nashville and the other half to reinforce the garrison at Donelson. In common with most of his contemporaries, Grant had expected Johnston to prove himself the most formidable opponent the Confederacy would produce. Later he changed his opinion. "I once wrote," he said, "that nothing occurred in his brief command of an army to prove or disprove the high estimate that had been placed on his military ability; but after studying the orders and dispatches of Johnston, I am compelled to materi-

[4] After the victory Foote sent his three wooden gunboats up the Tennessee as far as Muscle Shoals, Alabama. They destroyed shipping, military stores, and the only railroad bridge connecting Bowling Green with Columbus.

ally modify my views of that officer's qualifications as a soldier. My judgment now is that he was vacillating and undecided in his actions."

If Johnston's division of his army was unfortunate, his choice of the senior officers at Fort Donelson was equally unhappy. The commanding officer was General John B. Floyd, a prominent Virginian, one-time governor of that state and son of a governor, but as late as December of 1860 a strong opponent of secession. When Buchanan became president he appointed Floyd Secretary of War. In this office he was under suspicion of having sent an undue proportion of arms and munitions to United States military stations in the South. He was charged also with irregularities in a transaction with the Department of the Interior, and for this Buchanan demanded his resignation. The second in command at the fort was General Gideon Pillow. He claimed credit for the nomination and election in 1844 of President James K. Polk, who appointed him a brigadier general of volunteers in the Mexican War. Grant, who had served with him in the Mexican War, held him in such contempt as a military man that the day after the fall of Fort Henry he made a reconnaissance with some of his staff and a small body of cavalry and infantry up to the very defenses of Fort Donelson. Although Floyd was the commanding general, Grant was sure that he would "yield to Pillow's pretensions" and let Pillow direct matters; therefore he felt it safe to march within gunshot of any entrenchments the Southerner was given to hold.

The only real soldier among the chief officers at the fort was Simon Bolivar Buckner, who had been Grant's classmate at West Point. When Grant arrived in New York from the Pacific coast in 1854, without funds and under a cloud, Buckner befriended him and gave him money to reach his home. Grant never forgot that kindness. After the battle, Grant sought him out on the headquarters boat and, taking him aside so that none would notice, offered him his purse. Buckner had been offered a brigadier generalship by both Lincoln and the Confederacy. Oddly enough, it was only when his own State of Kentucky declared for the Union that he espoused the cause of the South.[5]

A few days before the attack on Fort Donelson, Grant held a singular council of war. He sent a staff officer to each division and brigade commander, saying, "General Grant sends his compliments, and requests to see you this afternoon on his boat, the headquarters steamer, *New Uncle Sam*." It was a strange council of war. General Lew Wallace, who was present in command of a division, said that during the meeting "Grant smoked, but never said a word. Each officer retired when he was ready, but knowing that the march would take place the next day, probably in the morning." [6]

On the afternoon of February 14th, the defenders of Fort Donelson, looking down the river from the high bluffs on which the batteries were posted, saw pillars of black smoke ascending skyward. Soon Foote's flotilla came into view. Squat, ugly, and shapeless were these monsters of the river; yet within their black hulls was packed tremendous power. The width of the gunboats, floating on the smooth, unruffled waters of the river, gave their batteries almost the stability of land forts. As they steamed slowly up the tawny Cumberland, they invaded a vast solitude. A profound silence, unbroken save for the flight of startled waterfowl, brooded over the wilderness.[7]

Suddenly, as Grant and his staff watched from the top of a hill, there was a burst of flame from the bow of one of the

[5] Although the battle at Okinawa in World War II was fought eighty-three years after Buckner surrendered to Grant, it was his son by a second marriage, Simon Bolivar, who commanded the American troops and fell in that battle.

[6] Wallace, Lew, "The Capture of Fort Donelson," *Battles and Leaders of the Civil War*, I, 404, 405. In his *Autobiography* Wallace gives quite a different account of this council of war.

[7] Just fifty years after the battle at Donelson, standing on the deck of a river steamboat on a beautiful April Sabbath morning, I was impressed by that same silence and solitude. In the distance, as the steamboat rounded a bend of the river, the nation's flag appeared above the tree tops, keeping watch over the graves of boys from Illinois, Wisconsin, Indiana, and other western states, who there "adventured their lives" on the high places of the field.

gunboats as Foote's flotilla went into action. It was not long, however, before both Foote and Grant discovered that attacking Donelson was a far different matter from attacking Fort Henry. This was due in part to the series of natural fortifications sur-rounding the fort on the land side, augmented by an abatis of fallen trees, with limbs trimmed to a spear-like point; but chiefly to the high elevation of the batteries which, in contrast with the low-lying batteries at Fort Henry, crowned the river bluffs and made it difficult for the guns of the ships to reach and penetrate them. Slowly the gunboats came on until they were only four hundred yards from the fort. The four ships leading the attack, line abreast, were from left to right, *Louisville*, *St. Louis* (flag-ship), *Pittsburg*, and *Carondelet*. Because of the navy's victory at Fort Henry, there was apprehension on the part of the fort's defenders and confidence on the part of Foote and Grant. To his great disappointment, Grant saw the Union gunboats one by one drop out of control down the river and drift out of action. The Confederate gunners had fled from the lower batteries where the guns of the fleet had created havoc; but on the heights the guns were taking a heavy toll of the ironclads, every gunner picking out one of the four gunboats and concentrating his fire upon it throughout the battle.

On the *Carondelet* a 128-pounder smashed the pilot house to pieces. In the excitement on board a rifled gun was loaded too hastily and exploded. When one of the gunners, more scared than hurt, recovered consciousness and saw the gun lying in pieces on the deck, he heard a cry that the ship was on fire, and ran to the pumps. There, two shots killed four men around him. As they were borne past him, three with their heads off, the sight sickened and horrified him. The master's mate ordered him and those who had accompanied him back to their station. Told that the gun had burst and that the upper deck was on fire, the mate said, "Never mind the fire; go back to your quar-ters!"

The three other gunboats were faring no better than the

Carondelet. The *Louisville,* disabled by a shot which carried
away her rudder chains, became unmanageable and drifted out of
action. The *Pittsburg,* also in trouble, in trying to turn and get
away struck the *Carondelet* and broke her rudder. The flagship
St. Louis was a chief target for the artillerists on the bluffs. In
the midst of the battle the flag officer went into the pilot house
to see that the ship was maintained in the proper position. There
he found the pilot, nervous and excited under the heavy fire
directed against the ship. Foote had just laid his hand on the
pilot's shoulder to encourage him, when a shot crashed into the
pilot house, killing the pilot and painfully wounding the flag
officer in the left foot and left arm. At the same moment a
misdirected shot fired at the fort by the *Tyler,* one of the wooden
gunboats which had been kept in the rear, smashed the steering
gear of the *St. Louis,* and the flagship went whirling out of action. As the *Carondelet* was falling back, but bow-on to the fort
and maintaining its fire, the shots from the fort, now concen-
trated on her, could plainly be seen skipping and ricocheting
over the surface of the river before striking the ship. Whenever
the gun captain at the starboard bow gun saw a shot coming
over the water, he would shout "Down!" This warning saved
many lives, although some in a spirit of bravado disregarded the
warning cry and were decapitated.

The hills and forests about Fort Donelson were silent once
more. There was sorrow on the river and there was sorrow on
the land. For the unusual spring weather had suddenly turned to
intense cold, only ten degrees above zero; woods and river were
swept with a hail of sleet. In the Union lines, where no fires
could be lighted and the men were without shelter, the suffering
was intense. On the march over from Fort Henry in the bright
sun and the balmy air, the improvident soldiers had thrown away
their overcoats and blankets as needless impediments.[8] There

[8] Discarding heavy clothing on a march is often spoken of as a piece of folly
committed only by new and inexperienced soldiers. But that was not so. An
aged Virginian, whose house stood on a hilltop close to Germanna Ford, where

was little cheer for Grant or Foote, for the soldiers or the sailors that cold and stormy night.

The repulse of the fleet, however, turned out not so serious as it at first appeared, for none of the gunboats had suffered major damage. What necessitated their withdrawal was injury to their steering apparatus, and that could soon be repaired. The *Carondelet,* under Henry Walke, the first in the fight and the last out of it, sustained the heaviest losses, five killed and twenty-eight wounded; the total casualties in the fleet were eleven killed and forty-three wounded. Although the fleet had to withdraw, it had inflicted some damage on the forts and contributed greatly to the victory of the army the following day. In his report to the Navy Department Foote said that he had taken the ships against Donelson at the "urgent request of General Halleck and General Grant, who regarded the movement as a military necessity, although not in my opinion properly prepared." In a telegram to his wife he said: "I will not go so near again, although at Fort Henry I produced an effect by it. We ought to have been victorious at Donelson, as we fought harder than at Henry. I went into it against my judgment by order of Halleck."

When the flotilla withdrew, General Floyd sent off a dispatch to Richmond announcing a great victory. To Grant, who had been watching the battle between the ironclads and the fort intently, it appeared that the gunboats had been put out of action for some time. "The sun went down on the night of the 14th of February, 1862, leaving the army confronting Fort Donelson anything but comforted over the prospect. I retired that night not knowing but that I would have to intrench my position, and bring up tents for the men or build huts under the cover of the hills."

At 2 o'clock the next morning Grant was called out of the

Grant's army crossed the Rapidan on a May day in 1864 to begin the battle of the Wilderness, told me how he had seen the road from Culpepper, over which Grant's army had marched to the ford, blue with the discarded overcoats which the soldiers had thrown away. These were not new and raw troops, but the seasoned veterans of the Army of the Potomac.

log house where he had sought refuge from the storm by a message from Foote, asking him to meet him on his flagship four miles down the river, as his wound prevented him from going to see Grant. After notifying all the division commanders of his absence and instructing them to do nothing to bring on an engagement without further orders, Grant set out to meet Foote, whose flagship was anchored in the middle of the river. Foote explained to him the condition of his ships, and said that certain repairs which were imperative would take about ten days. When they parted, it was with the understanding that Grant would hold and strengthen his lines until Foote came back from Cairo with the flotilla.[9]

Grant had no idea that the enemy would take the initiative for, despite the withdrawal of the fleet, his own position was much stronger than it had been before. He had been reinforced by a division of troops under General Lew Wallace, and 2,600 men of Smith's division, left behind at Fort Henry, had now joined the army. But when he stepped ashore from Foote's cutter he received a rude shock. One of his staff, "white with fear, not for his personal safety, but for the safety of the National troops," told him that early that morning the Confederates had come out of their defenses and attacked and scattered McClernand's division. As fast as his horse could carry him over the rough and frozen roads, Grant galloped to the front. McClernand's division had occupied the right of the Union line; to reach the point of disaster, Grant had to pass through the divisions of Smith and Wallace. There he was somewhat reassured, for he saw no signs of excitement or panic; but when he reached McClernand's division it was a different story. The men had fought bravely for a time until the ammunition in their cartridge boxes gave out, when they broke and fled. The soldiers were milling about, holding their muskets, but with nothing to shoot, although heaps of ammunition were lying all about. No officer appeared to be giv-

[9] Foote had created a navy yard at Cairo, largely afloat on river craft. Later it was moved ashore at nearby Mound City.

ing any orders or directions. Grant was relieved, however, to discover that the Confederate troops had withdrawn within their intrenchments. The road of escape to Nashville had been opened; but Floyd, flushed with what he thought was a great victory, ordered his troops back into the fort and its doom was sealed.

For Grant it was the hour of testing, the turning point in his career. Had the Confederate garrison escaped, or had Grant, alarmed at what had happened, settled down to a slow siege, it might have been the end of his war career. But he was equal to the fiery trial. When he reached the place where the line had been broken, he found McClernand in conversation with General Lew Wallace. After hearing their report, Grant, his face slightly flushed, with a sudden grip which betokened his determination, crushed the papers in his hand and said quietly to the two generals, "Gentlemen, the position on the right must be retaken." That sentence and that decision made Grant. Had he faltered or hesitated then, the country would never have heard of "Unconditional Surrender" Grant.

At midnight of the 15th of February, after Grant had not only regained the lost intrenchments but had established positions within the Confederate lines, the three generals in the fort held a council as to their future course. Buckner told the civilians, Pillow and Floyd, that their lines could not hold if the Union forces made an attack. The arrogant Pillow denied this and insisted that they could cut their way out if it became necessary. Buckner replied that, while this was possible, it would cost them the majority of their troops, and that no commander had the right to sacrifice three fourths of his men in order to save the remainder. To this Floyd agreed and suggested capitulation. "But, gentlemen," he said, referring to the charge of disloyalty made against him when he was Secretary of War, "I cannot surrender; you know my position with the Federals; it wouldn't do; it wouldn't do." Pillow then said, "I will not surrender myself nor the command; I will die first." Floyd then turned to Pillow and said, "I turn the command over to you, sir." To which Pillow replied, "I pass it." Buckner answered, "I assume it. Give me pen, ink and paper, and send for a bugler." He then wrote a note to Grant, asking for terms, and sent it into the Union lines with a white flag and a sounding trumpet; but it was for the garrison the trumpet of defeat, not of victory. It was then that Grant sent him the answer which made his name ring throughout the land, "Unconditional surrender." The surrender agreement was signed at a meeting in the dining room of the little Dover inn. When one of the Confederate officers said something about the "old flag," Buckner, bringing his fist down on the table, exclaimed, "The Old Flag! I followed it when most of your thousands out yonder were in swaddling clothes, in Mexico, on the frontier—and I love it yet."

By the time Foote returned from Cairo with his gunboats, Donelson had fallen. Grant had informed Halleck of the victory, and that unless he received orders to the contrary he would take Clarksville on the 21st of February and Nashville by the 1st of March. With two gunboats Foote left Donelson and proceeded up the Cumberland to Clarksville, which he occupied on February 20th, and planned to go on to Nashville. At midnight on the 20th Grant and Foote were together making plans for the movement up the river to Nashville when a telegram arrived from Halleck forbidding the gunboats to go higher up the Cumberland than Clarksville. After that they were to return to Cairo. Both Grant and Foote were much disappointed. It was Grant's opinion that immediately after Donelson "the way was opened to the National forces all over the South-west without much resistance. If one general who would have taken the responsibility had been in command of all the troops west of the Alleghenies, he could have marched to Chattanooga, Corinth, Memphis and Vicksburg with the troops we then had." But almost two years were to pass and thousands were to fall in battle before a unified command, not only in the west, but over all areas of the war, was established and Grant himself made the general in chief.[10]

After the fall of Fort Henry and Fort Donelson, the next bastion of the Confederacy to come under attack by Foote's flotilla was Island No. 10 in the Mississippi, an island which no longer exists, for it has long since been washed away by the rushing river. It lay at the beginning of a great horseshoe bend described by the erratic river where it turns on its long journey to the Gulf and flows northward to the town of New Madrid, Missouri; there it again turns southward. Island No. 10 and New Madrid were both strongly fortified. The garrison at New Madrid was commanded by Lieutenant General Leonidas Polk, who before the war had been the Episcopal bishop of Mississippi and had exchanged the surplice for the sword. General John Pope, later to meet disaster in the East at the hands of Lee and Jackson, lay before New Madrid with ten thousand men. He could have taken the place by assault only with heavy loss of life and wisely decided to lay siege to it. On the 3d of March his army marched against Point Pleasant, twelve miles below New Madrid. This cut off all supplies for the Confederate garrison; in ten days it surrendered.

But Island No. 10, though now isolated, still remained a plug in the river. Could the Federal forces pull that plug, the Mississippi would be free for further exploitation. Pope placed artillery on the Missouri shore to deny the river to Southern supply boats. That left the 7,000 men in the fortress dependent on a single supply road which passed through the swamps on the east bank of the river from Tiptonville, Tennessee, fifteen miles to the South.

To cut the road Pope had to get across the river. But all his transports were north of Island No. 10, separated from the

[10] In July, 1862, Halleck was called to Washington as military adviser to the President and given the title of general in chief. In this position, however, he was little more than a chief of staff. McClellan, who had succeeded Scott as general in chief in November, 1861, was unfortunately stripped of that title in March, 1862, and left in command of the Army of the Potomac only.

Union troops by that very stronghold they wished to overcome. To get those transports below the fortress, an engineer regiment, working in relays of three hundred men, hacked and sawed a canal through the sloughs and bayous and a submerged forest from a point on the river some miles north of the Southern fortress to a point near New Madrid. This tremendous piece of work, a channel six miles in length, fifty feet wide, and four and a half feet deep, perhaps the most successful accomplishment of its kind during the war, was finished in just nineteen days. By way of this huge ditch Pope's transports reached New Madrid in safety. Pope now had his transports with him; but still he could not get his troops across the river, for not only were strong Confederate batteries posted along the Tennessee shore where he planned to take his army across, but the river below Island No. 10 was patrolled by enemy gunboats. To deal with those batteries and gunboats he required the help of Foote's ironclads. The Federal warships, however, could not pass through the canal through which the transports had steamed, for not only was the channel too narrow, but it was only four and a half feet deep, while the gunboats drew six feet of water. Although always ready to cooperate with the army, Foote had misgivings about sending his gunboats past the formidable enemy position. Bold and dashing at Fort Henry and Fort Donelson, he was now very deliberate in taking his fleet down the Mississippi. The reason for this caution was clear: when he attacked the forts on the Cumberland and the Tennessee, he had taken his ships up-river, against the current. In contrast, on the Mississippi he would be going downstream, with the current. In case of injury to a ship, it could not be backed out of the fire zone, but would drift down before the guns of the enemy. When the flotilla lay at the Cairo navy yard after the campaign against Forts Henry and Donelson, Foote had experimented with the gunboats to see if they could be backed up the river against the current. He found that the combination of the strong current with the gunboats' awkward steering qualities made it impossible.

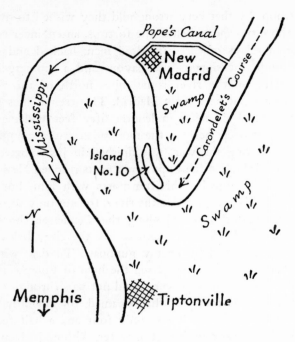

When Foote's brother, the Hon. John A. Foote, reminded him that what the people wanted was "dash and close fighting, something sharp and decisive," Foote answered: "Don't you know that my gunboats are the only protection you have upon your rivers against the rebel gunboats—that without my flotilla everything in your rivers, your cities and your towns would be at the mercy of the enemy? My first duty then is to care for my boats, if I am to protect you. Now when I ran up the Tennessee and the Cumberland and attacked Fort Henry and Fort Donelson, the current took care of me, carrying me away from the enemy's works. But all this is changed when I descend the Mississippi. Then my boats, if they become unmanageable, are carried directly into the hands of the enemy." Nevertheless, in spite of the hazard, Foote at length decided to send at least two of his ships down the river.

A few days before he made this decision, Foote held a council of war on his flagship. When the proposal to run by Island No. 10 was discussed, all the commanders except Henry Walke were against it, holding the opinion that any ship which attempted to pass would be sunk. After the vote was taken, Foote asked Walke if he was willing to undertake the attempt. He was much relieved when Walke eagerly accepted.

For several days before Walke started on his dangerous exploit, the flotilla bombarded at long distance Confederate batteries on and near the island. While the ships were thus engaged, Elihu Washburne, the influential Congressman from Illinois who was Grant's chief backer, and James B. Eads, the builder of the gunboats, paid a visit to Foote on the *Benton*, his new flagship. They were standing on the deck by the side of Foote, who, glasses in hand, was watching the flight of the big shells. While he was thus occupied, an officer handed him a package of letters. Out of the package Foote selected one and opened it. After reading only a few lines, he turned to Eads and said: "I must ask you to excuse me for a few minutes, while I go down to my cabin. This letter brings me the news of the death of my son, about thirteen years old, who I had hoped would live to be the stay and support of his mother." After a little he returned to the deck perfectly composed, as strong in his hour of affliction and sorrow as he was in the midst of the battle. Only a few days before, Foote had written a letter to his old friend and former commander, Commodore Smith, whose son Joseph had perished on the *Congress* when she was destroyed by the *Merrimac* at Hampton Roads. Acknowledging Foote's letter, Smith wrote: "We must bow our heads in the dust and say, 'Though he slay me, yet will I trust in Him.' I was relieved by receiving the mutilated remains of my son, and I deposited them with those of his mother. We are looking most anxiously for the reports of your success at Island 10. God give you victory."

Another devout officer, Commander Walke conducted divine service on the *Carondelet* before he cast off. Careful preparation had been made to protect as far as possible the vital parts of the ship from the fire of the batteries. A barge laden with hay was secured to the port quarter of the gunboat to protect the boilers; where there was no iron plating, the ship was protected with bales of hay and lumber. Chains and cables were coiled about the pilot house to a thickness of eighteen inches. In his final instructions to Walke, Foote told him that if he was successful in passing the batteries he felt certain that the government would "appreciate and reward" him for a service which would enable the army to cross the river and attack Island No. 10. In the event of disaster, Walke was to destroy the machinery and, if possible, set fire to his ship or sink her to prevent her from falling into the enemy's hands.

At 10 o'clock on the night of April 4th, 1862, when the moon was down, the *Carondelet* cast off and began to drift with the current through the Union ships. The vessel's ports were closed and the guns run in, with the gunners sitting close to them. The only light was a lantern, invisible from the outside, in the engine room; no one was permitted to speak above a whisper. The noise of the engines was muffled by passing the escaping steam through the wheel house[11] instead of through the smoke stacks.

Just as the *Carondelet* started, a wild thunderstorm broke over the river, and vivid flashes of lightning intermittently lighted up the water. When the ship had cleared the first point of land and opened up with all the power of her engines, the soot in one of the smokestacks, not moistened now by the steam, caught fire; the flames leaped up like a colossal torch. Immediately all the batteries on the island and those on the Tennessee shore began to flash and flame, the thunder of the artillery answering the crashes of the artillery of the heavens. The Union squadron, lying in the river above the island, began to hurl its shells against the Confederate batteries. The sound of

---

[11] The wheel house in this case meant the covering over the paddlewheel, three quarters of the way aft, and not the pilot house.

this firing and the meteor-like flight of the shells from the mortars furnished great encouragement to brave Walke and his crew.

At midnight the *Carondelet* passed the last of the batteries; the great feat, one of the most daring exploits of the war, had been accomplished, and with no loss of life or injury to the vessel. A second gunboat, the *Pittsburg,* was sent down two days later. Between them the ironclads silenced or destroyed the Confederate batteries on the Tennessee side of the river. The light Southern gunboats, unable to stand up to the bigger Federal ships, made no attempt to interfere with Pope's crossing.

The garrison at Island No. 10 knew the game was up once the *Carondelet* had gotten below the fortress. They abandoned their works and attempted to evacuate by way of the Tiptonville Road. But Pope got there first and captured the lot of them, including three generals, without the loss of a single Union soldier. The Mississippi was now open nearly to Memphis.

The *Carondelet's* exploit not only contributed greatly to the capture of the river stronghold, but also demonstrated that gunboats could run past river forts and batteries. Looking back, it may now seem strange that Grant waited for almost a year, laboring at divers experiments and expeditions to get at the Confederate stronghold at Vicksburg, digging canals, diverting streams from their channels, and sending Porter's gunboats and Sherman's troops through bayous and morasses in dangerous and futile attempts to get into the rear of Vicksburg, before he adopted what now would seem to be the obvious course of passing the gunboats and transports down the river under the fire of the batteries, after which he could begin the land operations which resulted in the capitulation of the long-beleaguered fortress. Porter's feat in running the batteries at Vicksburg received much more acclaim and publicity than that of Foote at Island No. 10; but nothing could have surpassed the daring and importance of what the *Carondelet* and the *Pittsburg* did there.

Although Foote himself was not with them, for it was on April 6th, the very night the *Pittsburg* ran the batteries at Island

No. 10, two of his wooden gunboats, the *Lexington* and the *Tyler*, played an important part in the great battle at Shiloh on the Tennessee River between Grant's army and the Confederate army under Albert Sidney Johnston. At a critical hour in the late afternoon of April 6th, after Grant's army had been driven from position to position and far back toward the river, the two gunboats went into action and every fifteen minutes hurled their heavy shells into the Confederate onrush which threatened to drive the Union army into the river: "At a late hour in the afternoon," wrote Grant, "a desperate effort was made by the enemy to turn our left and get possession of the landing, transports, etc. This point was guarded by the gunboats *Tyler* and *Lexington*, Captains Gwin and Shirk, U. S. Navy, commanding, four 20-pounder Parrott guns, and a battery of rifled guns. As there is a deep and impassable ravine for artillery or cavalry, and very difficult for infantry, at this point, no troops were stationed here, except the necessary artillerists and a small infantry force for their support. Just at this moment the advance of Major General Buell's column (a part of the division under General Nelson) arrived, the two generals named being present. An advance was immediately made upon the point of attack and the enemy soon driven back. In this repulse, much is due to the presence of the gunboats *Tyler* and *Lexington*, and their able commanders, Captains Gwin and Shirk."

At the time the two gunboats went into action, the Confederate officers and soldiers were confident that within an hour victory would be theirs and that General Johnston's prediction to his staff as he mounted on the morning of the battle, "Tonight we will water our horses in the Tennessee River," would be fulfilled. A Texan with the Confederate cavalry said of this critical moment in the battle, "Another hour, and we would have driven them into the river. I was with the cavalry on the extreme right, and could see thousands of panic-stricken Union soldiers cowering under the protection of the cliffs at the river's edge.

Another hour, sir, and we would have had them in the Tennessee." [12]

Foote's days in command of the gunboats were now numbered. He heard the thunder of his guns for the last time in an engagement with Confederate ships near Fort Pillow, some distance above Memphis. After their victory at Island No. 10, Foote and General Pope, losing no time, started down the Mississippi with the gunboats and transports carrying twenty thousand troops, which were landed north of the Confederate fort. On April 13th five Confederate ships under command of Commodore George Hollins, a veteran of the War of 1812, steamed up the river to oppose the advance of Foote's squadron. But after a few shots were fired the Confederate vessels were driven back to the protection of the guns of Fort Pillow. This engagement, the last in which Foote took part, was fought on the Sabbath. When the hour came for the regular Sunday worship, Foote silenced his guns and mustered the crew on the deck of the flagship, where he read the service and made an extemporaneous prayer. He explained to the crew why duty to the country made it necessary for them to fight a battle on the sacred day. The men were then piped back to their stations. Several Confederate shells burst over the flagship during this extraordinary lull in the battle. This is the only instance in the history of the United States Navy when an engagement was broken off that divine service might be conducted. There was, however, a somewhat similar incident in the Confederate Army in the Seven Days Battle in June of 1862. [13]

[12] A veteran's conversation with the author in 1918. It should be noted, however, that important as the fire of the gunboats and the timely arrival of Buell's advance guard were, Beauregard, who succeeded to command after Johnston's mortal wound, had ordered the Confederate troops, with victory almost in their grasp, to withdraw.

[13] In the Seven Days Battle, when McClellan's army was retreating down the Peninsula before the army of Lee, "Stonewall" Jackson's failure to carry out the part assigned to him in the battle at Savage Station stemmed from his reluctance to fight a battle on the Sabbath. Jackson said to one of his officers

On May 9th, soon after the brush with Hollins' fleet Foote was temporarily relieved of his command by Commodore Charles H. Davis, an old friend, and the replacement for whom he had asked. He retained titular command, however, until June 17th. It was Davis, therefore, who led the ironclads to victory over the Confederate river squadron in front of Memphis on June 5th. This led to the surrender of the city to the Federal forces. Fort Pillow, with the Union fleet in the river and the Army of the Tennessee in its rear, was evacuated.

The wound Foote received at Fort Donelson was now giving him great distress and affected his health. He was confined much of the time to his cabin, and when he did go on deck it was on crutches. He felt it to be his duty to inform the Navy Department fully as to his condition, leaving it to the Secretary to make the decision whether to relieve him or not. It was a hard struggle for him to relinquish the command of the river flotilla which he had created, and which under his leadership had rendered so great a service to the nation. In a letter to Fox, who had written him that he had no right to risk his life except in an engagement with the enemy, Foote said: "I have been in agony about the question of leaving to save my life, or dying in harness at my post. But here the idea of suicide flitted across my mind, and this, with the connection that the effectiveness of the flotilla required a man at its head of health—strength of body and mind, rather than one in his bed—able only to move on crutches, and daily failing, led me reluctantly to yield. It was a severe struggle, but it was officially and morally right, although it is hard, at this moment, to reflect that after struggling as I have in working at this flotilla, I find myself deprived from reaping the full harvest of its victories. I have this consolation, however, that from your generous treatment and assurances hitherto, Secretary

---

that day that he had other important duties to perform than to support Jones of Magruder's command. The "other important duty" was attendance upon divine service.

Welles and yourself will not let me suffer in consequence of this Providential dispensation." [14]

When he left his squadron, Foote went at once to the home of his brother, Judge John A. Foote, at Cleveland, where he could enjoy a period of rest, and at the same time, in accordance with the desire of the Department, exercise general supervision of the operations of the fleet under Davis. The citizens of Cleveland desired to honor him with a public reception. He declined the invitation because of the impaired state of his health, and because he did not feel it consistent with his views of duty to receive honors at a public reception when "my brave comrades may this day be engaged in deadly strife for the vindication of our flag." During his stay at Cleveland Foote pondered the question whether or not to relinquish completely the command of the river squadron. It was the earnest hope of his friend Welles that he retain general command of the fleet, and then, when sufficiently recovered, resume active command. However, another old friend, Commodore Joseph Smith, now a bureau chief in Washington, urged him to give up his command: "You are not bound to 'die in harness.' Nobody would thank you for doing so in your present condition, and, as I said before, the country may require you another day." [15]

Foote made the final decision on June 13th. On that day he forwarded to the Secretary of the Navy the report of his two physicians to the effect that he could not return to active duty with the fleet without seriously jeopardizing his health. He left it to the Department to decide whether he was to return at once to duty with the fleet, receive a three months' leave of absence, or be detached altogether from the river command. Under these

[14] When Foote, a firm Calvinist, used the word "suicide" in his letter to Fox, he was not thinking of taking his life because of his bodily distress, but rather that remaining with the fleet in his present state of health might cost him his life.

[15] When Smith said that the country might require him "another day," he was not thinking of future service on the Mississippi, but in a war with England which the Commodore then felt was imminent.

circumstances Welles very reluctantly detached him from command of the fleet on June 17th. In addition to the official notification, Welles sent him a personal letter, in which he said: "The country feels and acknowledges its indebtedness to you; but few know as I do the difficulties you have been compelled to encounter and overcome, in first creating the flotilla, and then carrying it into a series of successful actions, which have contributed so largely to the suppression of the rebellion throughout the southwest."

In the same letter in which he reported the state of his health to Welles and suggested that he be detached from command of the squadron, Foote reverted to the great evil, slavery, which he had combatted both on the West Africa coast before the war and in action on the western rivers: "If it will not be considered premature, I wish further to remark that when this rebellion is crushed, and a squadron is fitted out to enforce the new treaty for the suppression of the African slave trade, I should be pleased to have command; but so long as the rebellion continues, it will be my highest ambition to be actively employed in aiding its suppression."

In the last week of June Foote returned to his home in New Haven, where he was received with every token of esteem and honor. On July 16th, in answer to a suggestion from the President, the Congress tendered him their thanks, and on the 30th of the same month he was appointed Rear Admiral on the Active List. The appointment dated back to the 16th, the same day on which Du Pont and Farragut were made Rear Admirals. Public honors, however, were no balm for a wounded heart. His only son, William, had died when he was in the midst of the campaign against Island No. 10; early in the autumn two daughters, one of them blind and therefore all the dearer to him because of her affliction, died within ten days of each other. In July of that same year Foote was made Chief of the Bureau of Equipment and Recruiting. His experience in manning and out-

Andrew Hull Foote
1806—1863

Samuel Francis Du Pont
1803—1865

fitting the western flotilla, and the prestige of his name, hardly second to that of Farragut, highly qualified him for this work. But soon he was assigned to a more active post.

The failure of Admiral Du Pont to take Charleston and, as it seemed to the Secretary of the Navy, his "determination that the Navy should not take Charleston," prepared the way for his removal and the appointment of another in his place. Apparently sufficiently recovered for active duty at sea, Foote was one of the two or three officers under consideration; but when Welles first spoke to him about the matter, early in the autumn of 1862, Foote had such regard for Du Pont, an old friend and shipmate, that he expressed the wish that he might not be called upon to supersede him in command of the South Atlantic Squadron. But the months passed and Du Pont, after his attack in April, 1863, met with repulse, made no further effort to take Charleston. Welles finally decided to put Foote in his place. The appointment was made the following June 4th. Of this occasion Welles said: "To relieve Du Pont, who had court friends and admirers, would be likely to cause commotion, though he had indirectly invited it. Foote had shown his ability for the position, and possessed in an eminent degree, beyond any other officer suggested except Farragut, the confidence of the country."

In a letter to Du Pont, written two months before Foote was chosen to take his place, Commodore Charles Davis expressed great shock and surprise at what he had heard about the conduct of his "dear friend" Foote, and asked Du Pont to exercise the "Christian virtue of forgiveness" toward their mutual friend. The inference would seem to be that Foote had been seeking to have himself chosen for Du Pont's place. In this, however, both Davis and Du Pont were mistaken, for the Secretary of the Navy had sounded out Foote as to whether he would be willing to assume the command, with the particular duty of attacking Charleston. Foote was on his way to take command of Du Pont's fleet when he was stricken with illness and died at the

Astor House in New York on June 26th, 1863. Professor Alexander Bache, noted physicist, adviser to the President and the Navy Department, and associated with the medical staff of the New York Navy Yard when Foote had been the commandant, dreaded to tell the admiral that his was a fatal illness, for he knew the admiral's heart was set upon capturing Charleston. But when he gave Foote the verdict, the admiral answered that he was ready to go, and was glad to be through with guns and war.

In one of the finest tributes ever paid an officer of the United States Navy, the Secretary of the Navy bade farewell to his old Cheshire Academy schoolmate in a General Order to the officers and men of all ships:

"A gallant and distinguished officer is lost to the country. The hero of Fort Henry and Fort Donelson, the daring and indomitable spirit that created and led to successive victories the Mississippi Flotilla, the heroic Christian sailor, who in the China Seas and on the coast of Africa, as well as the great interior rivers of our country, sustained with unfaltering fidelity and devotion the honor of our flag and the cause of the Union—Rear Admiral Foote—is no more."

Foote was never a complainer, never a seeker after high place, and never unhappy at the promotion of others. He loved himself last; the only ends he aimed at were his country's, his God's, and the truth's. General Sherman, who was frequently associated with him in the campaigns in the Mississippi Valley, said of Foote: "To me he resembled Farragut in the simplicity of his mode of life, his intense love of country and profession, and the extraordinary personal courage that made him an example to all the commanders of the vessels in his squadron."

If Foote had not been fatally stricken just as he was to take command of the South Atlantic Squadron, Fort Sumter and the other defenses about Charleston would have experienced much more hard fighting than they ever actually did. Ships might have been lost, the admiral himself might have gone down; but if

Sumter did not fall until the march of Sherman's army across South Carolina compelled the evacuation of Charleston in the spring of 1865, the reason would not have been lack of aggressiveness on the part of the fleet.

IV

DU PONT

In certain respects, Du Pont was the McClellan of the Navy. His contribution to the cause of the Union, although notable, was not comparable to that of McClellan, who organized the Army of the Potomac and imbued it with a spirit which no defeats or reverses ever quenched; who re-organized that army on the march after the disaster at Second Bull Run; and won the battle on the banks of the Antietam. Yet between McClellan and Du Pont there was a definite similarity. Both were men of superior intelligence, high professional ability, aristocratic background, and great social charm. Both gathered about them a group of officers, a "clique" as the Secretary of the Navy called them, who idolized their commander; and both, perhaps more than any other Northern military leaders, won the affection of those who served under them.

In the mountains of western Virginia at Rich Mountain and Laurel Mountain, McClellan won victories which, though insignificant compared with those which followed, nevertheless stirred the nation and won for him the sobriquet, "The Little Napoleon." At Port Royal, off the South Carolina coast, Du Pont won a victory which roused great enthusiasm after the disappointment of Bull Run and other early reverses and made his name ring throughout the land. At the head of a splendidly drilled and equipped army, McClellan continually demanded more troops; Du Pont, given the pick of the officers of the Navy and a squadron larger than any ever assembled under the na-

tional flag up to that time, unceasingly requested more ships
and more men. Both quarreled with their superiors, the Secretary of War and the Secretary of the Navy; McClellan blamed
Stanton for his difficulties, while Du Pont maintained that he
had been unjustly treated by Welles. Both disappeared from the
stage of the mighty conflict before the war was over, McClellan
after Antietam in 1862, when he was superseded by Burnside,
and Du Pont soon after his repulse in the assault on Fort Sumter
the following year, when he was replaced by Dahlgren. But
there the similarity ends. Ninety-four years after he turned his
army over to Burnside on a snowy November day in 1862,
McClellan, sitting his horse with incomparable grace and authority, has emerged out of the smoke and mists of yesterday
and refuses to take a second rank. By contrast Du Pont, the first
victor on the sea and for a brief season the hero whose name
was on the lips of all, has passed into eclipse.

Samuel Francis Du Pont was born September 27th, 1803
at Bergen Point, New Jersey. His father, Victor Marie Du Pont,
was the head of an importing house in New York, and his uncle
had established the gunpowder factory associated with the Du
Pont name at Wilmington, Delaware. The most distinguished
member of the Du Pont family was the admiral's grandfather,
Pierre Du Pont de Nemours, a prominent French statesman, who
was a friend of Thomas Jefferson, with whom he carried on
correspondence. He asked Jefferson to secure a midshipman's
appointment for his grandson. Jefferson promised that he would
write to the then president, James Madison, and expressed the
hope that the grandson would become "one of our high admirals." Through Jefferson's influence, the lad of twelve received a
midshipman's warrant and a simultaneous appointment to West
Point. Like Admiral Foote, who also had received parallel appointments, Du Pont chose the navy. The War of 1812 had just
come to an end, and the fame which enshrined some of its sea
captains no doubt played a part in his preference for the navy.

As a midshipman, Du Pont saw much of the world in the

cruises of the frigates on which he served, especially in the Mediterranean, the navy's favorite training ground. When serving aboard the *Ohio*, under command of Commodore Isaac Hull, famous for his victory in the battle between the *Constitution* and the British frigate *Guerrière*, Du Pont and other midshipmen were engaged in a brawl at Port Mahon by toughs who attacked them at a ball given for the officers of the *Ohio* and the *Brandywine*. A mob had gathered about two midshipmen. A powerful youth, Du Pont went to their assistance. He also was assaulted, and narrowly escaped death when a member of the Civil Guard, who took the part of the mob, lunged at him with a bayonet, while the alcalde of the town stood by watching the fight. When Commodore Hull heard the midshipmen's story, he publicly reprimanded four of them, Du Pont among them, on the deck of the *Ohio* and sent them home, alleging that they had shown him disrespect. The commodore was incensed at Du Pont in particular because he had asked permission to send his account of the brawl to the Congressional representatives of Delaware, his home state. On their return, the Secretary of the Navy listened to their story, then exonerated them of all blame and misconduct and returned them to the squadron.

In the war with Mexico Du Pont, then a commander, served on the *Congress* under Commodore Stockton on the Pacific coast. Later in command of a sloop of war he transported John C. Frémont's battalion from Monterey to San Diego, and thence proceeded to the Gulf of California, which he cleared of hostile ships.

After the Mexican War Commander Du Pont served on a board of officers to revise the regulations and courses of study at the Naval Academy. In 1855 he became a member of an even more important board, appointed by Secretary of the Navy James C. Dobbin under the provisions of an Act of Congress which, for the first time in the Navy's history, provided for the retirement of superannuated or unfit officers. The thankless task of this board was to clear the Navy List of those who were no longer fit for active service. Out of a total of 712 commissioned officers, 49 were dropped as incompetent or unworthy and 152 were placed on the new "reserved" (retired) list. When the board's report was approved by President Franklin Pierce and the names published, the storm broke. Almost without exception the officers affected by the decision protested violently. Many of them managed to stir up so much Congressional support for themselves that they were restored to the active list. Du Pont appears to have been the moving spirit of the board, though he was far from being the senior member. At any rate, the resentment of the officers concerned centered upon him and followed him through the remaining years of his life.

At the outbreak of the Civil War, Du Pont held the rank of captain and was stationed at the Philadelphia Navy Yard. As the clouds of war gathered, he never felt a moment's hesitation in deciding to stand by the flag. One of the most stirring declarations of loyalty to the nation and to the navy came from his pen at that time. In a letter to his friend and fellow officer, Captain Foote, in command at the New York Navy Yard, Du Pont said:

What has made me sick at heart is to see the resignations from the navy. I had occasion to go to Washington the last week in November, and was astounded to see the extent of the demoralization, not only in every department of the government, but among the officers of the navy. I spoke out plainly, I tell you; told them I had never believed I had been serving two masters; that I had been nourished, fed and clothed by the general government for over forty years; paid whether employed or not; and for what? Why, to stand by the country whether assailed by enemies from without or from within; that my state had no part or lot in this support; that my oath declared allegiance to the United States as one to support the Constitution. I stick by the flag and the national government as long as we have one, whether my state does or not, and well she knew it.

Du Pont's declaration of loyalty was in keeping with the position his family had already taken. Some time before the war, large orders for gunpowder had been arriving at the Wilmington factory from state arsenals in the South and from private firms. At great sacrifice the company refused to fill these orders, believing that any explosives delivered might be used against the national army and navy. Two days after the fall of Fort Sumter, the head of the Du Pont Company, Henry Du Pont, wrote to their agent at Richmond, where a heavy powder order for Virginia had just been filed, saying: "Presuming that Virginia will do her whole duty in this great emergency and will be loyal to the Union, we shall prepare the powder, but with the understanding that should the general expectation be disappointed, and Virginia, by any misfortune, assume an attitude of hostility to the United States, we shall be absolved from any obligation to furnish the order." This entailed additional financial sacrifice, for the Du Pont mills manufactured more than a third of the gunpowder produced in the United States. In May, 1861, the Governor of Delaware commissioned Henry Du Pont major general in command of all Delaware troops. One of his first acts was to order that every officer and man of the Delaware home forces take the oath of allegiance to the United States. This occasioned no little stir. When Du Pont reported to General John A. Dix, in command at Baltimore, that many of the men of the Delaware home force had refused to take the oath, and asked that Federal troops be sent into Delaware, General Dix promptly sent a detachment into the state. Thus Delaware was held for the Union. During the war she sent 13,651 men into the armed forces of the nation, almost one out of every eight of the state's combined white and Negro population.

When the war began, Captain Du Pont was summoned from his post at the Philadelphia Navy Yard to head the Commission of Conference appointed by the Secretary of the Navy to devise plans for the naval warfare. The commission recommended the establishment of a large naval base off the Atlantic coast line of the Confederacy, and chose the location favored by Du Pont: Port Royal on the South Carolina coast, midway between Charleston on the north and Savannah on the south.

Hardly heard of then and, except for the battle fought there in 1861, almost unknown today, Port Royal was no misnomer, for it had a truly royal harbor, so commodious that all the navies of the world could comfortably ride at anchor inside it.

Gustavus V. Fox, the Assistant Secretary of the Navy, who was well acquainted with the personnel of the navy, strongly urged that Du Pont be appointed to command the expedition to seize Port Royal and destroy the Confederate forts there. With this in view, Du Pont was chosen to command the South Atlantic Blockading Squadron. He was given a free hand in selecting his staff and, combing the Navy Register, chose the best officers then in active service. On the 29th of October, 1861, Du Pont's fleet of seventy vessels, consisting largely of transports for 14,000 troops under command of General T. W. (Tim) Sherman, set sail from Hampton Roads. Including seventeen warships, it was the largest American sea force yet assembled under one command. The fleet was a heterogeneous one, embodying everything from the heavy frigates to Hudson River ferryboats, reinforced and armed. For his chief of staff on the flagship *Wabash*, Du Pont selected Charles H. Davis, one of the ablest and most courageous men in the navy. Du Pont also picked another officer who was to win great renown in the war, Percival Drayton, a South Carolinian, who commanded the *Pocahontas* and subsequently was Farragut's flag captain at the battle of Mobile Bay. Both of these men were close friends and admirers of Du Pont.

On the voyage down to Port Royal, the fleet was scattered by a storm off Cape Hatteras, the graveyard of ships; but the next day, save for a couple of auxiliary vessels, the fleet was reunited and proceeded to its station off Port Royal. The Southern newspapers, which were as well-posted on the squadron's movements as those in the North, learned of the gale which had struck the fleet and rejoiced at the tidings, reminding their readers of the fate which had befallen the Spanish Armada in the English Channel in 1588. But at noon on the 5th of November the fleet crossed the bar into Port Royal harbor. It was Du Pont's intention to attack the forts that afternoon, but his flag-ship was grounded for a time, and the attack was postponed. The next day was windy and stormy and the fleet remained at anchor.

The bay and harbor of Port Royal were defended by two forts on the two islands, Bay Point and Hilton Head. The for-tress at Bay Point to the east, was Fort Beauregard, named after the victor at Bull Run and the South's current hero. The other was Fort Walker at the end of Hilton Head. The com-mander at the forts was General Thomas F. Drayton, brother of Captain Percival Drayton. Thus two brothers, both South Car-olinians, fought on opposing sides at Port Royal. In addition to the forts, there was also at Port Royal a rather nondescript col-lection of Confederate warships under the command of Captain Josiah Tattnall. Du Pont, Tattnall, and Buchanan were the most distinguished officers of the United States Navy when the war began. The year after the Port Royal engagement Tattnall com-manded the *Merrimac* following her battle with the *Monitor*. In 1859, when commander of the East India Squadron, he was on the China coast negotiating a treaty with China, and wit-nessed the repulse of the British fleet at the mouth of the Pei-Ho River. In violation of the neutrality of the United States, Tattnall gave what aid he could to the British ships. Asked to explain his action, he replied, "Blood is thicker than water." [1] His superiors upheld his action and he received the thanks of the British government. When Tattnall was in want in his old age, British officers, remembering his assistance at Pei-Ho, con-tributed money for his relief.

Two days before the attack on the Port Royal forts, after

[1] The saying in different forms goes far back. It occurs in Sir Walter Scott's *Guy Mannering*, Chapter 38. It received new currency and popularity at Manila Bay after the defeat of the Spanish fleet. When Admiral Dewey was having difficulty with the commander of the German ships in the bay, the commander of the British fleet moved his ships to a location where, should a crisis arise, he could give aid to Dewey. In defense of his action he quoted Tattnall's adage.

the fleet had crossed the bar and anchored, Du Pont, now serving as flag officer, then the highest rank in the navy, summoned the commanders of all his ships on board his flagship where he outlined his plan of action and the position each ship was to take; also he explained the role of the reserve ships which were to guard the troop transports against a possible attack by the Confederate ships.

The morning of November 7th dawned bright and fair. The placid sea, unruffled by a single ripple, was a gunner's delight, lending to the ships' batteries a steadiness almost equal to that of land-based platforms. At nine-thirty the signal to weigh anchor rose to the masthead of the *Wabash*, and in a few minutes Du Pont's warships, steaming slowly at six knots and only a ship's length apart, moved in toward the forts. So as not to afford the forts the advantage of a stationary target, Du Pont had ordered his ships to keep moving, steering a middle course between the two forts, hurling their broadsides against Fort Walker on the left and against Fort Beauregard on the right. At a point two miles beyond the forts the fleet was to turn to the left and approach closer to Fort Walker. After passing the fort a second time, the ships were to turn again to the left and once more move up the channel, firing at both forts as they passed them. These circles, always to the left, were to be repeated until the forts were silenced and the Federal soldiers could land.

As the fleet went into action, Tattnall showed that he truly believed that "blood is thicker than water" by a moving display of sentiment for the old flag and his former associations. When he saw the *Wabash*, Du Pont's flagship, moving in, Tattnall said to his quartermaster, "Dip my broad pennant to my old messmate." In obedience to the order, the Confederate commodore's pennant was dipped twice.

As the fleet advanced in orderly array on that beautiful November day, it presented a brave sight, each ship's crew standing at their appointed stations and the national flag flying from every topmast. On the first circle Du Pont was disappointed with the fire of the ships, and that of the flagship in particular;

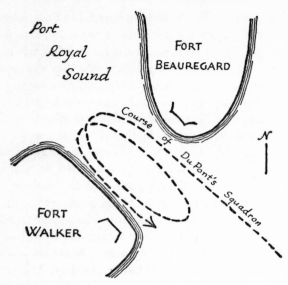

but of the second circle he later said that nothing in naval history could approach the effectiveness of the flagship's repeated broadsides. A correspondent of the *London Daily News,* looking shoreward, saw long columns of dust rise from the earth and the forts, "as if we had suddenly raised from the dust a grove of poplars." On one of the circles Du Pont narrowly escaped death when a solid shot from one of the forts passed between him and his aide, Captain Rodgers, as they stood together on the bridge of the *Wabash.* On the ships there were no places of refuge, no bombproofs, no headquarters far behind the firing line. The commanders shared equal peril with the lowest ratings. Many army generals on both sides were killed in action or mortally wounded, among them "Stonewall" Jackson at Chancellorsville; Leonidas Polk at Kennesaw Mountain; Albert Sidney Johnston at Shiloh; John Sedgwick at Spottsylvania; John F. Reynolds at Gettysburg; and A. P. Hill at Petersburg. By contrast, it is a singular fact that, although exposed in battle to far greater peril than were the generals of armies, not a single naval officer of the rank of captain or higher was killed or mortally wounded.

At 1:15, as Du Pont's squadron was about to commence a third circle past the forts, one of the ships signalled that the Confederate soldiers were leaving Fort Walker. After firing two pivot guns on the flagship, and raising no answering fire, Du Pont sent Captain Rodgers ashore with a flag of truce. When Rodgers landed he found that the defenders had fled, and raised the national flag over the fortress. The moment the flag appeared, the cheers of the seamen on all the ships of the fleet rolled over the waters.

The success cost the fleet almost no casualties. Yet the victory, its importance not to be measured by the number of the slain, was the navy's first triumph and one of the most important of the war. Naval men are all agreed that Du Pont's tactics in keeping his ships moving and circling the forts was superb. Henceforth Port Royal was the base of all the operations in that area of the coastline of the Confederacy. Du Pont himself, in writing to a friend, gives the best summary of the victory's significance: "The occupation of this wonderful sheet of water with its tributary rivers, inlets, outlets, entrances and sounds, running in all directions, cutting off effectively all water communications between Savannah and Charleston, has been like driving a wedge into the flanks of the rebels between these two important cities." The victory, coming after the depressing reverses at Bull Run and elsewhere, awakened tremendous enthusiasm in the North. The next day Du Pont was a national hero.

Du Pont followed up his victory at Port Royal by sweeping the coast from North Carolina down to Florida, seizing forts and towns and sealing up harbors. The chief ports of entry on the Atlantic coast for the blockade runners were Wilmington, North Carolina, which was not in Du Pont's area, and Charleston, South Carolina. The capture of Charleston was greatly desired by the government and the people of the North, not only because it was the second city of the South in size, but also because it was the cradle of secession. The state of which it was the port had been the first to drop out from the Union, and it was at Charleston that the flag was first fired on. For all these reasons, the capture of the proud and aristocratic capital was desired above that of any other Southern city, none excepted. Nevertheless, some Union military leaders doubted that Charleston had the strategic importance to warrant such long and costly efforts as were made to take it. After the repulse of Du Pont's first attack on the city in April of 1863, the Secretary of the Navy expressed his doubts in his *Diary* in the entry for April 20: "I am by no means confident that we are acting wisely in expending so much strength and effort on Charleston, a place of no strategic importance." Although the Secretary was correct, the nation's sentiment paid little heed to strategy. Where the flag had been first fired upon and first lowered, there the flag must be raised again. That objective was eventually accomplished, but not until the very end of the war and after the sacrifice of many lives and the expenditure of vast treasure.

Charleston was defended by an imposing series of forts and batteries, much more powerful than the defenses of other cities taken by the Union fleets and armies. After Farragut had run by Fort Jackson and Fort St. Philip, seventy miles down the Mississippi from New Orleans, there was nothing of a formidable nature to stop him from taking the city. But with Charleston it was a different matter. If, when the threat of war was hanging over the country, the government had adopted vigorous methods and had strengthened and reinforced Sumter, Moultrie, and other defenses at Charleston, the history of the first months of the conflict might have been different. During the last months of Buchanan's administration, the nation was adrift. Lincoln was not to blame for the extraordinary, almost incredible, state of the national defense, for it was a legacy which he inherited from the outgoing administration. On the night of his inauguration day, the new president was advised by General Winfield Scott, the commander of the army, whom he had asked to keep him posted as to the military situation, that neither Fort Pickens at Pensacola, Florida, nor Sumter at Charleston could be held.

The commander at Fort Moultrie was Major Robert Anderson. On the night of December 22nd he transferred his troops from the indefensible Moultrie to the far stronger Fort Sumter, an unfinished fortress with walls forty feet high and eight feet thick. This change of base excited and angered Charleston and all South Carolina and was, in a sense, the "overt act" which precipitated the conflict. Although he showed courage and enterprise in taking his troops from Moultrie to Sumter, it cannot be said that Major Anderson manifested great zeal in the defense of the latter fort. He had been urgently demanding supplies for the fort, but when the *Star of the West,* which had been sent down by Lincoln, appeared in the harbor and was fired on by the Confederate batteries, he would not permit Doubleday, the second in command, to fire a single gun. Thus, when the batteries opened on Sumter, the garrison had a very limited supply of food. Anderson's lack of zeal in defending the fort is proven by the letter he sent to the Adjutant General of the Army, Alonzo Thomas. Gustavus V. Fox, soon to be the Assistant Secretary of the Navy, had proposed a boat attack by which Sumter could be stocked and reinforced. In his letter to the Adjutant General Anderson raised objections to the plan as hazardous. "We shall strive to do our duty," he wrote, "though I frankly say that my heart is not in this war." Battles are not won nor strong defense made by commanders who say they have "no heart in the war." It was the opinion of the able and courageous Abner Doubleday, afterwards a distinguished general, that if Anderson's brother Charles, a former lieutenant governor of Ohio who had unflinchingly faced a mob and a halter in Texas, had been in command, he "would have made more than a technical defense of his post."

Two years had passed since the flag came down at Sumter before Du Pont made his attack on that fortress. These two years gave the defenders of Charleston time and leisure, under the able leadership of General Beauregard, whose batteries had fired the first shot at the fort, to enlarge and strengthen the bastions of the city. The chief defenses of Charleston were ancient Fort Moultrie and other batteries on Sullivan's Island; Castle Pinkney, at the mouth of the Cooper River; Fort Johnson on James Island; Fort Wagner on Morris Island; the batteries at Cumming's Point, at the very tip of Morris Island; and Sumter standing in the midst of the harbor. In addition to these batteries and forts, the channels had been sown with mines, or torpedoes as they were then called. To silence these forts and take Charleston was a most formidable undertaking. The man upon whom the government and the people counted to do this was Du Pont, now a Rear Admiral, whose superb management at Port Royal had cheered the hearts of the nation with its first significant victory. Now the great opportunity was presented to Du Pont. Had he been equal to the undertaking and captured Charleston, his fame would not have been second to that of Farragut.

The navy had been quick to learn the lessons taught by the battle between the *Monitor* and the *Merrimac* and had built not a few monitors. A good many were available when Du Pont made his attack on Charleston, and they comprised the bulk of his fleet. Fox, the Assistant Secretary, had the utmost confidence in their power, both for offense and defense; he entertained perhaps too high an opinion, higher, indeed, than that of Ericsson himself, who built the first and most famous of them all. Writing to Ericsson about the expedition against Charleston, Fox said: "Though everybody is despondent about Charleston, and even the President thinks we shall be defeated, I must say that I never had a shadow of doubt as to our success, and this confidence arises from a study of your marvellous vessels." To this Ericsson responded: "The most I dare hope is, that the contest will end without the loss of that prestige which your ironclads have conferred upon the nation abroad. A single shot may sink a ship, while a hundred rounds cannot silence a fort."

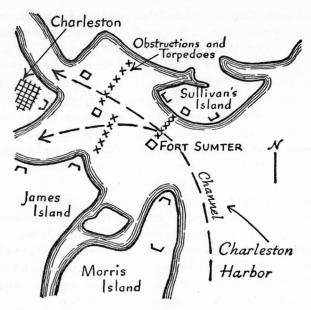

This shows that Ericsson considered the monitors more formidable against ships than against shore defenses.

As early as October of 1862, almost a year after Du Pont's victory at Port Royal, the Secretary of the Navy was beginning to have doubts as to Du Pont's ability and character, for he entered this note in his *Diary:* "Admiral Du Pont arrived today; looks hale and hearty. He is a skillful and accomplished officer. Has a fine address, is a courtier with perhaps too much finesse and management . . . like many naval officers, is given to cliques—personal, naval clanship. This evil I have striven to break up. . . . But all that I have yet seen is, if not exactly what is wished, excusable. Certainly, while he continues to do his duty so well, I shall pass minor errors and sustain Du Pont." At that time, however, Welles had no thought of relieving Du Pont and putting another in his place, for when Dahlgren visited him and asked to be assigned to the special duty of capturing Charleston, he told him that Du Pont had had that object in view for more than a year and had made it his study, and he could not supersede him in this work. Du Pont was not unaware of the fact that Dahlgren coveted the opportunity to take Charleston, for he wrote to Fox: "I forgot to tell you the other day, because I never had a chance to see you alone, that Foote and Wise had made a most extraordinary appeal to me to give up my command to Dahlgren. I was astounded; but as to what passed I will reserve until we meet. . . . Simply observing that Dahlgren is a diseased man on the subject of preferment and position . . . As I told Foote, he (Dahlgren) chose one line in the walk of his profession, while Farragut and I chose another; he was eating cream while we were eating dirt and living on the pay of our rank. Now he wants all the honors belonging to the other, but without having encountered its joltings." Thus, alas, did the desire for fame and high position corrode the bonds of friendship. Dahlgren would have been surprised and deeply grieved had he known that his old friend and shipmate had spoken of him in such derogatory terms. When Du Pont died none paid him a warmer or higher tribute than Dahlgren. As for Dahlgren "eating the cream" while Farragut and Du Pont were "eating dirt and living on the pay of their rank," Du Pont should not have forgotten that his victory at Port Royal had been won with the gun Dahlgren invented.

As the weeks and months passed by and the attack on Fort Sumter and Charleston was still postponed, the Secretary of the Navy and President Lincoln entertained increasing doubts as to Du Pont's ability and determination to take the city. Lincoln said it was McClellan over again. One reason for the delay was doubt on the part of Du Pont as to the monitors' efficacy against fortifications. In January of 1863, in order to test the monitors' powers of offense, Du Pont ordered an attack on Fort McAllister near Savannah, by the *Montauk*, commanded by John Worden. For four hours the *Montauk* hurled her shells against the fort, expending all her ammunition. The monitor, although repeatedly hit, was uninjured. On the other hand, no serious damage was done to the fort. After these experiments it was Du Pont's conclusion that "whatever degree of impenetrability they might have, there was no corresponding degree of destructiveness as against forts." In this opinion he was sustained by one of his ablest officers, Captain Drayton. On March 30th Drayton with three monitors bombarded Fort McAllister for eight hours. After the engagement he reported to Du Pont that "no injury was done which a good night's work would not repair." As early as February of 1863, two months before the assault on Sumter, reports which came to Welles from the fleet convinced him that Du Pont dreaded the conflict which he had sought, and yet was unwilling that any other should undertake it, for fear that his reputation would suffer.

But now at last the long delay and wait were over. On April 6th, 1863, the fleet led by Du Pont's flagship, the *New Ironsides,* crossed the Charleston bar and came to anchor. The next morning the sky was clear, the sea calm. The Union soldiers watching at their posts where they had landed on Morris Island expected that before the sun went down Sumter would be a pile of ruins. It was noon before the signal to weigh anchor flew from the flagship; because of tide conditions, the pilots had refused to take the ships in before that hour. No commander ever took his ships into action with abler officers than those who commanded the nine ironclads. On the flagship was Du Pont's chief of staff, Captain C.R.P. Rodgers, who had served with him at Port Royal as captain of the *Wabash.* On the *Passaic* was Percival Drayton, the South Carolinian who stood by the Union. Later he was to be Farragut's fleet captain at Mobile Bay. In the conning tower of the *Weehawken* was John Rodgers, who had also been at Port Royal and who bore one of the most famous names in the history of the United States Navy; and on the *Montauk* was John Worden, the hero of Hampton Roads.

Du Pont's squadron consisted of the flagship, the *New Ironsides,* an extraordinary looking, awkward, but powerful ironclad; the monitors *Catskill, Montauk, Nahant, Nantucket, Passaic, Patapsco,* and *Weehawken;* and the strange *Keokuk,* her sides protected with strips of railroad iron. Like Farragut at New Orleans and Mobile Bay, Du Pont had determined to lead the attack in his flagship, but yielded to the remonstrance of his captains, and surrendered that position to Captain John Rodgers in the *Weehawken.* The start was somewhat delayed when a heavy chain on the *Weehawken* became entangled with the raft at the ship's bow designed by Ericsson to pick up torpedoes. Slowly and silently the ships came in toward Sumter, watched by thousands of Charleston's anxious citizens, as well as by the Union soldiers of General David Hunter's army on the southern end of Morris Island. The batteries at Fort Wagner on Morris Island remained silent as the ships passed; but at 3 o'clock the Confederate and Palmetto flags were raised over Fort Moultrie, far to the right of Sumter, and the first shot was fired, answered immediately by the *Weehawken* and thereafter by the other monitors.

Because of steering difficulties, it was necessary to anchor the *New Ironsides* for a time to get her head into the tide. This caused some confusion among the ships directly behind the flagship, with which two of the ships collided, but without serious damage. Before the *New Ironsides* got under way again, she stood for a time directly over a mine made of a boiler filled with gunpowder and wired to Fort Wagner; but those at the fort were not able to produce a spark and the flagship passed over without injury. When 1,500 yards from Sumter, the *New Ironsides* had to anchor a second time to hold her direction. A torpedo went off, but without damage, under the *Weehawken.* Nearest to Sumter was the *Keokuk,* which was riddled like a sieve by fire from the fort and damaged so badly that she sank the next morning.

Late in the engagement, Du Pont inquired of C.R.P. Rodgers, his chief of staff, what time it was. Told that it was nearly five o'clock, he said, "Make signal to the ships to drop

out of fire; it is too late to fight this battle tonight; we will renew it early in the morning." Du Pont had withheld the fire of
the *New Ironsides,* hoping to get close to the walls of Sumter
before he delivered a broadside. Thus it was that in the engagement the flagship, although struck ninety-five times herself, did
not fire a single shot. But just as she was turning to withdraw,
Du Pont's gunners came to him and begged permission to fire at
least one broadside. Their request was granted and a single
broadside of eight guns was hurled at Fort Moultrie.

When darkness descended that night, with the fleet still inside the Charleston bar, Du Pont summoned his captains on
board the flagship. Until then, he had fully intended to renew
the conflict the next morning; but what he heard from his captains about the condition of their ships caused him to change
his mind. Early the next day he said to his chief of staff: "I have
decided not to renew the attack. During the few minutes we
were under the heaviest fire of the batteries we engaged, half
of our turret ships were in part or wholly disabled. We have
only encountered the outer line of defense, and if we force our
way into the harbor, we have not men to occupy the forts we
may take . . . We have met with a sad repulse; I shall not
turn it into a great disaster."

It was indeed a "sad repulse," one of the saddest in the history of the navy. During the forenoon of the next day the captains again came on board the flagship and, unasked by Du
Pont, expressed the opinion that it would be useless with their
present force to make another attack. With these officers, as
with those who surrounded McClellan in the army, their commander could make no mistake. "The iron-clad captains," wrote
the chief of staff, "stood like a wall of iron about Admiral Du
Pont's reputation, and there was no joint to be pierced in their
armor."

If Du Pont was genuinely convinced that a second attack
the day after the first abortive attempt would "turn a sad repulse into a great disaster," he showed high moral courage in

deciding not to make it, for he certainly knew the criticism which would fall upon him, from the barbs of which even his most loyal captains could not protect him. In the Mine Run Campaign in 1863 General Meade showed similar courage. He had started the Army of the Potomac on a carefully planned campaign against Lee's army in Virginia. Through the failure of one of his corps commanders, French, to carry out his assignment, the chances of success were greatly reduced. Knowing that his withdrawal might cost him his post, Meade nevertheless called back his army and retired to the line he had been holding since the battle of Gettysburg. In his life of Meade, Governor Pennypacker quotes him as saying: "I would rather a thousand times be relieved, charged with tardiness or incompetency, than have my conscience burdened with a wanton slaughter uselessly of brave men, or with having jeopardized the great cause by doing what I thought wrong." It takes high moral courage to adopt the course which Meade pursued and which Du Pont followed when, after the first repulse, he decided not to make a second attempt.

This "sad repulse" was a deep disappointment to the government and to the people of the North. However, although he lamented the failure, it was not a surprise to Lincoln; only five days before the battle he had told the Secretary of the Navy that "the long delay of Du Pont, his constant calling for more ships, more ironclads, was like McClellan calling for more regiments." He thought the two men were alike and said he was "prepared for a repulse at Charleston." Welles must likewise have been prepared, for on April 9th, the news of the battle of the 7th not yet having reached him, he made this entry in his *Diary:* "These great and prolonged preparations weigh heavily upon me—Providence delights to humble man and prostrate his strength. For months my confidence has not increased, and now that the conflict is upon us, my disquietude is greater still."

Prepared though he was for failure, the Secretary's scorn

and anger when he learned of the defeat were intense: "We learned that after all our outlay and great preparation, giving him [Du Pont] all our force, and a large portion of the best officers, he intends making no further effort, but will abandon the plan and all attempts to take it. A fight of thirty minutes, and the loss of one man, which he witnessed, satisfied the admiral." By the 25th of May the Secretary's scorn found expression in these words: "Du Pont is determined Charleston shall not be captured by the navy, and that the navy shall not attempt it." And then, very ungenerously and unjustly, this: "Thinks it dangerous for the vessels to remain in Charleston Harbor, and prefers to occupy his palace ship, the *Wabash,* at Port Royal, to roughing it in a smaller vessel off the port. His prize money would doubtless be greater without any risk. All officers under him are being affected by his feelings.—But I perceive that in all things he never forgets Du Pont. His success at Port Royal has made him feel that he is indispensable to the service."

As soon as Lincoln learned of the repulse of the fleet at Charleston, he telegraphed the following order to Du Pont: "Hold your position inside the bar near Charleston; or, if you shall have left it, return to it, and hold it till further orders. Do not allow the enemy to erect new batteries or defense on Morris Island. If he has begun it, drive him out. I do not herein order you to renew the general attack. That is to depend on your own discretion or a further order." The next day, April 14th, the President sent a second telegram addressed to both Admiral Du Pont and General David Hunter, commanding the land forces. In this message he said: "No censure upon you, or either of you, is intended. We still hope that by cordial and judicious co-operation you can take the batteries on Morris Island and Sullivan's Island and Fort Sumter. But whether you can or not, we wish the demonstration kept up for a time— We wish the attempt to be a real one, though not a desperate one, if it affords any considerable chance of success— Once again before Charleston, do not leave till further orders from here."

Already mortified by the failure of his assault on Sumter, Du Pont was stung by what he considered to be criticism and censure in the President's telegrams. Two days later, he wrote to the Secretary of the Navy requesting that the Department relieve him by appointing an officer "who, in its opinion, is more able to execute that service in which I have had the misfortune to fail—the capture of Charleston." Obeying the President's order, he took the fleet back across the bar to its anchorage off Morris Island, although he was convinced that the movement would be attended by great risk to his vessels. Lincoln had assured the admiral that no censure was intended, but it was not strange that Du Pont considered it as such, especially in what the President said about his desire that the next attack by the fleet be a "real one," as well as by his order to bring the fleet back into the harbor, "if you shall have left it."

In the course he took in not ordering a second attack, Du Pont was upheld by his chief officers, most, if not all, of whom had an invincible prejudice against the monitors. Five of the high officers of the fleet at Charleston submitted to the Navy Department a statement strongly condemning the monitors as unseaworthy and too slow in firing their guns.

A witness of the attack made by Du Pont's fleet on Fort Sumter was Chief Engineer Alban C. Stimers, who had been on the *Monitor* in her battle with the *Merrimac* at Hampton Roads. Stimers was now inspector general of all the monitor type of vessels, in commission or building. He had gone to Charleston with a crew of mechanics to make what repairs might be necessary after the expected battle. In a report he made to the Navy Department seven days after the battle, Stimers said he boarded every vessel the next morning and was "agreeably disappointed" to find how little serious damage the ships had suffered. "There were," he said, "no clear passages through the decks and no penetrations through the sides of the vessels, or the pilot houses . . . In consideration of the vast importance to our country that that stronghold of rebellion should be reduced, I take the liberty to express to the Department my firm opinion that the obstructions can be readily passed with the means already provided, and our entire fleet of ironclads pass up successfully to the wharves of Charleston, and that the monitor vessels still retain sufficient enduring powers to enable them to pass all the forts and batteries which may reasonably be expected." This was in direct variance with Du Pont's report that "five of the ironclads were wholly or partially disabled; disabled too (as the obstructions could not be passed) in that which was most essential to our success— I mean in their armament, or power of inflicting injury upon the enemy by their guns."

On May 12th Du Pont requested the Navy Department to arrest Stimers and send him to the fleet at Charleston for trial. The charges were that, on his return journey to New York on the *Arago*, Stimers had said at the table, in the presence of the officers of the ships and others, that he had been told by one or more of the commanders of the ironclads engaged in the battle of April 7th that the attack ought to have been renewed, and that they were "hot for renewing the engagement"; also that "with the intent to disparage and injure the professional reputation of his superior officer, Rear Admiral S. F. Du Pont, he had criticized the professional conduct of Admiral Du Pont," and had said the monitors were in as good condition the day after the battle, after slight repairs, as they had been the day before when they commenced it. Welles did not grant Du Pont's request that Stimers be tried at Charleston, but ordered the court to convene at the New York Navy Yard. The court was made up of Rear Admiral Silas H. Stringham, Rear Admiral Francis H. Gregory, and Commodore William C. Nicholson, all old and distinguished officers.

In answer to the charges made against him, Stimers denied that he had said that commanders of the ironclads had told him that the attack of the 7th of April ought to have been renewed, and that they were "hot" for another assault. As for the charge that he had criticized in terms unbecoming an officer the professional conduct of Admiral Du Pont by saying that the monitors, after slight repairs, were in as good condition to renew the battle as they had been to commence it, he answered that he had been careful and restrained in his comments on the admiral; but if he had stated all that was charged, it was no more than he was authorized to say. He had been charged by the government with the duty of inspecting the monitors when they were being built and, in addition, had had the good fortune of being on the *Monitor* in her fight with the *Merrimac*. Therefore, he claimed the right to express an opinion as to *the value* and *capacities* of the monitors and what condition they were in after the attack on Sumter, even if his opinion differed from that of Du Pont. "I was bound," he said, "neither by courtesy nor by any rule of the service with which I am acquainted to withhold or conceal it." The real purpose of the charges and prosecution, he asserted, was not an inquiry into his conduct or language, but under that pretext to justify the failure of Admiral Du Pont. After a session of four months the court reported that "there is no necessity or propriety for further proceedings in the case."

Two weeks after the Charleston battle Du Pont had written the Navy Department complaining of an account of the battle of April 7th which had appeared in a Baltimore paper, and intimating that the report had been inspired by Chief Engineer Stimers. Secretary Welles replied that he thought the press of the country had been "generally lenient and indulgent toward him and the censures, under a great disappointment, had been comparatively few." In his reply Du Pont took strong exception to the word "lenient" as a true statement of the attitude of the public toward him. In the long and acrimonious exchange of letters between the Secretary and the unhappy admiral, Welles, on the whole patient and forbearing, reminded Du Pont that after the attack on Sumter he had been dissatisfied with his flagship, the *New Ironsides,* dissatisfied with the monitors, dissatisfied with Chief Engineer Stimers, dissatisfied with the President for the telegram he had sent him after the battle, dissatisfied with the Department for not more promptly acknowledging and publishing his reports. Then came these caustic sentences:

> If these complaints and reports, wherein the admiral of the squadron devoted so large a portion of his time to his personal matters and so little toward marshalling his force for the occupation of the harbor of Charleston and the capture of the city, were not received with the patience to which they were entitled, it was my misfortune. I do not deny that it would have been more acceptable to the Department to have witnessed the zeal manifested in hunting down newspaper editors, engineers, and surgeons, directed against rebel enemies and to the destruction of their works.

Two months after the repulse at Charleston, and while Du Pont was still in charge of the fleet, one of his monitors performed a feat which nullified at least some of the criticism directed against them. This was the capture of the powerful Confederate ram *Atlanta* on June the 17th. Reports had reached Du Pont that the ram, one of the most formidable ships constructed by the Confederacy, would soon go down the Wilmington River from Savannah to raise the blockade of Warsaw Sound. The *Atlanta* was known as the "Ladies' Gunboat" by reason of the fact that the money to build her had been supplied by gifts of jewelry by ladies of Savannah. Originally an English iron ship, the *Fingal*, and for a time a blockade runner, the *Atlanta* had been altered into a ram by surmounting her deck with a shield or casement, after the fashion of the *Merrimac* and the *Arkansas*, arming her, and plating her sides with four inches of English railroad iron.

To stop the ram from coming out and, if possible, destroy her, Du Pont dispatched two of his monitors, the *Nahant* under Commander John Downes and the *Weehawken* under Captain John Rodgers, to Warsaw Sound. As soon as the monitors appeared, the *Atlanta* started down the river to meet them, accompanied by excursion steamers filled with spectators eager to witness the destruction of the Federal ships. When the two monitors saw the *Atlanta* approaching, they first steamed outward toward the end of Warsaw Island, creating the impression on the *Atlanta* that they were in flight; but when all was ready they turned about and headed for the ram. When Rodgers had the *Weehawken* in the position he desired, he opened fire with his big 15-inch gun. This first shot went through the iron shield of the *Atlanta* and strewed the deck with splinters of iron and wood. Three other shots followed in quick succession; one of them tore off the roof of the pilot house; another opened a hole in her plates near the water line. Meanwhile, the *Atlanta* had been able to fire just one shot. Then she raised the white flag of surrender. In his report of the engagement to Du Pont, Captain Rodgers said: "The first shot took away their disposition to fight; and the third their ability to get away." The excursion steamers which had brought the crowds down for a June outing hastily turned about and steamed back to Savannah. One of the objections Du Pont had raised against the monitors was that they would not be able to cope with ironclads then building at Savannah. The most formidable of these had now surrendered to the *Weehawken* after a battle of only fifteen minutes.

Du Pont remained in command of the South Atlantic squadron for two months longer, but his sun had set, for the Secretary of the Navy was giving anxious thought to the selection of a new commander. The noble and courageous Foote was named for the post, but he died in New York on his way to join the fleet. On July 6th, 1863, Rear Admiral Dahlgren raised his flag on the *Wabash* and Du Pont went into final retirement, with death not far off. He died in June of 1865.

Every war has its tragedies, as well as casualties, among its leaders. Du Pont is one of those tragedies. After he took Port Royal his name for a time shone in the brightest colors until, after Farragut's greater achievement at New Orleans and his own repulse at Charleston, he passed into eclipse. He was still supported, loved, and admired by the higher naval officers; but with the people at large his star had paled.

Receiving word of the death of Du Pont on June 23rd, 1865, Welles took this farewell of him:

Du Pont possessed ability, had acquirements, was a scholar rather than a hero. He challenged me to remove him, and felt confident I would not do it.—As it was, I made no haste, and only ordered Foote and Dahlgren when I got ready. Then the step was taken. Du Pont was amazed, yet had no doubt the navy would be roused in his favor, and that he should overpower the Department. He procured two or three papers to speak for him, but there was no partisanship in the navy for him, except with about half a dozen young officers whom he had petted and trained, and a few mischievous politicians. Returning to Delaware, he went into absolute retirement. None missed or called for him.[2]

Perhaps the most surprised, if not the most disappointed, of all at Du Pont's failure at Charleston was the Assistant Secretary of the Navy. Fox had selected many of the commanders of the ships and had unbounded faith in the monitors, even telling Du Pont that the original *Monitor* could enter and depart from Charleston Harbor alone and unscathed! Just a month before the battle at Charleston, Fox wrote Du Pont: "Every hour of the day and far into the night, and at earliest dawn I think of you and wish myself near you at the great attack, the prelude of the downfall of this infernal confederacy. Our flagstaff [at the Navy Department] stands surmounted by its gilded eagle, waiting patiently for the downfall of Charleston to fling forth our beloved flag." A week later he sent a final note of encouragement to Du Pont, saying: "Farragut has had a setback at Port

[2] The unhappy correspondence between Welles and Du Pont makes it clear that a chief complaint of the Secretary of the Navy was that the admiral had never intimated to him in any way that he regarded the attack on Sumter and Charleston a hopeless undertaking. This he revealed only *after* the "sad repulse." If Du Pont felt, as he said afterwards he did, that the Department was driving him into an assault which he was convinced would fail, he ought to have done one of two things: secure a postponement or relinquish the command.

Hudson and lost the noble old *Mississippi*. It finally devolves upon you by great good fortune to avert the series of disasters that have fallen upon the Navy. That you will do it most gloriously I have no misgivings whatever."

The downfall of the "infernal confederacy," as Fox called it, had to be postponed for two more years; the navy flagstaff with its gilded eagle waited in vain to fling forth the banner of victory. Although Fort Wagner was taken by Gillmore's troops and Sumter reduced to a heap of ruins by the bombardment of Dahlgren's guns, Charleston was not captured by either fleet or army until General Sherman's march across the Carolinas compelled its evacuation.

On the evening of that memorable 7th of April, 1863, the thousands of Charlestonians who had been watching the duel between the forts and the Union fleet rejoiced greatly as they saw Du Pont's ironclads go smoking down the harbor to their anchorage. On the tip of St. Michael's steeple, the pride of Charleston, the golden ball which was the first glimpse of home to seamen entering the harbor and the last slow-fading vision to ships outward bound, still shone and flashed in the setting sun.

When one comes to the end of Admiral Du Pont's story and the repulse of the powerful fleet which had been prepared for him, inevitably the question arises: what would have happened if Farragut, Porter, or Foote had been in command? None of those illustrious three was afraid to take the chances of battle, without which great victories are never won. When Farragut's flagship grounded almost under the guns of Fort St. Philip in the attack on New Orleans and was set on fire by a Confederate fire raft, and Farragut was fearful that the end of the *Hartford* and the failure of the attack had come, he too might have turned back and would have been sustained in so doing by his captains, as Du Pont was by his. Again at Mobile Bay, when the *Tecumseh* at the head of the line went down after striking a mine and the *Brooklyn* was backing into the *Hartford*, throwing the whole battle line into confusion, Farragut might have signalled for the fleet to retire. Instead, he gave the order for full steam ahead and, passing the *Brooklyn*, took his flagship over the very field of mines where the *Tecumseh* had gone down, and went on to glorious victory and everlasting fame. This much is certain: if Foote or Porter, but especially Farragut, had been in command of the Union fleet that April afternoon at Charleston, the flagship would never have retired without firing a single shot into the walls of Sumter, nor would the fleet have retreated until it had suffered greater damage and left deeper scars on the grim walls of the fortress.

There was a report in navy circles that near the end of the war Admiral Du Pont in conversation with Farragut gave several reasons for his "sad repulse." At the end of Du Pont's recital of factors which made success impossible, Farragut is reported to have said: "Admiral, there was one other reason why you did not take Charleston,—you didn't think you could." Whether or not Farragut actually said that, there can be little doubt that Du Pont failed to take Charleston chiefly because of his lack of faith in his own ability.

V

DAHLGREN

LIKE EVERY true navy man in time of war, John Dahlgren longed for glory on the sea, but like many others, he failed to achieve it. During the first two years of the war he was too valuable to be spared from the Bureau of Ordnance and from his post as commandant of the Washington Navy Yard. When at length his chance came to gain distinction in battle as commander of the South Atlantic Blockading Squadron, like Du Pont before him he failed in the great objective of that squadron, the capture of Charleston. He did not win the fame which came to Farragut, Du Pont, Foote, Worden, and Winslow, but he played an important part in the victories they won, for it was his invention, the Dahlgren gun, which smashed the defenses at Port Royal, New Orleans, Fort Henry, and Wilmington, and spoke with authority from the deck of the *Kearsarge* when she sent the *Alabama* to the bottom of the sea.

In the persons of two inventors, Sweden made a notable contribution to the cause of the North in the Civil War. John Ericsson gave the navy the *Monitor* which freed the Atlantic coast from the menace of the *Merrimac* and revolutionized naval warfare; Dahlgren, son of the Swedish consul at Philadelphia, gave the navy its most powerful weapon.

John Adolphus Bernard Dahlgren was born at Philadelphia on November 13th, 1809. His highly educated father had fled his native country because of his advocacy of democratic principles

and had come to Philadelphia in 1806. There, restored to favor
with the Swedish government, he served as consul until his
death in 1824. The future admiral attended a Quaker school; he
enjoyed also a close intimacy with the minister of Old Swedes
Church, serving him occasionally as an amanuensis. From the
windows of his father's house he could see the tall masts of the
ships as they passed up and down the Delaware. On Saturday
afternoons he would sometimes walk down to the Philadelphia
Navy Yard, where he looked with wonder and desire on the
Pennsylvania, the pride of the navy, a huge three-decker, destined to end her career ingloriously by being burned when the
navy yard at Norfolk was abandoned by the government at the
beginning of the Civil War.

Although his sponsors spoke of him in the highest terms, his
first application to the Navy Department was rejected. He could
have had a lieutenant's commission in the Colombian Navy, but
wisely refused the offer. While waiting and hoping for a midshipman's warrant, in order "to obtain a knowledge of my intended profession" he sailed before the mast in a merchant ship
trading with the West Indies, and narrowly escaped disaster and
death in a hurricane off the Florida coast. When he returned to
Philadelphia he wrote an article relating his experiences in the
storm which was published in *The Saturday Evening Post*. At
length his ambition was realized when he received his commission as Acting Midshipman on February 1st, 1826. His first
cruise was made on the *Macedonian*, a frigate captured from the
British in the War of 1812 and whose figurehead stands today
as a monument on the grounds of the Naval Academy at Annapolis. Dahlgren's journal gives interesting accounts of this first
cruise and the countries he visited. Of Rio de Janeiro he writes:
"In the course of my rambles my attention was attracted by a
pretty ring set with nine diamonds—value forty Spanish dollars.
Where could that look better than on the hand of my dear
mother, thought I; and in a few minutes my determination was

put into practise." His father died when he was only fifteen, and he pays frequent tribute to his devoted mother, from whom he thought he inherited his talent for drawing and designing.

His next cruise was on the *Ontario* in the Mediterranean, which at that time might well have been called the navy's training school. A favorite calling place for the ships was Port Mahon, on the island of Minorca, in the Balearic group. On this cruise Dahlgren had for a shipmate Lieutenant Samuel Francis Du Pont, whom he was to succeed as commander of the South Atlantic Squadron many years later. At the end of the cruise the captain of the *Ontario* commended Dahlgren highly to the Board of Examination as one "possessing in an eminent degree those attributes of the officer and seaman which will, I trust and believe, eventuate in much future usefulness to his country and reputation to himself." Of the seventy acting midshipmen who had received temporary commissions in 1826, only thirty-one passed the examination in 1832, and in this list Dahlgren stood ninth.

In 1834 he was ordered to duty with the Coast Survey, an appointment which had an important bearing on his future career, for the superintendent under whom he served was the Swiss scientist, Ferdinand Hassler, who immediately recognized Dahlgren's mathematical ability and made him second assistant of the Survey. Three years later, threatened with blindness brought on by his arduous labors on the Coast Survey, and relieved from active duty, he spent several years on a farm in Bucks County, Pennsylvania. At this time of trial and discouragement, a brother officer wrote him these prophetic words: "Keep up your spirits, and remember that Heaven has given you talents of no ordinary kind, and these talents may still reap both fame and honor to you." By 1843 he was able to report for active duty, and sailed for the Mediterranean on the *Cumberland*, where he had for a shipmate Andrew Hull Foote, later to win fame on the Tennessee and Mississippi rivers. On his return from this cruise, during which he visited most of the countries of the Mediterranean and the Near East, he received an appointment to the Bureau of Ordnance. There his genius was given full rein, and he soon gained fame and recognition as a scientist and inventor. In this bureau and at the Washington Navy Yard he served for nearly two decades, until July of 1863, when he succeeded Du Pont as commander of the South Atlantic Squadron.

His years in the Bureau of Ordnance were marked by two outstanding inventions. The first of these was a new kind of howitzer for small boats. The other, and more important, was the Dahlgren gun. The bursting of a gun on the *Princeton* in 1844, which killed the Secretary of State and the Secretary of the Navy, and the subsequent bursting of one of the standard thirty-two-pounder guns, gave force to his request that he be allowed to submit plans for a gun of his own design. He first designed a nine- and then an eleven-inch gun. His chief innovation consisted in enlarging and strengthening the gun at the breech, thus making it possible to use a much heavier charge and hurl a more destructive missile. There was much opposition to these heavy and ugly weapons, which were called "Bullfrog" guns because of their width at the breech. In order to demonstrate their practicability, Dahlgren secured from the Navy Department a modest-sized sloop of war, the *Plymouth*, and was given a free hand to arrange her armament. Many navy men entertained the belief that even the heaviest frigate would be torn to pieces by the shock and concussion of firing such a big gun. But on a cruise to Europe and return on the *Plymouth*, Dahlgren demonstrated that it could be fired without ill effect even from such a comparatively small vessel. Soon after this, all the important ships of the small American Navy, such as the *Merrimac*, the *Brooklyn*, and the *Hartford*, were armed with the Dahlgren gun.

When Captain Franklin Buchanan, commandant of the Washington Navy Yard, joined the Confederacy early in 1861, Dahlgren replaced him in office. In view of what had happened at Norfolk and at Pensacola when these yards were seized by the Confederacy, Dahlgren's post was one of the most important in the service. After the crisis of the first weeks of the war had passed, some of the navy captains asked for Dahlgren's post on the ground that a law passed in 1804 directed that only an officer with the rank of Captain could be commandant of the Navy Yard. But Lincoln declared, "The Yard shall not be taken from the Captain [he was then only a commander]; he held it when no one else would; and now he shall keep it as long as he pleases." Until he went to sea in the summer of 1863, Dahlgren served successively as Commandant of the Navy Yard and then as Chief of the Bureau of Ordnance. Nathaniel Parker Willis, popular poet and dramatist and at that time a Washington correspondent, gives us this sketch of Dahlgren when he was at the Navy Yard: "He is a light complexioned man of perhaps forty years of age, slight, and of medium height; pale and delicate features. His countenance is exceedingly thoughtful and modest, and expresses complete unconsciousness of being observed; while his eye is inevitably keen, and his thin nostrils expand as he talks, with a look of great enthusiasm."

No officer of the Navy enjoyed a greater intimacy with Lincoln, or was held in higher esteem, than Dahlgren. He achieved a high place in the President's opinion and friendship partly through his convenient position as Commandant of the Washington Navy Yard and the energetic measures which he took to hold and strengthen it; partly because of his invention, the Dahlgren gun, which was such an important instrument of victory on river and on sea; and especially because at the outbreak of the war, when Captain Buchanan and all the other officers at the Yard resigned their commissions and joined the Confederacy, Dahlgren had remained loyal to the flag. He was one man upon whom Lincoln knew he could rely to the end. When McClellan came to Washington to command the Army of the Potomac and then to direct all the armies as general in chief, Dahlgren at once established a friendly and confidential relationship with him. In the naval officer's journal one can trace Secretary of

War Stanton's growing enmity and treachery toward McClellan. While assuring the general that he was his true friend and would give him full and loyal support, Stanton simultaneously made scornful references to him and his plans in the presence of the President and other high members of the government and officers of the army and navy. Dahlgren tells of a visit he paid the President at the White House at the time McClellan was starting his campaign up the Peninsula from Fortress Monroe toward Richmond, and relates how Stanton made slighting remarks to Lincoln about the general in chief.

On the morning of "Black Sunday," March 9th, 1862, Lincoln appeared at Dahlgren's office with Senator Browning of Illinois, saying he had "frightful news." The *Merrimac* had come out and sunk the *Cumberland* and the *Congress*. The President was not stunned by the news, "but was in his usual suggestive mood." At a meeting held that day at the White House, the Secretaries of State, War, and Navy, General Meigs, General McClellan, and Dahlgren were present. Meigs was "desponding and silent; McClellan was concerned about the troops at Newport News. Seward alone was composed." Dahlgren advised that Port Royal, the great naval base on the South Carolina coast which had been won by Du Pont's victory the previous November, should be on the "look out"; that the *Wabash*, Du Pont's powerful flagship, should go at once to Hampton Roads; and that preparations should be made for blocking the Potomac. That same afternoon Dahlgren, who, with McClellan and Meigs, had been directed by the President to arrange for the blocking of the river, went down the Potomac with the Secretaries of War and State and pointed out the places where the *Merrimac* might be expected to appear if she attacked Washington. At ten o'clock that same night the Secretary of the Navy informed Dahlgren of the four-hour battle between the *Merrimac* and the *Monitor* and reported that the dreaded "monster" had withdrawn to Norfolk.

On the night of this memorable day of fear, excitement, and eventual rejoicing over the news of the *Monitor's* battle with the *Merrimac*, Dahlgren notified the Secretary of the Navy that he had obtained a number of boats and was filling them with sand and gravel for the purpose of blocking the Potomac so that the *Merrimac* could not reach Washington. The Secretary replied that he had issued no orders for such a proceeding. At a meeting with the President the next morning, Stanton said that it was he who had given the order to Meigs and Dahlgren with the President's approval. Lincoln confirmed this, saying that even though the sinking of barges filled with stone at Kettle Shoals or elsewhere in the river might do no good, it could do no harm. To this Welles replied that he had labored with General McClellan and the War Department to keep the river open to navigation, "and we ourselves were now to shut ourselves off by these obstructions." The President then forbade the sinking of the barges in the channel until it was known for a fact that the *Merrimac* was approaching. Although the *Merrimac* had withdrawn to Norfolk after the battle with the *Monitor*, obviously the ram was still a foe to be dreaded. Some weeks later a long line of barges along the Maryland shore attracted the attention of the President and members of the government as they were proceeding down the Potomac in a steamer. In answer to an inquiry as to the purposes of these barges, Lincoln said: "Oh, that is Stanton's navy—Welles was incensed and opposed to the scheme, and it has proved that Neptune [Lincoln's favorite name for Welles] was right. Stanton's navy is as useless as the paps of a man to a sucking child. They amuse the child, but they are good for nothing for service." [1]

Dahlgren's journal throws light upon Lincoln's apparently casual way of conducting the nation's affairs in the midst of a great crisis. At almost any hour of the day or night the President might appear at Dahlgren's office at the Navy Yard or summon him to the White House. He frequently invited him to take a cruise down the Potomac. One day Dahlgren was at the Navy Department conferring with Fox about naval matters when the

[1] From an article written by Welles some years later and incorporated in his diary.

President came in. Lincoln sat and talked with them for some time, saying, among other things, that Admiral Du Pont "showed an over-sensitiveness" and had taken unwarranted offense at a letter he had written him. After a short time, the President arose, and as he left said: "Well, I will go home. I had no business here; but, as the lawyer said, I had none anywhere else." And with that circuit-riding anecdote, the tall gaunt form of the President vanished.

New military devices and weapons, whether brought to him by experts through the proper departmental channels or not, were examined by Lincoln with interest and curiosity. On one occasion he sent for Dahlgren for advice about a new kind of powder which had been submitted to him. The President told Dahlgren that he had burned a little of the powder, and that there seemed to be too much of a residuum. Saying to Dahlgren, "Now I'll show you," he poured some of the powder on a piece of paper and ran to the fireplace with it; there he picked up with the tongs a live coal, "blew on it and clapped it to the powder, and away it went." After the flame had disappeared Lincoln pointed out that "there is too much left there." Dahlgren later remarked on how peaceful was the President's mind, "so easily diverted from the great convulsion going on, and a nation menaced with corruption."

At a critical stage of McClellan's 1862 campaign on the Peninsula against Richmond, Lincoln, alarmed for the safety of Washington, held back the powerful corps of General McDowell, the unfortunate commander at Bull Run, with almost disastrous consequences to McClellan's army.[2] One day Lincoln invited Dahlgren and Stanton to go down the Potomac with him to visit McDowell's corps, then stationed at Aquia Creek, where it flows into the Potomac. When they reached McDowell's headquarters the general wished to show them a trestle bridge which his

[2] McClellan's plan was to have McDowell's corps join the right wing of the Union army in its advance on Richmond. The holding back of this corps enabled Lee to make the successful attack which began the Seven Days' Battle of June 26th-July 2nd, 1862.

engineers had thrown across a creek, and invited his visitors to accompany him. When they reached the bridge, Lincoln said, "Let us walk over it." The floor of the bridge consisted of a single plank, one hundred feet above the creek. Lincoln went first, McDowell next, then Stanton, and after him Dahlgren. Halfway over, Stanton became dizzy, and stopped, fearful lest he fall. Although he was likewise far from comfortable, Dahlgren took the fiery Secretary of War, now completely tamed, by the hand and led him across the bridge. Lincoln, the frontiersman, accustomed to such experiences in Indiana and Illinois, felt no discomfort. On the way back to Washington, the President took from his pocket a volume of Fitz-Greene Halleck's poems, and with much feeling read to his companions, whose thoughts were far removed from verse, the poem on Marco Bozzaris, the Greek patriot who fell in a victorious battle with the Turks.

The President was a man of dreams and premonitions. One feels impelled to wonder whether, when he read Halleck's lines to Stanton and Dahlgren, he had a premonition of the tragic end which would deprive him of his hope of seeing the nation united. After the poet has described the different ways and ages in which death comes to men, he says:

> But to the hero, when his sword
> Has won the battle for the free,
> Thy voice sounds like a prophet's word;
> And in its hollow tones are heard
> The thanks of millions yet to be.

From the very first day of the war, Dahlgren had been making a great contribution to the final, though long deferred, victory through his work at the Bureau of Ordnance and as Commandant of the Navy Yard, and perhaps most of all through his invention. But as month after month passed by, and the nation rejoiced over the victories of Du Pont at Port Royal, of Farragut at New Orleans, of Foote on the Tennessee and the Mississippi, and of Worden at Hampton Roads, Dahlgren grew restive; he longed to exchange the blueprints of guns, the ordnance testing

grounds, and the routine at the Navy Yard for active duty with
a fleet, and he repeatedly sought service at sea. A few days
after the engagement between the *Monitor* and the *Merrimac,*
at a meeting of the Cabinet he asked the Secretary of the Navy
to give him command of the *Monitor,* since Worden, her
captain, was disabled from the wound received in the battle.
Welles would not grant his request, telling him that he was too
valuable in his present position and that he would not run the
risk of having him injured. In July of that same year, at the end
of McClellan's unsuccessful campaign against Richmond, Lincoln
consulted Dahlgren about the feasibility of keeping the James
River open. Dahlgren told him he could do it if the President
would give him the means and place him in command. But
when Dahlgren, at Lincoln's direction, applied to Welles for the
appointment, he was told that he could not be spared, and that
his services were of greater importance where he was. Dahlgren protested that it would be his last chance to become a flag
officer and command a squadron, but Welles would not be
moved. Later Dahlgren asked to be assigned to the special mission of capturing Charleston; but Welles was not yet ready to
have him supersede Du Pont, who was ambitious to seize that
citadel of nullification and secession.

After the repulse of Du Pont's attack on Fort Sumter in
April of 1863, the Secretary of the Navy began to consider whom
he could put in Du Pont's place. His first choice, which reflected
the sentiment of the country, was Farragut. That officer, however, was already employed in important work in the Gulf. To
replace Du Pont with Porter, who was doing notable work on
the western rivers, also seemed unwise. Although Porter had
great dash and daring, he was boastful, occasionally reckless,
and had not yet gained the President's regard. Dahlgren was
Lincoln's choice. It was thought, however, that his elevation
would create discontent among navy officers because he had had
no active war service. Dahlgren had felt slighted when the command of the Western Flotilla on the Mississippi was given to

David Porter. "Dahlgren," wrote Welles in his *Diary* for June 23rd, 1863, "is grieved with my action in his case. He desires beyond almost any one the highest grade honors of his profession, and has his appetite stimulated by the partiality of the President, who does not hesitate to say to him, and to me, that he will give him the highest grade if I will send him a letter to that effect, or a letter of appointment. Titles irregularly obtained cannot add to Dahlgren's reputation; yet he cannot be reasoned with. He has yet rendered no service afloat during the war—has not been under fire—and is not on the direct road for professional advancement. But he is a favorite with the President and knows it."

Welles, at the close of one of his busy days, pondering the important decision he must soon make thus appraised Dahlgren:

My intercourse and relations with Dahlgren have been individually satisfactory. The partiality of the President has sometimes embarrassed me and given Dahlgren promotion and prominence which may prove a misfortune in the end. It has gained him no friends in the profession, for the officers feel and know he has attained naval honors without naval claims or experience. He has intelligence and ability without question; his nautical qualities are disputed; his skill, capacity, courage, daring, sagacity and comprehensiveness in high command are to be tested. He is intensely ambitious, and, I fear, too selfish. He has heroism which proceeds from pride, and would lead him to danger and death; but whether he has the innate, unselfish courage of the genuine sailor and soldier, remains to be seen.

The Secretary of the Navy's comments on Dahlgren are less unjust and neither so severe nor so satirical as those he wrote on Du Pont. Dahlgren was ambitious for glory in active service; but so, and properly, were all the other high officers. If, indeed, he had "rendered no service afloat during the war" and "had not been under fire," that was no fault of his, for he had repeatedly sought service at sea and invariably had his application refused by Welles on the ground that his services in the Bureau of Ordnance and at the Navy Yard were too valuable to justify risking his death or disablement in battle.

Soon after the repulse of Admiral Du Pont's squadron, Admiral Foote was selected to replace him. Perhaps to satisfy the President's desire for Dahlgren's promotion, Welles offered him the second place in the fleet, the command of the ironclads, with a special view to the capture of Charleston. When Fox first broached the matter to Dahlgren, he was strongly averse to such an arrangement, saying that two admirals in the same fleet would produce trouble. He consented, however, to go to New York and have a talk with Admiral Foote. Foote, an old friend, was quite willing to have Dahlgren in command of the ironclads; but just as he was preparing to sail he was stricken with his fatal illness. Dahlgren called to see him at the Astor House; when he called again the next day he found Foote, the brave hero of Ft. Henry, Ft. Donelson, and Island No. 10, in a coma. "Alas!" wrote Dahlgren in his journal, "he was unconscious, and had in reality taken his leave of earth."

On a Sunday morning in June, 1863, Dahlgren was summoned from church to the Navy Department, where the Secretary informed him that he was to succeed Du Pont as commander of the South Atlantic Blockading Squadron. As he was about to sail from New York to join the fleet, Dahlgren called once again, and for the last time, to see the dying Foote, whose misfortune had given him his opportunity. The government and the people had been sorely disappointed at the failure of Du Pont. Now the naval scientist and inventor was presented with his hour of great opportunity. Notified that he was to be succeeded, Du Pont did everything possible to put the fleet in readiness for battle when Dahlgren took over the command. In private correspondence Du Pont had referred scornfully to Dahlgren as a man who "ate cream" while the fighting admirals were "eating dirt." That, however, was at a time when Du Pont was soured by disappointment and stung by criticism. Now his better nature asserted itself and he greeted his successor with courtesy and kindness and as a friend whom he had long honored and loved.

On July 18th, just four days after he succeeded Du Pont in command of the South Atlantic Blockading Squadron, Dahlgren, with his flag on the *Montauk,* led the ironclads across the Charleston bar to bombard Fort Wagner on Morris Island in preparation for an attack by the army under General Gillmore. First at a distance of 1200 yards from the fort, and then, as the tide changed from ebb to flood, as close as 300 yards, from noon until 7:45 P.M. the ships rained shells on Wagner. General Taliaferro, the Confederate officer commanding the fort, estimated the number of shells at 9,000. Dahlgren thought he had silenced the batteries. They were indeed silent; not, as the sequel showed, because they had been destroyed, but because the gunners had taken refuge in the bombproofs, ready to man the guns again when an attack was made.

On a blank leaf Dahlgren received a penciled note from Gillmore that he was now ready to make the assault with his soldiers. The ships then ceased firing, lest they kill friend as well as foe. In the waning light, those in the fleet could see the masses of troops moving along the beach toward Fort Wagner. Then darkness shut them in, and only the flashes of artillery could be seen. The assault was a ghastly failure, costing the army 1500 casualties. The heaviest losses were in the 54th Massachusetts Regiment, made up of colored troops, led by the young Bostonian, Robert Gould Shaw, who was buried in a ditch with his men. Saint-Gaudens' stirring equestrian statue of Shaw stands on Boston Common, just across from the State House. Thus ended the second major attack on the defenses of Charleston.

From the day of his first attack on Fort Wagner in July until October, Dahlgren, in conjunction with the army under General Gillmore on Morris Island, maintained periodic bombardments of Fort Sumter, Fort Wagner, and the other defenses of Charleston; day after day, shifting his flag from one vessel to another, he led the ironclads in against the forts. The fierce heat of the South Carolina summer and long confinement on the poorly-ventilated monitors impaired his health; at times he was prostrated in body and depressed in spirit. He knew the disappointment the people of the North experienced when Du Pont failed to take Charleston, and he was well aware of the criticism which was falling upon him because he had achieved no greater success. The entries in his journal for this period reflect his state of mind and body:

August 4.—News from poor Ully. Poor child! He had to lose his foot to save his life.[3]

August 13.—I am better today, but the worst of this place is that one only stops getting weaker. One does not get stronger.

August 15.—Nothing but the *will* has kept me up.

August 21.—Sumter is now completely dilapidated at the gorge. So I decided to try a hand at completing the work, and assembled the captains of ironclads to explain my plan. At 10½ were to move. The hour came; I went to the *Weehawken;* she had not moved. Simpson alone understood and acted rightly, hence the catastrophe. Comes a scout and says the *Passaic* is aground. No one knows where. I took instant measures; but so much time had been lost by the time she was off, that there was too little of the night left. So I had to abandon the attempt.

August 26.—One of those debilitating days, such as I have seen nowhere else. I was so feeble that I could hardly rise from the chair and walk across the room. Through the day preparing to force the obstructions, and called the captains of ironclads on board to explain. Rowan is a great drawback,—full of objections and can suggest nothing. Shows no interest, and is ready to cavil at anything.

August 28.—My debility increases, so that today it is an exertion to sit in a chair—I do not see well. How strange,—no pain, but so feeble, it seems like gliding away to death. How easy it seems! Why not, to one whose race is run?

Thus with Dahlgren passed the weeks and the months: plans, thundering bombardments; hopes and disappointments; sickness, anxiety about his son; disputes with General Gillmore.

[3] His son, Ulrich Dahlgren, lost his leg in a cavalry skirmish at Hagerstown, Maryland soon after the battle of Gettysburg.

Yet there was progress; Wagner fell on September 7th, and Sumter, although still held by the Confederates, was a mass of ruins. During all these engagements with the forts there were few casualties on either side. There was, however, one serious loss in the fleet. In the attack on Wagner on August 17th, the fleet captain, Commander George Washington Rodgers, was standing in the pilot house of the *Catskill* when a shot from the fort struck it, instantly killing Rodgers and the paymaster and wounding the pilot and the quartermaster.

During these months of bombardment Dahlgren made one attempt to take Sumter by a landing party. This was a boat attack on the night of September 8th. The recent Southern evacuation of Fort Wagner suggested to the admiral that this success be followed up by an effort to take Sumter by storm. Dahlgren called for five hundred men to make the assault under a courageous officer, Commander Thomas H. Stevens. So little confidence did Stevens have in the success of the proposed venture that he asked permission to decline the duty. But this Dahlgren refused, saying to him, "You have only to go and take possession. You will find nothing but a corporal's guard."

During the war there occurred other instances of a lack of cooperation between attacking forces, but none so flagrant or incredible as between the army and the navy that night in Charleston harbor, for General Gillmore, commanding the land forces on Morris Island, planned a similar attack for the same evening. How complete and appalling was the lack of cooperation at this critical time is painfully illustrated by the following telegraphic exchange between Dahlgren and Gillmore during the afternoon and evening preceding the assault:

Dahlgren to Gillmore, 1 P.M.—I will assault Sumter tonight.

Gillmore to Dahlgren, 7 P.M.:—Your dispatch by signal that you intended to assault Sumter tonight reached me about an hour after I had sent one of my staff informing you that I intended to do the same thing. In an operation of this kind there should be one commander to insure success and prevent mistakes.

Dahlgren to Gillmore, 8:10 P.M.:—I have assembled five hundred men and I cannot consent that the commander shall be other than a naval officer. Will you be kind enough to let me know at what time you will move, and what the watchword will be, to prevent collision.

Gillmore to Dahlgren, a little later:—You decline to act in concert with me or allow the senior officer to command the assault on Sumter, but insist that a naval officer must command the party. Why this should be so in assailing a fortress, I cannot see. I am so fearful that some accident will take place between our parties that I would recall my own if it were not too late. We must trust to chance and hope for the best, no matter who gets the fort first, if we plant our flag over it.

Dahlgren to Gillmore, 10 P.M.—Will you name the hour. I am waiting.

Finally, at 11:30 P.M. Dahlgren notified Commander Stevens to proceed with his boat attack, as he had been unable to agree on a plan with the army.

From the very beginning everything went wrong. The five hundred men were towed near to Sumter by a tug; as soon as the boats were cast off, the tug circled about as if it intended to abandon the sailors to their fate, and there was the greatest confusion among the many boats. It was planned that one division under Lieutenant Higginson create a diversion at the northwest front of the fort, and that the main division close up and wait for the order to attack on the opposite face. Partly because they did not understand what was expected of them and partly because of a commendable spirit of gallantry, many of the boats of the main division dashed toward the fort before Higginson's division had gained the enemy's attention. The defenders had hours before been warned of a coming attack by the assembly of so many boats, and met the assault with a fierce fire of musketry, grape, cannister, and hand grenades. The few men who succeeded in landing came ashore under rugged walls, and, with no means of scaling them, were easily dispersed. So great was this confusion among the Federal attackers that the men who had landed were fired on by their own comrades still in the boats. Among the more than one hundred prisoners taken by the

Confederates, two accepted bribes and gave full information about the fleet.

Seldom was an attack so poorly planned, so poorly supported, and so certain of failure. Here were a brigadier general and a rear admiral, both able and intelligent men, both standing high in their profession, both devoted to the cause for which they were fighting, yet completely unable or unwilling to reach either an understanding or a compromise. The sentiment Gillmore expressed in his last message to Dahlgren to the effect that it mattered little who reached the fort first, so long as the flag of the nation was placed upon it, was the only commendable aspect of the attack. Yet neither would yield to the other, each hoping that the honor of taking Sumter, the victory desired by the nation above all others, would fall to him. Thus were precious lives sacrificed in vain.

On October 22nd Dahlgren called a council of war to discuss the question of whether or not to enter the inner harbor of Charleston. Besides the admiral, there were present eight captains of ironclads and two staff officers. Dahlgren records that the object of the council was not to get advice for himself, for his own mind was made up, but "to comply with the request of the Secretary, who asked for the opinion of these officers." The conference lasted from eleven in the morning until five in the evening. The four junior officers voted for an attack with seven ironclads. The six senior officers voted against the attack. "The intelligence," wrote Dahlgren, "was largely with the latter. One of the juniors seemed hardly to know what he was about. So my views were sustained." These "views," according to Abner Doubleday, were that the fleet could "steam in and make a promenade of the harbor, suffering much damage and inflicting little. Then retire. To remain in would be only a useless expenditure of valuable vessels which could not be replaced." Like Du Pont before him, Dahlgren had been eager to gain the honor of taking Charleston and, like Du Pont he was unwilling to take the risks that precede great achievements and victory.

Had Admiral Dahlgren passed Sumter, forced the obstructions, entered the inner harbor, and steamed up to the Battery at Charleston, what would have been the outcome? We have seen how Chief Engineer Stimers, who was on the *Monitor* in her battle with the *Merrimac* and then was inspector general of all the monitors, was in Charleston at the time of Du Pont's unsuccessful attack on Sumter, and examined all the ironclads the day after the battle. His opinion was that the ironclads had suffered no serious injury, and that if a second attack had been made they could have passed Sumter and the obstructions in the harbor and steamed up to the wharves of Charleston. This was not the opinion of a layman, but of one who perhaps knew as much about the monitors and their powers of offense and defense as any officer in the navy. If Dahlgren had not been content with only periodic bombardments of Sumter and the other forts, but had entered the harbor, he probably would have lost some ships; there was also the probability that he would have won the victory. One of the secrets of General Grant's success lay in the fact that he always thought more about what he could do to the enemy than what the enemy might do to him. Both Dahlgren and Du Pont, highly intelligent though they were, belonged to the school who thought more of what the enemy might do to them than what they could do to the enemy.

In the fall of 1863, while the powerful ironclad *New Ironsides,* was lying off Charleston, a daring attempt, prophetic of the submarine attacks of the two World Wars, was made to sink the ship with a torpedo. Dahlgren's journal gives this account of what happened:

Quite early a frightened wretch was brought to me as taken out of the water after escaping from the torpedo. He gave a full statement. The vessel was about fifty feet, made like a cigar; five to six feet in diameter, with an engine which would drive her eight to ten knots. At the bow was a bar ten feet long, with a torpedo at the end holding sixty pounds of powder, with four nipples to act by percussion. There were four persons in the boat, and they stood on the bottom with their heads out of the hatch. They left Charleston at dusk, passed our vessels in the dark, then returned and attacked the *Ironsides*. He could not tell whether the captain or the pilot fired at and wounded the officer of the deck. The immense jet of water that came down put out the fire of the *David*. It seems to me that nothing could have been more successful as a first effort, and it will place the torpedo among certain offensive means. The Captain was also picked up. His name is Glassel, and he was formerly a Lieutenant in our Navy, and is now in that of the Confederates. I did not see him, as I could get nothing from him. What became of the other two and the boat, no one could say; they may have perished or not.

A fuller account of this daring and almost successful attack by the *David*, probably named after the youth who attacked mighty Goliath with his sling, is given by General Beauregard, who commanded the defending forces at Charleston. According to Beauregard's story, the *David* struck the *New Ironsides* with a torpedo six feet under water; but the fact that the torpedo struck one of the ironclad's inner bulkheads saved the ship from destruction. The explosion of the torpedo cast up a great pillar of water which almost swamped the *David* and put out her fires. The little craft then drifted seaward with the ebbing tide, under heavy musketry and grape fire from the Federal flagship. The four men in the boat, thinking that she was sinking, leaped into the sea. After being in the water for an hour, Lieutenant Glassel was picked up by a Northern boat, taken on board the guard ship, and later transferred to the *Ottawa*, lying outside the bar. Dahlgren ordered him to be put in irons and, if he resisted, to be "double ironed." But the captain of the *Ottawa* was a friend of Glassel, and through his intercession the lieutenant, on giving his word that he would not attempt to escape from the ship, was spared the indignity of being shackled.

After the explosion of the torpedo, the fireman of the *David* took refuge on the rudder of the *Ironsides*. When discovered, he was put in irons and kept in a dark cell until he was sent to New

York with Glassel to be tried for using a weapon not recognized by civilized nations. After an imprisonment of several months at Fort LaFayette and later at Fort Warren at Boston, the two men were exchanged for the captain and a seaman of a captured Union gunboat. Two other men on the *David*, Engineer Tomb and Pilot Cannon, swam about for a time after the discharge of the torpedo and then, seeing the *David* floating nearby, managed to get aboard her, relit the fires with a bull's-eye lantern and steamed back to Charleston, fired at on the way by several gunboats and monitors.

Another equally daring, but tragic, attack by a torpedo boat was made by a Lieutenant Payne of the Confederate Navy on the wooden screw-sloop *Housatonic*. Payne's craft was called the "fish" boat because it was equipped with fins which, when depressed, enabled it to dive and, when elevated, to surface. As the boat was about to start from the wharf at Fort Johnson, the wash of a passing steamer caused it to capsize and sink; two of the crew were drowned. After she was raised, a second crew volunteered for the perilous enterprise. On a practice dive in the harbor, the boat failed to rise and all hands perished. When she was raised the second time, the spectacle of the unfortunate crew "contorted into all kinds of horrible attitudes" was so terrible to behold that General Beauregard forbade further use of the craft. However, a Lieutenant Dixon of Mobile finally persuaded Beauregard to let him make a second attempt on the *Housatonic*, which was on the watch for blockade runners; but Beauregard's consent was conditioned by an order that she was to attack the Federal ship on the surface, as the *David* had attacked the *New Ironsides*, and not as a submarine. The attack was a complete success; the *Housatonic* sank almost immediately after the discharge of the torpedo. Unfortunately for the torpedo boat, she went down with her victim. Thus, in the pioneer days of the torpedo and the submarine there were young heroes on both sides in the great conflict who, for the sake of their cause, "loved not their lives unto the death."

In the first week of March, 1864, in response to an invitation from Welles, Dahlgren left his squadron for a time and went to Washington. On the 4th of March he received a card from Lincoln saying that his son, Colonel Ulrich Dahlgren, was missing after a raid against Richmond.

This gifted son had served on the staff of Generals Sigel, Hooker, and Meade. In the Gettysburg campaign of 1863 he captured a Confederate courier carrying a dispatch from Jefferson Davis to General Lee. The dispatch said that it would not be possible to gather another army at Culpepper, Virginia to threaten Washington and thus draw off part of the Union army then confronting Lee at Gettysburg. In a fast thirty-mile ride over the mountains Dahlgren carried this message to Meade, arriving at his Gettysburg headquarters at the close of the second day's battle, July 2nd. This intelligence is supposed to have had some influence on Meade's determination to fight it out in the position he then held. After Gettysburg, while serving with a cavalry unit harassing Lee's retreating army, Ulrich lost a leg in an encounter at Hagerstown. For gallantry in this and previous actions, though only twenty-one, and without having served as a major, he was commissioned a colonel. When he was brought to his father's house at Washington, Lincoln paid him honor with a visit. Toward the end of his convalescence he spent several happy weeks on his father's flagship, the *Philadelphia*, off Charleston.

The raid against Richmond did not originate with General Meade, but with the fiery Hugh Kilpatrick, who commanded a cavalry division in the Army of the Potomac. "I trust," Meade wrote to his wife, "they will be successful; it will be the greatest feat of the war if they succeed, and will immortalize them all. Young Dahlgren, with one leg, went along with them." The chief objective of the raid was to release the Union prisoners held at Belle Isle in the James River and at Libby Prison in Richmond. With 4,000 troopers Kilpatrick moved around the right wing of Lee's army and headed straight for Richmond. At

Spottsylvania Courthouse, south of the Rapidan, he detached
Ulrich and five hundred men from the main body with instructions to cross the James north and west of Richmond, then re-
cross it, release the prisoners, and rejoin the main force. As he
was about to start on his fateful ride, Ulrich said to his men: "If
there is any man here who is not willing to sacrifice his life in
such a great and glorious undertaking, let him step out, and he
may go home to the arms of his sweetheart and read of the
brave who swept through the city of Richmond." To his father
he had written, "If we do not return, there is no better place to
give up the ghost."

Led astray by their guide, young Dahlgren's detachment became lost, and, like the main body, had to retreat. Near King
and Queen Court House they were ambushed by hostile home
guards, and Ulrich was killed.

On March 8th, the day after Lincoln learned of Ulrich's
death, he sent for the admiral. Too tender-hearted to tell the
father that his son was dead, and still hoping that there might be
better news, Lincoln told the admiral to go down to General
Benjamin Butler's headquarters at Fortress Monroe and find his
son if he could. There the heart-broken father learned that
his son was dead. Despite the efforts of Lincoln and Butler and
an appeal to Jefferson Davis by the admiral, the body of Ulrich
could not be found. A funeral was held in the First Presbyterian
Church at Washington, and was attended by a great throng, for
the young colonel's death had aroused deep feeling in the nation.

In the meantime the Confederates recovered the body, and
claimed to have found on it two orders, one signed, the other
not. The signed order read: "We hope to release the prisoners
from Belle Isle first, and, having seen them fairly started, we
will cross the James River into Richmond, destroying the bridges
after us, and exhort the released prisoners to destroy and burn
the hateful city; and not allow the rebel leader Davis and his
traitorous crew to escape." The order was signed, "*U. Dalhgren,*"

not with the proper spelling, "*Dahlgren*." The unsigned document read: "Once in the city, it must be destroyed, and Jeff Davis and his Cabinet killed. Pioneers will go along with combustible material."

The publication of these alleged orders caused a storm of rage to sweep over Richmond. General Braxton Bragg, then acting as military adviser to President Davis, wrote the Confederate Secretary of War, James A. Seddon, that the prisoners captured with Dahlgren ought to be hanged. Seddon forwarded the papers to General Lee with the recommendation that at least some of the prisoners be hanged. Lee, a much wiser man, answered: "I cannot recommend the execution of the prisoners—I think it is better to do right, even if we suffer in so doing, than to incur the reproach of our conscience and posterity." He reminded the Secretary that recently Confederate soldiers had robbed Union prisoners on a train and that "the enemy might claim to treat them as highway robbers." From his correspondence with Seddon, and later with General Meade, one gathers the impression that Lee doubted the authenticity of the orders purportedly signed by Ulrich.

As soon as Meade read in the Richmond papers the copies of the supposed orders, he ordered an investigation. General Kilpatrick reported to him that the unanimous testimony of the officers and privates who had accompanied Dahlgren on the raid was to the effect that Dahlgren gave no address to his men, nor any written instructions. However, Dahlgren had submitted to him an order, or address, which he, Kilpatrick, endorsed in red ink with the word, "Approved." This address conformed to the one published in the Richmond papers except for the sentence exhorting the released prisoners to burn and destroy the city and kill Davis and his cabinet. "All this," wrote Kilpatrick, "is false, and published only as an excuse for the barbarous treatment of the remains of a brave soldier."

Two weeks later, General Lee sent to Meade copies of the alleged orders, and inquired if these instructions of Colonel Dahlgren had been authorized by the United States Government, or by his superior officers, or were now approved by them. For answer, Meade sent Lee Kilpatrick's report and added, "Neither the United States Government, myself, nor General Kilpatrick authorized, sanctioned or approved the burning of the city of Richmond, and the killing of Davis and his Cabinet, nor any other act not required by military necessity, and in accordance with the usages of war." General Lee, of course, knew Meade and the policy of the United States Government well enough to be certain that neither the Army of the Potomac nor the Government could have sanctioned such orders. In a letter to his wife, Meade, who did not entertain a high opinion of Kilpatrick, said: "This was a pretty ugly piece of business, for in denying having authorized the burning of Richmond or killing Mr. Davis and his Cabinet, I necessarily threw odium on Dahlgren. I however enclosed a letter from Kilpatrick in which the authenticity of the papers was impugned; but I regret to say, Kilpatrick's reputation, and collateral evidence in my possession, rather go against this theory."

If the South was outraged by the alleged orders, the North was not less shocked at the manner in which the body of the fallen Dahlgren was reported to have been treated. The survivors of the ambushed detachment made their way to a Federal ship on the James river. There they reported that the colonel's body had been stripped and left naked, and that some of his fingers were cut off to obtain the rings on them.

Taken to Richmond, the mutilated body lay exposed for a time at the railway station. It was then clothed to prevent identification and buried in a secret grave. Writing seventeen years after the event, Jefferson Davis said: "Many sensational stories, having not even a basis of truth, were put in circulation to exhibit the Confederate authorities as having acted with unwarrantable malignity toward the deceased Colonel Dahlgren. The fact was that his body was sent to Richmond, interred in the Oakwood Cemetery where other Federal officers were buried, and decently buried. The enormity of the offense was not forgotten, but resentment against him ended with his life."

After the fall of Richmond in the spring of 1865, a Negro reported to the Federal authorities that he had seen Dahlgren's body at the railway station and that his mistress, loyal to the Union, had instructed him to see where the body was buried. This he did. That same night he guided a farmer sympathetic to the Union to the grave, where they removed the body and reburied it on the farmer's property.[4]

The death of Ulrich and the uncertainty surrounding the disposal of his body was a terrible blow to the admiral. He always regarded the orders said to have been found on his son's body as a forgery, pointing out that his son never signed himself *U. Dahlgren*, but always *Ulrich Dahlgren.* "This is not my son's writing," he said, "or even his name," referring to the misspelling. Unless some clerk wrote the order for the colonel and misspelled his name, this would seem to indicate that the orders were a forgery.

The body was recovered, and a second funeral was held, attended by President Johnson and the Cabinet. Henry Ward Beecher made one of his stirring addresses, in the course of which he said: "Dahlgren! Once he dwelt in a house made with hands, and only one; now he dwells in thrice ten thousand. Wherever children are reared to duty and heroism, there his example lives. As long as history lasts, Dahlgren shall mean truth, honor, bravery, and sacrifice."

[4] Siviter, Anne Pierpont, *Recollections of War and Peace,* 276-283. Before the full story of the first burial of his son's body, its disinterment, and the reburial on the farm was given the admiral by Francis H. Pierpont, provisional governor of Virginia, he had been informed that friendly hands had buried the body, but in a place where it could not be reached until Union soldiers had possession of the neighborhood. In his journal for April 26, 1864, two days after the first funeral in Washington, Dahlgren wrote this entry: "In the evening a countryman came, who said that my Ully's remains were on his farm. They had been removed privately by one or two persons. He says the body cannot be removed until our troops get that far."

At length came the 14th of April, 1865. President Lincoln had ordered that at noon on that day, the fourth anniversary of the surrender of Fort Sumter, the flag which Major Anderson had lowered and saluted four years before should be raised by Anderson's hands over the fallen fortress. A distinguished company was assembled at Charleston for the celebration. At dawn that morning the harbor and the streets of Charleston echoed with a familiar sound, the thunder of the guns of Dahlgren's fleet; but this time they were saluting the end of the war and the return of the national emblem to Fort Sumter. That night, the nation's rejoicing was suddenly turned into mourning by the flash of John Wilkes Booth's pistol. While Dahlgren's ships were glowing with joyous illumination, the admiral's firm friend lay dying in a narrow chamber at the house on 10th Street. When Dahlgren heard the tidings, he bade Lincoln farewell with these words: "I can say from an intimate acquaintance with the President, that he was a man of rare sagacity, good genial temper, and desirable firmness; that he possessed qualities of the highest order as a ruler; indeed, we know of no man who was so well fitted to carry the country through her trial."

During the few post-war weeks that Dahlgren remained in command of the squadron, he had a visit from General Sherman to whom he rendered assistance in the capture of Savannah the previous December. Sherman was in a "magnificent passion" at the treatment he had received at the hands of Secretary of War Stanton and General Halleck, when the terms he had given General Joseph Johnston, commander of the Confederate army in the Carolinas, were made public. These terms stipulated that the arms of the Confederate soldiers were to be deposited at the State Houses of the various states, and that the state governments would be recognized when they took the oath of allegiance. The government immediately repudiated these terms and directed Grant to resume hostilities against Johnston's army. Halleck even went to the length of instructing Union officers in

North Carolina to disregard Sherman's orders. When Dahlgren boarded the *Russia*, on which Sherman had arrived, "the general exploded instanter about Halleck's orders, and Stanton's; most violent, too . . . Sherman, when he let loose, said Halleck had not been under fire once; that he could whip him and the Army of the Potomac; and read me a letter which he had addressed to me and my fleet. I reminded him of the uselessness of such measures, and that even Jackson would not resist a civil court, but paid its fine." Later, when he had cooled down, Sherman thanked him for the advice he had given him.

On June 17th Dahlgren lowered his flag on the *Philadelphia* and started homeward. The entries in his journal at the time of the evacuation of Charleston in February and the celebration at the raising of the American flag over Fort Sumter on April 14th do not reveal any great feeling of elation over the part the fleet had taken in the final victory. There can be little doubt that the admiral must have felt a degree of disappointment. The high hopes with which he had raised his flag as commander of the squadron had not been fulfilled. The operations of the fleet had indeed put an end to the blockade runners; Sumter had been reduced to rubble; but the Stars and Bars floated in defiance over its battered walls until the march of Sherman's army across South Carolina compelled its evacuation.

As he left his flagship, the admiral's thoughts were not of the victory and the end of the war; nor of the part his ships and his invention, the Dahlgren gun, had played in the war; nor of his friendship with Lincoln, but of his lost son, the adored center of the father's hopes and affections. As the admiral sat in the cabin of the *Pawnee*, the vessel which was to convey him to Washington, he put down these words: "At last, all things being ready, I left the old *Philadelphia*, rich with memories of the past, and none now dearer to me than those of my dear son; for in that cabin we spent together the last days permitted us. He liked to sit in the green cushioned chair of mine; back of him hung Darley's fine picture of his own exploit at Fredericks-

burg. There was the table; and just where he sat, a crutch resting on each side of the chair. He used to walk in the gangway,
and I often caught sight of his noble head and the jaunty little
military cap. How often his military figure filled that doorway!
Dear son, your memory will not die while I live." The lament
over his lost son, which echoes so frequently in his journal and
correspondence, recalls another father's lament over a far less
worthy son: "O Absalom, my son, my son Absalom! Would God
I had died for thee, O Absalom, my son!"

On the 12th of July, 1865, just two years after he had assumed the command, Dahlgren, to the sound of a thirteen gun
salute, hauled down his flag as commander of the South Atlantic
Squadron. After the war he had the South Pacific Squadron for
two years. This was followed by a second term as Chief of the
Bureau of Ordnance, where he had long before won his real
renown. His last service was as Commandant of the Washington
Navy Yard, the post he had held in the first two critical years
of the war.

His final years were solaced by his marriage to the gifted
Madeleine Vinton Goddard, who wrote the story of the admiral's
life in her *Memoir of John A. Dahlgren,* and also edited the
notes he had prepared in memory of his son Ulrich. On the last
night of his life, as he sat in his study at Washington conversing
with his wife about his career in the navy, he said, "The officer
should wear his uniform as the judge his ermine, without a
stain." Though the admiral's ambition for high distinction in battle
had not been achieved, he had measured up to his own standard.

VI

WORDEN

At 10:30 on Saturday night, March 8th, 1862, one of the saddest days in the history of the United States Navy, the waters of Hampton Roads, Virginia, were brightly illuminated by the flames of the burning U. S. frigate *Congress*. A mile to the east lay the stranded frigate *Minnesota*, and close to the *Congress* there appeared above the waters the tops of the masts of the sunken sloop-of-war *Cumberland*, her oaken walls a coffin for one hundred and twenty brave seamen, but her flag, never struck, still flying from the mainmast. As the soldiers at Newport News and the sailors on the *Minnesota* watched the flames, they saw a strange vessel, resembling nothing they had seen before, her deck only a few inches above water with a cylinderlike structure rising from it, come slowly up the Roads and cast anchor near the mud-bound *Minnesota*, in comparison with which she looked like a pigmy. The new arrival was the *Monitor*, with Lieutenant John Worden in command. Her appearance at the end of that tragic 8th of March was one of the timely arrivals of history.

It is not possible to understand the significance of what Worden and the *Monitor* did the next day without a recital of the events during and before the battle at Hampton Roads on March 8th, a battle far more dramatic and stirring, if not so epoch-making, as the duel between the *Monitor* and the *Merrimac*.

In the long history of the United States Navy there is no event of which the nation can be less proud than the surrender and abandonment of the navy yard at Norfolk, Virginia, the largest and most important of the government yards in the South. In that surrender the most humiliating incident was the needless abandonment of the splendid ship *Merrimac*. Chief Engineer Benjamin F. Isherwood, then stationed at Washington, had received full information of the purpose of the Confederates to seize the yard, and early called the attention of the Secretary of the Navy to the importance of removing the *Merrimac*, then undergoing repairs, from Norfolk to a place of safety. Because of conflicting reports as to the time it would require to put the ship's engines in order, the Navy Department directed Isherwood to proceed to Norfolk and take full charge of the repairs. Commodore Charles S. McCauley, Commandant at Norfolk, was ordered to put the ship in his hands so that the *Merrimac* could be removed to Philadelphia "with the utmost dispatch." Commander James Alden, who later commanded the *Richmond* in the battle at New Orleans and the *Brooklyn* at Mobile Bay, was to have charge of the ship when she was ready to leave Norfolk. If the Department had given Isherwood orders to remove the ship, as well as repair her, the *Merrimac* probably would have been saved for the Union.

Taking ship at Baltimore, Isherwood arrived at the navy yard on Sunday, April 14th. Early on Monday morning he had a force of mechanics at work on the engines of the *Merrimac*. On Wednesday afternoon, he reported to the Commandant that he was ready to fire the boilers and get steam up; but McCauley told him to wait until Thursday morning. The moment midnight had passed, the fires were lighted, and at nine o'clock on Thursday morning Isherwood reported to McCauley that the ship was ready to move. To facilitate a quick departure, Isherwood had replaced the chain cables which held the ship to the dock with rope hawsers which could be severed by a stroke of the axe. McCauley, however, still hesitated to give the word. He had been fifty-two years in the navy and was then sixty-eight years of age. Many of the officers at the navy yard were from the

South, but McCauley, apparently, was unable to believe that they would desert the navy and lift a hand against the flag. Moreover, he was perplexed by the instructions which he had received from Washington to remove the *Merrimac* "with the utmost dispatch," but also to take no step which might provoke Virginia into secession. Virginia seceded from the Union on Wednesday, April 17th; there was therefore no reason on Thursday, April 18th, to fear that the removal of the *Merrimac* would create an insurrection in Virginia, for the insurrection had already begun.

Isherwood kept the engines going all day Thursday, vainly hoping that McCauley would give the order for the removal of the ship. He described the commandant as a man "in a state of complete prostration," behaving "as though he were stupefied." By his own exertions, knowing that every obstacle was being put in the way of Captain Alden's getting men to man the ship, Isherwood had secured coal and other stores, and, with the promise of high wages, had secured a skeleton crew of wheelmen and firemen to work the ship as far as Newport News. When late on Thursday afternoon, McCauley gave the order to draw the fires and stop the engines on the *Merrimac,* Isherwood, watching sorrowfully their slackening revolutions, was tempted to cut the hawsers and take the ship out himself. "This," he said, "would have been my destruction, for then, the disasters which followed her detention, and which are my justification for the desire to take the matter into my own hands, would not have happened."

On Saturday morning, April 20th, Captain Hiram Paulding arrived at Norfolk on the sloop-of-war *Pawnee* with authority to abandon the yard. Convinced that the yard was lost, Paulding gave orders for the destruction by fire of everything that would burn, and the spiking of the twelve hundred cannon. Many of these guns, however, among them new Dahlgren guns, the most formidable weapon the navy possessed, were not ruined, and later dealt out death to Union soldiers and sailors all the way from Virginia to the Mississippi. Early on Sunday morning the *Pawnee,* with the sloop-of-war *Cumberland* in tow, departed from the flaming scene of disaster, devastation and national humiliation. As soon as the *Pawnee* was out of sight Confederate forces entered the yard in time to extinguish the powder train which had been laid for the destruction of the dry dock.[1]

Early in June of 1861, the Confederate Navy Department directed Commander John M. Brooke, distinguished as an inventor and naval scientist, to submit a design for an ironclad warship. At that time there were no engines in the South suitable for such a vessel; but as the hull of the burned and sunken *Merrimac* was found to be in good condition, and since haste was all-important, it was decided to raise her, repair the engines, and superimpose on the hull a structure plated with iron and pierced for ten guns. There was no little dispute about the credit for raising and reconstructing the *Merrimac.* As far back as 1846, Naval Constructor John L. Porter, then stationed at Pittsburgh where he was superintending the building of an iron steamboat, made a model for an ironclad warship. Sixteen years later, when the work of salvaging the *Merrimac* and converting her into an ironclad was committed to him, he followed the model made at Pittsburgh. Some months after the battle with the *Monitor,* the Confederate Government gave the credit to Brooke by granting him a patent number; but Porter wrote that no man but himself had anything to do with converting the *Merrimac* into an ironclad. But to whomever the credit should go—to Chief Engineer William P. Williams who, after examination of the hull and the engines, suggested that time and money would be saved by raising her; to Commander Brooke; or to Porter, who did the actual work of reconstruction—the job was well done. Imagine the roof of an old-time Pennsylvania

[1] For the best account of the disaster at the Norfolk Navy Yard, see *The Steam Navy of the United States,* by Frank M. Bennett, 230-242.

barn, cut off at the eaves and pierced with holes for ten guns, two at the bow and two at the stern and four on each side; a huge chimney protruding from the center of the roof; and the sides of the roof plated with an iron shield; and one has a fair idea of the appearance of the *Merrimac*. Her chief defects as a fighting ship were her unprotected rudder and propeller; her slow speed of five knots; the difficulty of steering her; and her great draft of twenty-two feet, which handicapped her for fighting in inland waters. In the battle with the *Monitor* these proved to be serious disadvantages.

The commanding officer of the *Merrimac*[2] was one of the most distinguished members of the old navy, Captain Franklin Buchanan. It was he who, in obedience to the orders of the then Secretary of the Navy, the historian George Bancroft, organized the Naval Academy at Annapolis in 1845 and served as its first Superintendent. At the outbreak of the war he was Commandant of the Navy Yard at Washington. Thinking that his home state of Maryland would secede, he resigned from the navy in April of 1861. When Maryland did not secede and he thought that a reconciliation between the States might yet come to pass, Buchanan requested permission to withdraw his resignation. This was not granted; he was dismissed from the service, and soon thereafter joined the Confederacy. If Secretary of the Navy Welles had not decided otherwise, Buchanan's services might have been retained for the nation. But his resignation, though followed by a request to withdraw it, cast a shadow on his full loyalty, and Welles was undoubtedly wise in the decision he made.

The attack which the *Merrimac* launched against the Union ships at Hampton Roads was as great and as inexcusable a surprise as the attack of the Japanese bombers on the United States ships at Pearl Harbor seventy-nine years later. Everyone knew that the *Merrimac* had been raised and was being converted into

---

[2] The ironclad was renamed *Virginia* by the Confederacy, but is best known by her old name.

John Adolphus Bernard Dahlgren
1809—1870

John Lorimer Worden
1818—1897

an ironclad, yet her appearance in the Roads found the Union fleet totally unprepared. A short time before the appearance of the *Merrimac* Lieutenant David D. Porter, destined to win great fame later in the war and at this time preparing his fleet of mortar boats to join in the attack on New Orleans, happened to be at Hampton Roads. As Porter was standing on one of the wharves, a man landed from a small boat and told him that he had escaped from Norfolk where he had been employed as a mechanic, and that the *Merrimac*, on which he had been working, was near completion. Porter sent him to Van Brunt, the Captain of the *Minnesota*, who rudely dismissed him as an impostor. But Porter had quite a different opinion, and at once wrote to Fox, the Assistant Secretary of the Navy, urging him to hurry the work on the *Monitor*.

Saturday, the 8th of March, dawned fair and warm. Five powerful Union vessels lay at anchor in the roadstead. Three of them, the *Roanoke*, with the senior officer of the fleet, Captain John Marston, on board, the *Minnesota*, like the *Roanoke* a sister ship to the original *Merrimac*, and the *St. Lawrence*, were anchored near Fortress Monroe. Two others, the *Congress* and the *Cumberland*, lay near Newport News, not far apart. Every officer on these ships knew that at Norfolk, only a few miles up the Elizabeth River, a Confederate ironclad was nearing completion. Yet, so far as any sign of preparation or vigilance on the part of the Union ships was concerned, the *Merrimac* might have been a thousand miles away. The shirts and trousers of the sailors' washing hung from the rigging of the ships and from lines stretched over the decks, small boats were hanging from the booms, and the ships swung lazily to and fro with the tide and an occasional gentle breeze. Disaster and tragedy seemed remote, indeed.

Suddenly there was great stir and excitement on the National ships; the shrill whistle of the boatswains and the sharp commands of the officers were heard; shirts and trousers were stripped from the lines; the boats were dropped; the ships stripped for action; the big guns uncovered and run out. The long-expected, yet unexpected, *Merrimac* was making her appearance, recognized in the distance by her big stack from which heavy black smoke ascended to the cloudless sky. Her approach was observed not only from the two ships nearest her, the *Congress* and the *Cumberland*, but also by the three ships several miles distant at Fortress Monroe. Of these, the *Minnesota* was closer to Newport News than the other two. The senior officer present, Captain John Marston of the *Roanoke*, at once signalled the *Minnesota* to go to the aid of the two ships at Newport News.

So sluggish was the *Merrimac* that four hours elapsed from the time she was first seen until she fired her first shot. When the Confederate vessel, accompanied by two smaller ships, was within three-quarters of a mile of Newport News, the *Congress* and the *Cumberland* opened on her with their heavy guns. The *Merrimac* did not deign to answer until she was within easy range, then there was a flash of flame from her side and a shell smashed into the *Cumberland*, killing and wounding most of the gunners at the after pivot gun. The shots of the two Union ships struck the side of the *Merrimac*, but made little impression on her iron plates, which were set at an angle of forty-five degrees to the vertical. Disregarding the heavier Union ship, the *Congress*, save to give her a broadside in passing, the *Merrimac* steered straight for the *Cumberland*. William Radford, the *Cumberland's* captain, was absent from his ship attending a court martial on the deck of the *Roanoke* at Fortress Monroe. When word came that the *Merrimac* was on her way, he was hastily rowed ashore. Mounting a horse, he galloped to Newport News, killing the horse but arriving just in time to see his ship sink beneath the waves. The officer next in rank, Lieutenant George U. Morris, commanded the *Cumberland* during the brief action with the *Merrimac*. The *Congress* was nearer to the approaching *Merrimac*, but the ironclad steered straight for the *Cumberland*. It has been surmised that the reason Buchanan temporarily ignored the *Congress* in favor of her consort was that his brother, McKean Buchanan, was paymaster on the *Congress,* and that he wished to spare his own flesh and blood. But that hardly fits in with the fact that, after he had disposed of his first victim, Buchanan riddled the *Congress* with his guns and then set her on fire with red-hot shot, a more terrible fate for the men than ramming would have been. In a few minutes the iron beak of the *Merrimac* crashed into the starboard side of the doomed *Cumberland,* whose towering masts trembled and tottered, but did not fall, as the ship careened over toward her antagonist.

Backing off to prepare for another thrust if necessary, the *Merrimac* lost the iron beak which she had driven into the vitals of the Union sloop. But a second blow was not required. Through an immense hole in her side, the sea flooded in and the *Cumberland* began to go down. Her courageous seamen and officers fought her to the very end; the last gun was fired just before the sea engulfed it. Her flag was not struck, and remained flying from the masthead after the ship settled on the bottom, as if in token of ultimate victory.

Having thus disposed of the *Cumberland,* the *Merrimac* turned her attention to the other vessel. When he saw the fate of the *Cumberland,* the young senior officer of the *Congress,* Lieutenant Joseph Smith, son of old Commodore Smith, tried to save his ship by running her inshore near the Federal batteries. To this end the *Congress* slipped her anchor, hoisted sail, and made an effort to escape the destroyer's path. In this she did not succeed, for she soon ran aground, and thus became a stationary target for the guns of the *Merrimac.* Lieutenant Smith was killed by a shot from the enemy ship and the command devolved upon Lieutenant Austin Pendergrast. In a hopeless situation, he fought his ship until her decks were strewn with the wounded and the mangled remains of the dead. Buchanan did not attempt to ram the Federal vessel, for she was aground, and nothing could be gained by such a maneuver; furthermore, the

Merrimac had already lost her iron ram when she drove into the side of the *Cumberland*.

At four o'clock the white flag of surrender was raised on the *Congress*, and Buchanan sent one of his gunboats, the *Beaufort*, to her side to take off her officers and wounded men, and let the crew escape. But when the *Beaufort* attempted to carry out this mission of mercy, the Union batteries on the shore under command of Brigadier General J.K.F. Mansfield maintained musketry and artillery fire, killing friend and foe alike. The *Beaufort* then drew off, but took with her the captured flag of the *Congress*. Buchanan, observing that the shore batteries fired on the *Congress*, and thinking that the raising of the white flag was an act of treachery, ordered the gunners of the *Merrimac* to open on the frigate with red-hot shot, which soon set the helpless ship on fire. Most of her crew and the wounded who were able to walk escaped safely to the shore; but many of the badly wounded who could not be carried to safety perished in the flames.

The *Minnesota* had started to the aid of the threatened ships as soon as the enemy ironclad was sighted but she went aground when a mile distant from the endangered vessels. The *Roanoke* and *St. Lawrence* also started to aid the victims of the *Merrimac*, but they, too, ran aground. The fact that four of the Union frigates ran aground during the battle would, on the surface, seem to suggest treachery or gross incompetence on the part of the pilots; in reality, the ships came to grief because a strong wind had driven the waters back and made hitherto safe channels too shallow for the passage of the frigates. Considering the fate of the *Congress* and *Cumberland*, this was probably just as well.

The *Merrimac* was now free to give her whole attention to the stranded *Minnesota*. Fortunately for that frigate, however, the ironclad's pilots refused to approach her for fear of being grounded themselves and also because, at that late hour of five o'clock, the change in tide would soon make it impossible for the

Merrimac to get back to shelter under the guns of Norfolk or Sewell's Point. Buchanan therefore withdrew, feeling confident that in the morning he could destroy the remaining Federal ships.

That night Buchanan, who had been wounded toward the end of the battle, sent one of his officers, Lieutenant John Taylor Wood, to Richmond to report to the Confederate Navy Department. News of the battle and the victory of the *Merrimac* had preceded Wood, and cheering crowds gathered about his train at every stop. At Richmond he reported to Stephen Mallory, the Confederate Secretary of the Navy; then, accompanied by prominent officers of the army and navy and the government, he proceeded to the Confederate Executive Mansion, where Jefferson Davis heard his account of the battle with great interest. The flag of the *Congress* was brought into the room as a trophy and symbol of victory; but when it was unrolled it was seen to be saturated with the blood of the Union seamen who had fought under its folds. This shocked those present, and the flag was hastily removed.

Word of the battle at Hampton Roads and the destruction of the Union warships reached Washington Sunday morning, March 9th and occasioned almost unbelievable fear and panic in the government and on the part of the naval and military leaders who assembled at the White House that day. The calmest and most self-possessed among them was Welles, the Secretary of the Navy. He told Lincoln and the others present that there was no likelihood that the *Merrimac* could lay waste New York and Boston, and that her deep draft made it impossible for her to navigate the Potomac to Washington. Despite this assurance, Stanton and Lincoln went repeatedly to the window to see if there were any signs of the *Merrimac's* coming up the river. Stanton, almost frantic, said that the dreaded ironclad's next move would be to come up the Potomac, disperse Congress, destroy the Capitol, and possibly go out to sea as far as New York and Boston to destroy those cities. He declared that McClellan's "mistaken move" (to the Peninsula), just under way, must be abandoned. When, in answer to Stanton's question about the number of guns on the *Monitor*, Welles told him "only two," the Secretary of War gave Welles a mingled look of "incredulity and contempt" which, wrote Welles in his *Diary*, could not be described. In his panic Stanton telegraphed the governors of the Northern states and the mayors of several cities warning them of the danger and advising them to protect their harbors with rafts of timber and other obstructions.

Welles describes that meeting of March 9th as the

most unpleasant and uncomfortable of my life. The events were momentous and portentous to the nation; the responsibility and the consequences of disaster were heavier on me than on any other individual . . . My Assistant, Fox, was absent at Hampton Roads in anticipation of the arrival of the *Monitor*, whither he had gone before the occurrence to meet her. Dahlgren and Meigs, by nature and training cautious, not to say timid, who had been called in, were powerless, and in full sympathy with Stanton in all his fears and predictions. In all that painful time my composure was not disturbed, so that I did not perhaps as fully realize and comprehend the impending calamity as others; and yet to me there was something inexpressibly ludicrous in the wild frantic talk, action and rage of Stanton as he ran from room to room, sat down and jumped up after writing a few words, swung his arms, scolded and raved. He could not fail to see and feel my opinion of him and his bluster—that I was calm and unmoved by his rant, spoke deliberately and was not excited by his violence.

Among those at the White House meeting that morning was Commodore Joseph Smith, whose son, Lieutenant Joseph Smith, Jr., had perished on the *Congress*. When he heard that the *Congress* had struck her flag to the *Merrimac*, he said quietly, "Joe is dead." Others present tried to comfort him, saying that perhaps his son had escaped death, or was wounded, but the Commodore answered, "No; Joe would never haul down his flag. He's dead."

Although it is distressing to read of the uncontrolled disquietude of some of the leaders of the Government, there was, nevertheless, good reason for deep concern. The performance of the *Merrimac* at Hampton Roads did not, as so many said after the battle, give the wooden warship its immediate coup de grace, for the following month Farragut and his wooden ships conquered the forts at New Orleans. But the battle did show that the odds were heavily against a wooden ship in an encounter with an ironclad; that the artillery of that day could do little damage to an armor-plated vessel; and that wooden hulls could not withstand an iron ram. The sinking of the *Cumberland* alone proved that. There was good reason to fear that the *Merrimac* could cripple or sink any wooden ship she encountered. It was not known then, save to some of her officers, that she was altogether unseaworthy, and that she might well sink if she attempted to round Cape Henry. The claims made in the South for her possible and probable achievements were as groundless and absurd as the dread and panic in the North.

In a letter to the *Merrimac's* first commander, Franklin Buchanan, the Confederate Secretary of the Navy, Stephen R. Mallory, expressed confidence that with a smooth sea the *Merrimac* could steam to New York, and that once in the harbor she could shell the city and burn the city. "Such an event," he wrote, "would eclipse all the glories of the combats of the sea— Peace would inevitably follow. Bankers would withdraw their capital from the city. Brooklyn Navy Yard and its magazines and all the lower part of the city would be destroyed, and such an event, by a single ship, would do more to achieve our immediate independence than would the results of many campaigns."

For the time being the hopes and fears of the North were centered in the little seven-hundred-ton vessel which had cast anchor alongside the stranded *Minnesota*. What could the *Monitor* do? Would she be able to stand up to the *Merrimac?* At the very hour when the anxious Lincoln was meeting with his Cabinet and military leaders, when Stanton was making his dire predictions, scornfully asking Welles if he thought a ship with just two guns could match one with ten, the *Monitor* under Worden's guidance was demonstrating in an unforgettable manner what she could do and what the *Merrimac* could not do.

As early as August of 1861, the Secretary of the Navy had appointed a board of naval officers to whom all plans for ironclad vessels were to be submitted. It was this board which, after much discussion and no little skepticism, accepted the plan for an ironclad which the Swedish engineer and inventor, John Ericsson, had submitted to Napoleon III at the time of the Crimean War. Lincoln, always interested in new devices and himself the inventor of a mechanism to raise flatboats over dams, summed up his opinion of the plan with one of his Illinois anecdotes, remarking, "All I have to say is what the girl said when she put her foot into the stocking: 'It strikes me there's something in it.'" The keel of the *Monitor* was laid on October 25th, 1861, at the Greenpoint yards at Brooklyn, N.Y., and the vessel was launched on January 30th, 1862, a three months' achievement. A larger ship would have been built, but it was a day when the "king's business required haste," for it was known that the Confederates were rebuilding the *Merrimac* at Norfolk, and that there was no time for constructing a ship of greater dimensions. The *Monitor's* deck, barely level with the sea, was inspired by a scene from Ericsson's youth; as a lad he had often seen lumber rafts with a house built on them going serenely down the Swedish coast while the waves rolled over them. This feature of the *Monitor* was to prove of no little advantage when she met the *Merrimac*, for the only targets which presented themselves to the Confederate gunners were her pilot house and turret. One of the most experienced naval constructors scouted the plan of the *Monitor* and dubbed her the "iron pot" which would sink when committed to the deep and prove to be an iron coffin for her crew. Captain Charles H. Davis, one of the members of the board which finally adopted the plan of the *Monitor* and one of the few scientifically-minded officers of the navy, told Ericsson's representative that he could take the plan of the ship home and worship it, for it was not like anything in the heavens above, or in the earth beneath, or in the waters under the earth, and therefore to do so would be no violation of the Second Commandment. The wisdom of the *Monitor's* sponsors was soon to be justified.

When the strange craft slid off the ways at the Greenpoint yard, Ericsson christened her *Monitor*. He said he chose the name for two reasons: first, because the aggressive and impregnable character of the ship would "admonish the leaders of the Southern Rebellion that the batteries on the banks of their rivers would no longer present barriers to the entrance of the Union forces, and thus the ironclad intruder would prove a severe monitor to those leaders"; and second, because the statesmen of Europe, and England in particular, would be "startled and admonished by the booming of the guns from the impregnable iron turret."

Who should command this new warship, untried in the sea and untested in the crucible of battle? The lot fell upon Lieutenant John Worden, then forty-four years of age. Commodore Joseph Smith, one of the members of the naval board for ironclads, was chiefly responsible for this happy selection. Worden is to be remembered, not only for commanding the *Monitor* in the battle with the *Merrimac*, but also for the fact that he was the first prisoner of war of the Confederacy.

At the beginning of the war Worden was assigned to special duty in connection with new discoveries in the field of naval warfare. He had requested duty afloat, but instead was dispatched on an important and secret mission for the Navy Department to Captain H. A. Adams, commanding the United States ships off Fort Pickens, at Pensacola, Florida, in the Gulf of Mexico. The holding of Fort Pickens was considered of such importance that Lincoln and Seward, the Secretary of State, without consulting either the War or Navy departments, had dispatched Lieutenant David D. Porter on the *Powhatan*, accompanied by a troop ship, to reinforce the Fort Pickens garri-son.[3] A few days after Lincoln's inauguration, Lieutenant General Winfield Scott, the aged and infirm commander in chief of the army, had sent orders to Captain Israel Vogdes of the army to land troops from the frigate *Brooklyn*, then at Pensacola, and strengthen the garrison at Fort Pickens; however, when the messenger arrived with these orders, Captain Adams, the naval commander, would not recognize them nor permit the troops to land. His reason was that in the last weeks of President Buchanan's administration, Secretary of War Joseph Holt and Secretary of the Navy Isaac Toucey had entered into an agreement, one which reflects the low state of the national morale at that time, not to reinforce Fort Pickens, provided the Confederates promised not to attack it. Somewhat troubled by his own refusal to permit troops to land, Captain Adams dispatched Lieutenant Gwathmey with a confidential message to the new Secretary of the Navy, Gideon Welles, asking for instructions. Lieutenant Gwathmey was a Southerner with Confederate sympathies, but he did not betray his trust. Traveling day and night, he reached Washington on April 6th. Not waiting to go to a hotel, he went at once to Welles and gave him the message from Adams which he had carried in a belt strapped about his body. When he had discharged this mission, Gwathmey tendered his resignation and joined the Confederacy.

Welles at once took Adams' message to Lincoln. Both agreed that a special message must be sent ordering Adams to land the troops and strengthen Fort Pickens. With so many surprises and disappointments involving the loyalty of his officers, Welles wondered to whom he could entrust this message. His first choice was Paymaster Etting, who was unwell at the time, but nevertheless willing to undertake the journey. Before sending Etting, however, Welles told him that in view of the state of his health he would relieve him of this mission if he could find another officer about whose fidelity there could be no question.

[3] See Chapter X on Porter.

At five o'clock that afternoon, two hours after the meeting
with Lincoln and the decision to send a messenger, Etting reported to Welles that Lieutenant John Worden had just arrived
in Washington, and that he was one on whose loyalty they
could count to the uttermost. As soon as Worden reported to
Welles, he was informed of the secret and, because of the excited state of opinion in the South, somewhat dangerous mission, and told that he must start that very night by the mail
train. Worden at once signified his willingness to go and was
given the communication addressed to Captain Adams at Pensacola. In view of the fact that he might be challenged and
searched, Welles advised Worden to commit the message to
memory; then, if an emergency arose, he could destroy the paper.

On his journey to Pensacola, a group of boisterous soldiers
on their way to join the Confederate force at Pensacola boarded
the train at Atlanta. Fearing that he might be arrested and
searched, Worden went into the water closet, carefully read
again the brief message of Welles to Captain Adams, and destroyed the order. He reached Pensacola on April 11th, and was
about to take a boat out to Adams' vessel when he was told
by a "prominent citizen" that he must first report to General
Braxton Bragg, commanding the Confederate troops. When he
saw Bragg, the general asked, "I suppose you have a dispatch
for Captain Adams?" Worden answered, "No; not a written one,
General, but a verbal communication." Bragg then gave him a pass
to go out to the Union warship. On the boat which carried him
out, he heard talk of Bragg's intention to send troops to attack
Pickens that very night, regardless of the truce. The commander
of the *Wyandotte*, to which Worden was first taken, refused to
take him out to the flagship that evening because of a storm
which had arisen. The next day he reached the flagship and delivered Welles' order to Captain Adams. That very night Adams
landed a company of the 6th Artillery at Fort Pickens. Thus
Bragg's attack on Pickens, if indeed he planned such a venture,

was frustrated, the fort was held for the Union, and the naval base itself was soon recovered.

Captain Adams ordered Worden to return at once to Washington; Worden replied that, if reinforcements were thrown into Pickens that night, as must be done, he would be arrested by the Confederates when he attempted to leave for Washington. Adams, however, thought it safe for him to go by land and he started on his journey. He was not molested until his train neared Montgomery, Alabama, when he was arrested and taken to the city, then the Confederate capital, where he was at once surrounded by a hostile crowd. He was kept at first in the home of a deputy marshal and then lodged in the city jail. The jailer was kind and took him for a time to his own home, under a pledge that he would not attempt to escape. During these days he walked about freely on the outskirts of the town. But one day a man told him that a vigilance committee wanted him back in the jail. The jailer was disconcerted, but decided that Worden would be safer behind protecting bars. The turnkey was given instructions that, should a crowd gather about the jail, he was to shut the outer gate and put Worden in the ironclad lock-up. While incarcerated, Worden occasionally received a basket of choice viands from the widow of a navy officer, a former shipmate, living in Memphis.

On November 13th, seven months after he was taken from the train and imprisoned, he was released and directed to report to Adjutant General Cooper at Richmond. Cooper sent him on to Washington, where he reported to the Secretary of the Navy. The firing on Sumter by the Confederate batteries at Charleston in April of 1861 was the act which precipitated the Civil War; but John Worden, taken from the train at Montgomery, and put in prison two days after the flag was fired on at Sumter, had the distinction of being the first prisoner of war.

The *Monitor* left New York on March 6th in tow of the tug *Seth Low*. No one knew how she would behave in a storm, but those on board soon learned. Some of the seamen later said that the trip down to Hampton Roads was a far more trying experience than the subsequent battle with the *Merrimac*. Off Chincoteague Shoals the *Monitor* encountered heavy seas; the deck was under water most of the time. Due to the breakdown of the blower system, the engine rooms were so filled with gas that it became necessary to bring the engine and fireroom crews up to the deck to be revived. At four P.M. on March 8th the *Monitor* passed Cape Henry Light; not long thereafter the men saw flashes in the sky and heard the distant thunder of artillery. Worden correctly surmised that the *Merrimac* was engaging the Union ships and immediately ordered the *Monitor* stripped and made ready for action. As they neared Fortress Monroe, a pilot boat gave them the tragic tidings of the havoc wrought that day by the *Merrimac*. Twenty-four pilots, either through fear of the *Merrimac* or because of adherence to the South, refused to take the *Monitor* through the Roads, pleading ignorance of the channels. Fortunately a very able and patriotic pilot, Acting Master Howard, volunteered his services and was taken on board.

The Commander of the North Atlantic Blockading Squadron, Flag Officer L. M. Goldsborough, was still off the North Carolina Coast, where he had co-operated with the army under General Ambrose Burnside in the successful attack on Roanoke Island in the early part of February; the senior officer present at Hampton Roads was Captain John Marston, on the *Roanoke*.

On his arrival at nine P.M. on March 8th, Worden at once reported to Marston. Captain Marston had received orders from the Navy Department to send the *Monitor* to Washington as soon as she arrived. Fortunately, in view of the critical condition of affairs at Hampton Roads, Marston had the courage and the wisdom to disregard this order and he directed the *Monitor* to go to the aid of the *Minnesota*. It is one of those interesting instances in the history of war where disobedience to orders paid a rich dividend.

The little ironclad reached the *Minnesota* about eleven o'clock, and Worden sent Lieutenant S. Dana Greene, his second in command, to report to Captain Van Brunt and assure him that the *Monitor* would stand by him the next day. The sailors who leaned over the rail of the big frigate and saw the *Monitor* revealed in the light of the burning *Congress* must have wondered what this little ship could do to help save them from the fate of the *Cumberland* and the *Congress*. Shortly after midnight, the men on the *Monitor* heard a great roar and saw a column of flame mount skyward. The magazine of the *Congress* had finally exploded. Thus the *Monitor* cast anchor amid the wreckage of the first day's calamitous encounter with the *Merrimac* and waited for the dawn and the battle which all knew was sure to follow. All that Worden had heard about the day's battle and the havoc wrought by the *Merrimac* was of a nature to give a less courageous and determined commander deep misgivings. That night he wrote to his wife: "I arrived here an hour since, and am going immediately to the assistance of the *Minnesota* near Newport News. The *Merrimac* has just caused sad work amongst our vessels. God bless you and our little ones. Devotedly, Worden."

In the battle of March 9th the *Merrimac* enjoyed certain advantages over the *Monitor*, not the least of which was the elation and confidence felt by her officers and crew after the successes of the previous day. The heaviest cannonade from the Union frigates, while it shot away the big smokestack and all equipment outside the iron shield, had not seriously damaged the ship. She had lost her iron beak, but her bulk of 3,500 tons, in contrast with the *Monitor's* 700, would have enabled her to push her adversary under the sea, provided she were able to ram the smaller vessel. As for guns, the *Merrimac* had ten, some of them Dahlgrens, compared with only two on the *Monitor*. But the *Merrimac* also fought under certain disadvantages. One was her draft of twenty-two feet, as against the *Monitor's* ten. Thus, when she desired, the *Monitor* could retire to shallow waters where the *Merrimac* could not follow her. The Confederate ship was also very sluggish in her movements and difficult to turn.

Both ships were commanded by able and courageous officers, devoted to their cause; but Lieutenant Catesby ap R. Jones, who now commanded the *Merrimac*, had been the executive officer on the Confederate ship in the battle the day before and knew by experience what he could expect of his ship, whereas the *Monitor* was untried in battle.

The crew of the *Monitor* had already fought a three days' battle with the sea on the voyage down from New York, a journey so tempestuous that it was impossible to obtain warm food or restful sleep; their arrival late on the night before the battle allowed the crew only a few hours of rest before the *Merrimac* made her second appearance. Nevertheless, the men on the little ship were full of spirit for the conflict, were devoted to their commander, and realized that the safety of all the other Union vessels depended upon them. The crew of the *Monitor* consisted of forty-six men, all volunteers, and twelve officers. In the pilot house, conning the ship, was Lieutenant Worden, and with him Acting Master Howard, the pilot who had volunteered for the battle. At the wheel was Quartermaster Peter Williams, and in the turret, operating the two Dahlgren guns, were Lieutenant Greene and Acting Master Stodder; First Assistant Engineer Isaac Newton handled the engines. The location of the pilot house, directly in front of the turret, was one of the constructional defects of the *Monitor*. Lest some of the shots from the eleven-inch weapons strike the pilot house, Lieutenant Greene himself fired the guns. Chief Engineer Alban Stimers operated the turret revolving gear.

At 4 o'clock on the morning of the 9th of March, just four hours after her arrival, the *Monitor*, misled by a false report, got under way; but soon returned to her anchorage alongside the towering *Minnesota*. At daybreak the *Merrimac*, anticipating an easy victory over the helpless *Minnesota*, left her anchorage at Sewell's Point and came up the Roads toward the stranded frigate. As she approached the *Minnesota,* the men on the Confederate ironclad spied what seemed a toy ship standing out to intercept the path of the *Merrimac.* It was a craft such as none of them had ever seen before. To the men on the *Merrimac,* the *Monitor* resembled a small water tank set on a shingle. To the men on the *Monitor,* too, the oncoming *Merrimac* was a strange sight, resembling a colossal turtle with smoke pouring out of a hole in its back.

Captain Van Brunt of the *Minnesota* had signalled the *Monitor* to attack the *Merrimac.* The signal was not seen on the *Monitor;* but she needed no orders and stood out to meet her antagonist, placing herself between the *Merrimac* and her intended victim. Captain Van Brunt, who had made all preparations to destroy his ship if worse came to worst, had expected that the *Monitor* would stand off and fight the *Merrimac* from a distance; to his astonishment, however, he saw her moving in to close quarters and, on occasion, lay herself alongside her antagonist. At 8:45 one of the two big guns on the *Monitor* spoke and the battle was on. On the deck of the *Monitor* there were white direction markers to let the men in the revolving turret know how to fire; but these marks were soon obliterated, and the guns, firing every seven or eight minutes, hurled their heavy shots at the *Merrimac* the moment they saw her through one of the gunports. The communication system soon broke down, and Worden, as he conned the ship, had to send his orders to the men in the turret by messenger. To the thousands who were watching the battle, as well as to the men fighting on both ships, it soon became apparent that neither vessel had yet inflicted serious injury on her adversary. Sometimes almost alongside, and at other times at a distance, the *Monitor* kept circling around her big opponent "like a cooper with his hammer going round a cask."

To the delight of Worden and his officers, the turret, which critics of the *Monitor's* construction feared would jam in battle under the impact of cannon shots, never broke down or ceased to rotate. At 11:30, after three hours of battle, the *Monitor* hauled off for fifteen minutes to hoist ammunition up to the gunners in the turret. This could not be done when the turret was revolving. Northern sympathizers watching the battle were downcast, thinking that the *Monitor* had received a serious blow and been forced to retire from the fight. Captain Jones on the *Merrimac* shared this belief and turned his ship toward the *Minnesota*, the destruction of which remained his chief objective. When she came within range, the *Minnesota* gave her a broadside which, said Captain Van Brunt, would have blown any other vessel out of the water. The heavy shots, however, rolled harmlessly off the *Merrimac's* iron back and sides.

Meanwhile, after the ammunition had been hoisted into the turret and Lieutenant Worden had emerged through a port of the pilot house to take the air and look around, the *Monitor* once more headed for the *Merrimac* and the duel was resumed. Since the rain of shells which had been fired at the *Monitor* had not been able to cripple her, and since she had suffered no injury when an attempt was made to ram her, Jones ordered the gunners on the *Merrimac* to concentrate their fire on her pilot house. Worden was looking through one of the slits in the armor of the pilot house when a shell from the *Merrimac* struck the bars through which he was peering, driving paint, dust, and splinters into his face, temporarily blinding him. He immediately sent a message to Lieutenant Greene in the turret, asking him to come to the pilot house. Greene found him standing at the foot of the ladder leading to the pilot house. "He was a ghastly sight, with his eyes closed, and the blood apparently rushing from every pore in the upper part of his face." Knowing that he was badly, perhaps fatally, injured, Worden directed Greene to take charge of the ship and withdraw from the battle, for he thought that the pilot house had been wrecked by the shot. In the interval between the wounding of Worden and Greene's arrival at the pilot house to minister to his suffering commander,

Quartermaster Williams had control of the ship; having no orders, he steered the *Monitor* out of the *Merrimac's* range.

Observing this, the commander of the *Merrimac* again concluded that he was at last rid of the *Monitor*, and headed once more for the *Minnesota*. For the second time his pilots refused to approach the stranded frigate too closely for fear of grounding, and he turned the *Merrimac* toward Norfolk. In the meantime Lieutenant Greene, having discovered that the *Monitor's* pilot house had suffered no great injury, was maneuvering the *Monitor* towards the *Merrimac*, when he saw her turn away and steam toward the Elizabeth River and Norfolk. The epochal battle had ended in a draw; nevertheless, the *Monitor* had proved what she could do, what she could withstand, and what the *Merrimac* could not accomplish.

As soon as the *Monitor* anchored after the engagement, Worden's friend, Lieutenant Henry A. Wise, a gifted author and an able naval scientist, boarded her and descended through the manhole into the cabin where he found Worden lying on a couch, with the surgeon bathing his eyes. Told that he had "fought the most glorious battle in naval history," Worden asked, "Have I saved that fine ship, the *Minnesota?*" "Yes," replied Wise, "and whipped the *Merrimac* to boot." "Then," said Worden, "I don't care what happens to me." With his devoted crew cheering him, the temporarily blinded officer was taken off the *Monitor* and carried by steamer to Baltimore, and thence by train to Washington, where he was put to bed in Wise's home. The next day Lieutenant Wise gave Lincoln and his cabinet an account of the battle. When he had finished, Lincoln asked, "Where is Lieutenant Worden now?" "At my house, sir," answered Wise. Reaching for his hat, Lincoln said, "I don't know what you gentlemen are going to do, but for my part I am going to pay my respects to the young man who fought that battle." As he entered the upper chamber where Worden lay, Lincoln wordlessly laid his hand on that of the wounded Lieutenant. "Jack," said Wise to Worden, "here is the President, who has come to see you."

"You do me great honor, Mr. President, and I am only sorry that I can't see you," said Worden. "You need no man to do you honor, Lieutenant," answered Lincoln, "for you have done great honor to yourself and to your country."

Messages of praise, congratulations, and sympathy poured in upon Worden during the long months of his convalescence, but none could have moved him more than the letter which he received from the crew of the *Monitor*. It read, in part, as follows:

> To our Dear and honored Captain—Dear Sir: These few lines is from your own Crew of the '*Monitor*.' Hoping to God that they will have the pleasure of Welcoming you Back to us Soon, for we are all Ready, able, and willing to meet Death or anything else, only give us back our Captain. Dear Captain we have got our Pilot-house fixed and all Ready for you when you get well again. . . . But we all join in with our Kindest Love to you hoping that God will Restore you to us again and hoping that your Sufferings is at an end now, and we are all glad to hear that your eye Sight will be Spaired to you again. . . . We remain until death, your Affectionate Crew, the *Monitor* Boys.

New York, proud of her Westchester-born son, presented him with a sword and a testimonial. The letter of thanks which Worden wrote to New York's Secretary of State reveals more about his character and personality than most of what has been written about him. In the letter he said: "I have looked fondly in many distant climes upon the emblem of her [the United States'] greatness, power and glory, floating from the masthead, and ever with the determination that it should never be sullied if my life could avert such a calamity. . . . The genius and skill of another land furnished the means by which, under the Providence of God, I have been enabled to act a part." Then, after saying that many of his comrades in the navy would have achieved the same end, he concluded: "But I hope I may be pardoned in rejoicing that the opportunity was given me to accomplish the greatest hope of my existence."

The immediate effect of the *Monitor's* battle was the neutralization of the *Merrimac*. The battle itself was a draw; but the *Minnesota* and the other vessels at Hampton Roads had been saved. The *Merrimac* was by no means out of commission; but wherever and whenever she moved, the *Monitor* would have been there to confront her. Had the *Monitor* been sunk in the battle or badly damaged, the *Merrimac* would have been a serious menace to the army of General McClellan which was just beginning its campaign up the Peninsula between the York and the James rivers.

The duel between the two ironclads was momentous in its influence on naval construction and warfare. The wooden war-ship had become a relic of the past. Commenting on the bat-tle, the *Times* of London said: "Whereas we had available for immediate purposes one hundred and forty-nine first-class war-ships, we have now two, these two being the *Warrior* and the *Ironside*. There is not now a ship in the English Navy apart from these two that it would not be madness to trust to an engagement with that little *Monitor*." The British Admi-ralty quickly began the construction of new ironclads to rein-force its *Warrior* and *Ironside*. In France, home of the first ar-mored ships, Napoleon III appointed a commission to oversee the rapid creation of a fleet of ironclads. But all these were built on the obsolete broadside system used on the *Merrimac* and the wooden ships. The United States had a clear lead in the construction of turreted ironclads, and by the end of the war this country had a formidable fleet which any nation would have been reluctant to challenge. Ericsson was not mistaken in his belief that the European nations "would be startled and ad-monished by the booming of the guns from the impregnable iron turret."

After her battle with the *Monitor*, the *Merrimac* went into drydock for repairs. A new and heavier ram was secured to her bow, 100 tons of ballast added, and the hull below the shield covered with 2-inch iron. These changes, while adding to her power of resistance, reduced her speed to four knots and in-creased her draught to 23 feet. Josiah Tattnall, one of the most distinguished officers of the old navy, was appointed her commander, with Lieutenant Catesby ap R. Jones, who had commanded her in the fight with the *Monitor*, as executive officer. Three times the *Merrimac* steamed down to the Roads; on the third descent she found the *Monitor* with two ironclads shelling the Confederate batteries at Sewell's Point and steered straight for her. But the *Monitor*, under orders to take no unnecessary risk, declined the challenge and withdrew to Fortress Monroe.

The evacuation of Norfolk by the Confederate army on May 9th left the *Merrimac* in a desperate situation. There were two courses her captain might attempt: first, he could run the Union Blockade, but after that, as his ship was not seaworthy and carried little coal or ammunition, he would soon be helpless; second, he could lighten the ship and take her up the James River to Harrison's Landing or City Point to assist in the defense of Richmond. If neither course were chosen, then all that was left was surrender or destruction. The plan which promised the best chance of success was to lighten the ship and take her up the James. By discarding ballast, stores, and water, the ship was lightened by three feet. But because contrary westerly winds cut down the tide, the ironclad was still two feet too deep to go up the river. Reluctantly, Tattnall gave the order to run the *Merrimac* ashore at Craney's Point and set her on fire. Her crew of three hundred were sent to take part in the defense of Richmond. There was no little anger and disappointment in the South when it was learned that the *Merrimac*, of which such great things were expected, had been destroyed. Tattnall became the object of unmerited abuse. He asked for a court of inquiry, and then a court-martial. The verdict of the court was that, in destroying the *Merrimac*, Tattnall had followed the wise and only possible course.

The end of the *Monitor* was as dramatic as, though more tragic than, her fight with the *Merrimac*. At daybreak on December 29th, 1862, the *Monitor*, in charge of Commander J. P. Bankhead, hove anchor and started for the blockade of Charleston, South Carolina. To increase her speed, she was taken in tow by the *Rhode Island,* a powerful side-wheel steamer. At noon on December 30th the two vessels were seventy miles at sea and off Cape Hatteras, the graveyard of many ships. A heavy sea was running and the waves poured over the *Monitor* as if it were a half-submerged rock in the midst of the ocean. At eight o'clock that night the first distress signals to the *Rhode Island* were burned. As soon as she saw the signals, the *Rhode Island* lay to, and for a time the *Monitor* rode the sea more easily. But the *Rhode Island,* to keep from drifting down on her, had to start forward again. Once, when she came close enough, Commander Bankhead shouted through his trumpet that the *Monitor* was sinking and asked for boats to rescue the crew. Because of the danger of being towed under, an order was given to cut the towing lines. In attempting to do this two seamen were swept to their death in the wild seas.

At ten o'clock that night the *Monitor* let go her anchor, and a red light notified the *Rhode Island* that the ship was to be abandoned. The towing hawsers were then cast loose by the *Rhode Island;* but when she tried to start forward it was found that one of the hawsers was afoul of the paddle wheel, so that when the *Rhode Island* was under way, the hawser wound up on the wheel and drew the two vessels together. At length a brave fireman went into the wheel at the risk of his life and cut the hawser loose.

On the deck of the doomed *Monitor* there were moving scenes. The Negro cook was cursing with loud oaths several terror-stricken, seasick cabin boys who lay on the deck. An ensign handed his watch, one of unusual value, to a Master's Mate, saying, "Here, this is yours; I may be lost." The Master's Mate took the watch in his hand, but, after a moment's glance at it, threw it on the deck, exclaiming, "This thing may be the means of sinking me." A helmsman saw a black cat crying disconsolately on the breech of a gun and, despite the sailors' superstition, took pity on her and placed her inside another gun.

It was with great danger and some loss of life that those on the *Monitor* got into the rescue boats sent over from her consort, and with still greater peril that they got aboard the *Rhode Island*.

At half-past-twelve on the night of December 31st, the red and white lights which hung from the pennant staff on the turret suddenly disappeared from the view of the anxious watchers on the *Rhode Island* as the *Monitor*, her last battle ended, sank to the bottom. Thus with the roaring of the wind and the moaning of the sea sounding her requiem, the *Monitor* went to her ocean grave. Recently, divers have located the *Monitor* lying in the sands ten fathoms down, and plans have been projected to raise her. It would seem more fitting to let her lie where she sank on that wild December night in 1862 than to have her raised from the depths and towed about, an ugly, rusted mass of iron, to be exhibited in the ports of the land.

VII

CUSHING

"GENERAL CONDUCT BAD; aptitude for the naval service not good; not recommended for continuance at the Academy." Such was the report for February, 1861 on a cadet then in his senior year. Yet that cadet, William Barker Cushing, was shortly, on five different occasions to receive commendation and thanks from the Secretary of the Navy, and for his most daring and successful exploit the thanks of Congress. In a conversation with the Secretary of the Navy soon after the end of the war, Admiral Farragut said, "While no navy had braver or better officers than ours, young Cushing was the hero of the war."

The "hero of the war" was dismissed from Annapolis for misconduct. The edict of dismissal was softened somewhat by the grant of permission to resign. Nevertheless, it was dismissal, and based on his February report that his aptitude for the naval service was not good.

It was a rather harmless prank which brought him into disfavor with the authorities at the Academy and played a part in his dismissal. On a January day in 1861, the professor of modern languages was crossing a street in Annapolis when a vicious horse bit him on the shoulder. When the professor entered the classroom for the first time after this mishap, he saw a group of cadets, all laughing, gathered about the desk of Cushing. Sensing that he was the object of their amusement, the professor demanded an explanation. Cushing then had to deliver over to him his textbook, on the fly leaf of which he had drawn a

sketch of the professor biting the horse on its shoulder. Unable
to see the humor of the sketch, the professor earnestly protested that the horse was the aggressor, and not he. This excited
additional amusement and was the beginning of the end for
Cushing. Soon after this incident the recommendation for
his dismissal was sent to the Superintendent of the Academy.

Cushing was born at Delafield, Wisconsin on November 4th,
1842, the youngest son of Dr. Milton Cushing. The family
later removed to Chicago, and then to Gallipolis, Ohio, where
Dr. Cushing died when William was five years of age. The wid-
owed mother, a cultivated and strong-minded woman from Boston, went to live at Fredonia, New York, where she established
a school and supported her family by teaching. In 1856 William
secured an appointment as a page in the House of Representatives, of which his uncle, Francis S. Edwards, was a member. At
Washington young Cushing attracted the attention of another
relative, Commodore Joseph Smith, and through him obtained
an appointment to the Naval Academy. Another brother,
Alonzo, was at the same time a cadet in the Military Academy at
West Point.

Cushing's letters from the Naval Academy reveal a youth of
high ambition and determination. In one letter he said: "I intend
to see every nook and corner of this little world that is to be
seen, if I live." On a cadet cruise on the *Plymouth* in 1860, at a
time when there was considerable war talk, he wrote: "If it
comes to blows between the North and South, I will shed the
last drop of blood for the State of New York." About the time
of his dismissal from the Academy, Southern cadets who were
resigning and "going South" urged him to accompany them,
but he never wavered in his allegiance to the nation—or at least
to the State of New York! Influential friends of the family
spoke in his behalf after he left the Academy; among them was
Ben Butler, who had been a schoolmate of Gustavus Fox. After
he had given Secretary Welles a personal pledge of honorable
conduct for the future, Cushing was assigned to the *Minnesota*

as an acting master's mate, and in October of 1861 was formally restored to the navy as an acting midshipman. Throughout the war, no officer was more frequently under fire or performed more deeds of valor in battle. From the *Minnesota* he reported to a cousin: "I am going to fight under the old banner of freedom. I may never return, but if I die, it shall be under the folds of the flag that sheltered my infancy, and while striking a blow for its honor and my own. . . . Wherever there is fighting, there we will be, and where there is danger in the battle, there will I be, for I will gain a name in this war."

The first sign that he was to fulfill his vow to "gain a name" was in an attack on the town of Franklin on the Blackwater River in North Carolina on October 3rd, 1862. The *Perry*, to which he had been transferred as executive officer, encountered barricades well up the river which made further progress impossible. As soon as the *Perry* and the other Union ships reached the barricades, the Confederates felled three trees below the ships; it seemed that the little squadron was hopelessly trapped. Admiral Porter, who had experienced the same immobilization on the Red River and Steele's Bayou in the west, wrote of Cushing's predicament: "There is nothing so harassing as to be caught in a narrow river under such circumstances." But Cushing and his skipper, Lieutenant C. W. Flusser, were equal to the occasion. At an opportune moment, the *Perry* and her two companions turned about and under a full head of steam rammed their way through the fallen trees; by nightfall they were out of danger. At one time the Confederate troops made an attempt to board the *Perry*, but Cushing and several volunteers ran out a gun and scattered the attackers with its fire. Although most of the men serving the gun were wounded, Cushing himself escaped without a scratch. This good fortune attended him throughout his extraordinary career, for never was he seriously wounded.

Cushing's next adventure, and one from which it seemed impossible to escape without experiencing capture or death, occurred the following November when, in command of a small gunboat recently captured from the Confederates, the *Ellis*, he attacked the town of Jacksonville, North Carolina, on the New River Inlet. On his way up the inlet he captured an outward-bound blockade runner loaded with cotton and turpentine. The ship had been set on fire when her crew abandoned her, but Cushing extinguished the flames and seized the vessel as a prize. At Jacksonville he captured a quantity of arms stored in the Court House, several Negroes, the postmaster, and two schooners. On his way back with his prizes, the *Ellis* went aground not far from a high bluff. Knowing that the Confederates would make an attack as soon as they discovered his plight, Cushing stripped the *Ellis* of everything valuable and loaded it on one of the captured schooners, leaving on his own vessel only coal, ammunition, and a pivot gun. Mustering his crew, he ordered them to board one of the schooners and make their way down the inlet and over the bar to safety. Before the crew left the ship, he asked for six volunteers to remain with him on the *Ellis* and with the lone gun fight the ship to the last. Although they all felt it meant certain death, six men immediately stepped forward. Early the next morning, the Confederates on the river bank opened fire on him with four heavy guns and the *Ellis* was soon in a hopeless condition. Faced with the alternative of surrender or a perilous attempt to escape, Cushing chose the latter. Before leaving his ship, he trained her gun on the enemy so that it would discharge when the fires he had started reached it. Then, with the flag still flying on the doomed vessel, Cushing and his six men clambered into a small boat and bent to the oars. Escaping a Confederate cavalry force which sought to intercept them at a bend in the river, they rowed safely down the inlet and out to sea. Just as they crossed the bar, they heard a distant roar as the *Ellis* blew up. Because he had lost his ship, Cushing asked for a court of inquiry; instead, he was commended for his courageous and successful escape.

He next made an attempt to capture the pilots who guided

the blockade runners in and out of Wilmington, North Carolina. The pilot station was near Fort Caswell on the Little River. With three cutters and twenty-five men, Cushing crossed the bar at eight in the evening and started for the station. He did not succeed in finding the pilots but, when fired upon from a bluff, he landed his little troop and charged the position whence the firing had come, not knowing whether it was defended by fifty or a thousand men. With loud shouts, Cushing and his men reached the walls of a fort illuminated by campfires. Hearing the shouts and the cheering of the twenty-five men, and believing they were under attack by a strong force, the defenders aban-doned the fort and fled precipitately, leaving everything behind them.

The record of these daring exploits by Cushing has the ring of romance, but every one of them reveals an amazing spirit of ingenuity, courage, and fortitude. "There were many other officers in the navy," said Admiral Porter, "who were equally brave, and with more judgment; but Cushing was of a peculiar temperament, always doing something to astonish his commanders, and, whether fortunate or not in his undertakings, he was sure to create a sensation." His name soon became as well-known among the Confederates as it was in the Union navy.

One of Cushing's daring, but unsuccessful, deeds was an attempt to capture some officers at Smithville, near Wilmington in February, 1864. The commanding general, who was playing cards in a house with one of his majors, managed to escape in the darkness. He hid in bushes near the house, but the major was captured. When Cushing asked his prisoner to identify him-self, he replied, "Major Brown, commanding the fortifications. Are you Captain Cushing?" "Yes," answered Cushing, "why do you ask?" "Well," replied the major, "I don't know of anyone else who attempts such things."

While William Cushing was achieving fame and winning one commendation after another, his older brother, Alonzo, was also making a name for himself in the army. He was brevetted a captain for gallantry at the bloody, disastrous battle of Fredericksburg; advanced to a major for meritorious service at Chancellorsville; and at the end of the first day's battle at Gettysburg was made a lieutenant colonel. The unit which he commanded at Gettysburg, Battery A of the 4th Artillery of Hancock's Corps, was stationed at the very center of the Union line. Soon after the Confederate artillery opened with its earth-shaking cannonade from Seminary Ridge on the climactic day of battle, Alonzo was painfully wounded in both thighs; nevertheless, even after most of his officers had been killed or wounded, he continued to serve his guns to the very last. He fell by the side of one of his guns just a few minutes before the brave Confederate General Armistead, at the head of Picketts' charge, leaped the stone wall and fell dead on the other side of the same gun. But while death laid his hand on Alonzo at Gettysburg, he stood aside and let William pass unscathed.

William was as spirited a writer as he was a warrior. In a letter to his mother, he thus describes a battle through which he had just passed:

Crash! go the bulkheads; a rifle shell has exploded on our deck, tearing flesh and woodwork. A crash like thunder is our reply—and our heavy shell makes music in the air and explodes among our traitor neighbors with a dull, sullen roar of defiance. Up goes the battle flag, the air is filled with the smoke of furious battle and the ear thrills with the unceasing shriek and whistle of all the shell and rifle bolts that sinful man has devised to murder his fellow creatures. Crash! Crash! Splinters are flying in the air; great pools of blood are on the deck, and the first cry of wounded men in agony rises on the soft spring air. The dead men cannot speak; but there they lie, motionless and mangled, who, a moment ago, sailed under the old flag that floated over them, and fought for its honor and glory.

Up to an October night in 1864, all Cushing's marvelous deeds and heroic exploits, his hairbreadth escapes, his daring attacks were only a prelude to, and a severe training school for, his great achievement, the sinking of the Confederate ram *Al-*

bemarle. This ship, named after Albemarle Sound, was built on a cornfield at Edwards Ferry, North Carolina, on the Roanoke River. Her builder, Gilbert Elliot, followed the plans laid down by John L. Porter, Chief Constructor of the Confederate Navy. The *Albemarle* was 122 feet long, 40 wide, and drew 8 feet of water. Her upper structure, or shield, was 60 feet long; the sides sloped to the deck at an angle of 45 degrees, an arrangement which made it difficult for hostile shots to penetrate her armor. Inside the iron-plated superstructure were two pivot guns, so placed that each could fire through any one of three portholes.

As early as September of 1863, Commander C. W. Flusser had warned the Navy Department that the Confederates were building a formidable ram on the Roanoke. Because of the difficulty of getting heavy gunboats over the bar and ascending the river, Secretary Welles suggested to the War Department that the army take over the task of destroying the ram. It was Admiral Porter's opinion that this could have been easily accomplished. The formidable ram was completed in April of 1864, nine months after Welles had asked the army to destroy her. The *Albemarle* did not wait long to display her powers. On April 18th, 1864, with mechanics still working on her, she set out down the Roanoke for the town of Plymouth, then held by Union forces, with orders to cooperate with the Confederate land forces in their attack upon the town. Because the swift current made it difficult to steer head-on, the ram went down the river stern foremost, with heavy chains dragging from the bow. Three miles above Plymouth, she anchored and sent out a scouting party which reported that it was not possible to pass the obstructions which the Union garrison at Plymouth had placed in the river. The builder of the vessel, Gilbert Elliot, was on board as a volunteer aide to Captain T. W. Cooke. Disappointed that the ram had halted, and convinced that this was her opportunity to render service to the Confederacy, Elliot obtained permission from Captain Cooke to make a personal reconnaissance. Taking a few seamen and a long sounding-pole, he dropped down the river at night in a lifeboat. To his great joy he discovered that, due to a recent freshet, there was ten feet of water over the obstructions, two feet more than the *Albemarle* required. With muffled oars, Elliot continued down the river until he reached a point opposite Plymouth, where he saw Union transports taking on women and children to escape the danger of the expected bombardment. He then returned to the ram and reported his discovery to Captain Cooke, who roused the crew, slipped the cables, and started down the river.

When the gunners on the Union vessels discovered the *Albemarle* approaching, they opened fire, but the cannon balls and shells glanced off her side like so many pebbles. The leader of the Union ships in the river, C. W. Flusser, had lashed his flagship *Miami* to the *Southfield* with long spars and chains, leaving considerable space between them. The purpose of this was to pin the *Albemarle* between the two ships where she would be unable to ram either. Captain Cooke avoided the trap by running close to the southern shore of the river. Then, turning quickly, with the current in his favor and at full speed, he drove the ram's iron prow into the side of the *Southfield*, which sank almost immediately. The *Miami* then opened fire on the ram with her heavy Dahlgren guns. In an exchange of shots Commander Flusser was killed, either by a direct hit or by a fragment of a Federal shell rebounding from the ram's iron back. With her captain dead, the *Miami* and two other Union ships then retreated down the river. The *Albemarle* pursued them for a short distance but, finding them too fast, gave up the chase and, well satisfied with the night's work, returned to Plymouth, which at once fell into Confederate hands.

After this defeat, the Navy Department sent Captain Melancthon Smith, who had served under Farragut at New Orleans and Port Hudson as captain of the *Mississippi*, to take command of the ships in Albemarle Sound and capture or destroy the *Albemarle*. Admiral S. P. Lee, then commanding the North Atlantic Squadron but soon to be succeeded by Admiral

David Porter, gave Smith detailed instructions on how to battle the ram, although so able an officer hardly needed such guidance. The Union ships were to center their fire on the *Albemarle*'s ports, whether the shutters were open or closed; after firing, the gunners were to lie prone on the deck and thus avoid the dangerous rebound of shell fragments as they struck the ram's iron plates. A position close to the *Albemarle* was to be maintained to obviate the threat of her ram.

At Edenton Bay, off the mouth of the Roanoke River, Captain Smith had with him eight vessels. One of them, the *Miami*, which had already tested her mettle against the *Albemarle*, was fitted with a torpedo to explode against the sides of the ram if an opportunity presented itself. At one o'clock on May 4th, four Union ships, accompanied by a transport, were going up the mouth of the Roanoke with the purpose of planting torpedoes, when the *Albemarle* was seen coming down the river. Sending the transport back to warn the flagship, the *Matabesett*, the other ships withdrew slowly, hoping to lure the ram as far as possible from the mouth of the river. As soon as he received word that the ram was on her way down, Captain Smith signalled his ships to engage her. He ordered the heavier ships to steer as close to the ram as possible without getting entangled with her, deliver a broadside, and then turn about for a second broadside. As the ram slowly drew near to the Union vessels, she opened the battle by firing her pivot gun at the *Matabesett*, smashing down her rails and spars and wounding several men. This was followed by an unsuccessful attempt to ram the flagship, which rounded the *Albemarle*'s bow and gave her a broadside at the distance of 15 yards. As the *Albemarle* turned to attack the flagship once more, she presented her side to the *Sassacus*, which gave her another broadside that skimmed harmlessly off her iron shield.

A little later in the engagement, at an opportune moment, Commander Roe of the *Sassacus* gave the order for ramming. As the *Sassacus* bore down on the *Albemarle*, the order rang out,

William Barker Cushing
1842—1874

John Ancrum Winslow
1811—1873

"All hands lie down!" Then with a loud crash the *Sassacus* drove her bow into the side of the ram, causing the Southern ironclad to keel over until her afterdeck was submerged. The engines of the *Sassacus* were kept going in the hope of pushing the ram deeper and deeper into the water. During the brief period the two ships were locked together, the men on the *Sassacus* hurled hand grenades at the hatches of the ram and tried to fire into her smokestack, which lay far over to one side. The *Albemarle's* stern had now swung around so that her gunners were able to fire one of their heavy guns into the *Sassacus* at pointblank range. The shot crashed through the side of the ship and exploded her boilers. Escaping steam turned the below decks of the *Sassacus* into an inferno whence issued agonizing screams and groans from scalded and dying men. In his account of this terrible scene on the *Sassacus* Admiral Porter says: "Only those who have witnessed the effect of a bursting boiler, with the steam rushing all over the ship, can appreciate the condition of affairs on board the *Sassacus*. The stoutest nerves are scarcely proof against the appalling sights which meet the eye, and the cries and groans which meet the ear." In the midst of the tumult, the cry went up on the *Sassacus*, "All hands repel boarders." Those of the crew who were able seized pistols and cutlasses to meet the attack, which was baffled by the musketry fire and hand grenades thrown from the rigging of the *Sassacus*.

During the death duel between the *Albemarle* and the *Sassacus*, the other Union ships stood by with silent guns, afraid to fire lest they kill friend as well as foe. At length the two ships drifted apart, and the *Sassacus* dropped out of the battle. At 7:40 o'clock, with darkness coming on, the engagement was broken off and the ram went up the river and moored under the guns of Plymouth.

How could this iron monster be destroyed? That was the problem which the navy must solve, for at any time she might sally forth from Plymouth and smash the fleet in the sound. One daring attempt to destroy her was made by five men from the

Wyalusing, who carried torpedoes on stretchers through the swamps near Plymouth. A little above the town a coal-heaver swam the river, pulling the torpedoes after him on a line. The plan was then to float them down with the current and fasten them across the bows of the ram. At a given signal, one of the five men stationed in the swamp was to pull a wire and explode the torpedoes. The coal-heaver succeeded in getting within a few yards of the *Albemarle*, when he was seen by a sentry and fired on. This compelled him to cut the guiding rope and abandon the attempt. After great hardships all five of the brave men reached the *Wyalusing* in safety.

This was the state of affairs when Admiral Lee, well informed as to the exploits of the young lieutenant, consulted Cushing, who submitted two plans of attack. The first was for a hundred men to carry rubber boats through the swamps, get within a few hundred yards of the ram, and then use the boats to board her and cut her loose. The other plan was to attack her with two steam launches equipped with torpedoes, one boat to stand by and make a second attempt if the first failed. This was the plan favored by Lee, who sent Cushing to Washington to submit the plan to the Navy Department. Fox, with whom he talked, entertained no high opinion of the plan, but finally directed Cushing to go to New York and obtain the launches.

At New York Cushing secured two screw-propelled open launches, thirty feet in length. A 12-pounder howitzer was fitted to the bow of each, and a boom, so fixed that it could be raised and lowered and swung to either side, was installed. A torpedo was fixed in an iron slide at the end of the boom; this device was the contrivance of a navy engineer. While the two launches were being prepared, Cushing visited his mother at Fredonia, New York. Taking her one day for a drive into the country, he said: "Mother, I have undertaken a great project, and no soul must know until it is accomplished; but I must tell you, for I need your prayers." When his brave mother learned of his project, she said: "My son, I believe you will accomplish it; but you cannot come out alive."

Toward the end of October, 1864, Cushing started south with his two launches, one of which was lost in a storm in the Chesapeake. By the time he reached Hampton Roads, where he reported to Admiral Porter (who had replaced Lee as Commander of the North Atlantic Squadron) his physical condition was such that Porter ordered him to bed for a rest, telling him not to report again until sent for. After he was well rested Porter gave him his orders to proceed to the Roanoke River and destroy the *Albemarle*. Commander W. H. Macomb, at that time in command of the Union vessels in the North Carolina sounds, was instructed to give Cushing all possible assistance; if he succeeded in blowing up the *Albemarle*, the fleet was to attack and recapture Plymouth. Just as Cushing was about to leave Hampton Roads, an order came from the Navy Department directing Porter to investigate certain charges lodged against Cushing by the Secretary of State for violating neutral rights in connection with the seizure of a British vessel. Fortunately, it was Porter and not some other commander who received this order, for Porter, himself a man of great courage and daring, admired these virtues in others. Instead of holding Cushing for a long investigation, he had him briefly interrogated and sent him on his way rejoicing.

Passing through a storm on the way down, Cushing at length reached the Union flotilla, fifty miles up Albemarle Sound, and reported to Commander Macomb on his flagship, the *Shamrock*. The vessel's executive officer, Rufus D. K. Duer, mustered the seventy-five men of her crew and addressed them as follows: "I want eleven men and two officers to accompany Lieutenant Cushing on a dangerous expedition, from which probably none will return. None but the young men without encumbrances will be accepted. Those who wish to volunteer will step over to this side." Every man of the seventy-five moved over. When Duer so reported to Commander Macomb, he said, "I thought so. Pick your men." So eager were all seventy-five men to accompany Cushing on this dangerous errand, that the eleven who were finally chosen were offered bribes to withdraw and let others go in their place.

The *Albemarle* was moored near Plymouth, eight miles up the Roanoke. At this point the stream was one hundred and fifty yards in width. A mile below the ram lay the wreck of the *Southfield*, sunk in the April battle. Captain A. F. Warley, now commanding the *Albemarle*, had stationed twenty-five pickets on the *Southfield* to give warning of the approach of any hostile craft. Cushing's first attempt was made on the night of October 26th. When the launch came near the mouth of the river, Union pickets who had heard the sound of the engine challenged her and almost fired into her. This warned Cushing that Confederate pickets on the *Southfield*, of whose presence he had been notified by "contraband," could be likewise alerted. He therefore returned to the *Shamrock* and had the ship's carpenter box-in the engine so as to render it almost noiseless.

The night of October 27th witnessed the bravest deed of the Civil War. The night was dark and rainy, most favorable for Cushing's project. In tow of the launch was the *Shamrock's* cutter with sailors aboard; if the launch was hailed when passing the wreck of the *Southfield*, these men were to dash aboard, capture the pickets, and so prevent the firing of a rocket to warn the *Albemarle*. Through the thick darkness the launch with its twelve men made its careful and almost noiseless way up the river; not even a whisper was permitted. Unseen by any eye and unheard by any ear, the launch reached and passed the *Southfield* without being challenged. Cushing had two plans in mind. One was to board the *Albemarle* and "take her alive," for on his two boats he had twenty courageous men armed with hand grenades, revolvers, and cutlasses. "To be sure," Cushing said, "there are ten times our number on the ship, thousands nearby; but a surprise is everything, and I thought that if her

fasts were cut at the instant of boarding, we might overcome
those on board, take her into the stream, and use her iron sides
to protect us from the forts."

He was about to land his men at a wharf a little below the
Albemarle, creep around behind the ram and board her from the
land, when there came a hail from the watch. Instantly Cushing cut loose the cutter with orders to go back down the river
and seize the pickets on the *Southfield*. Then, under full steam,
he headed up the river for the ram in the face of fire from both
the ship and the shore. Just as he was nearing the ironclad,
Cushing saw by the light of a fire which had been kindled on
the shore that she lay in a "pen" of logs, designed to protect
her against just such an attack as he was about to make. Cushing, however, had no thought of turning back. "Impossibilities,"
he said, "are for the timid," among whom he could never be
numbered. When first hailed by the watch on the *Albemarle*,
he answered, "We'll soon show you," and pulled the lanyard on
his howitzer. Although he was now under heavy and constant
fire, he ran along the side of the log pen to examine it more
closely. Then, sheering off for a hundred yards, he turned
about and headed straight for the logs, hoping that their long
submersion had made them slimy and would allow the launch to
slip over.

In that moment of quick decision, when he changed his plan
from an attempt to board the ram from the shore and bore
down on the logs which cradled the *Albemarle*, Cushing estimated that he had about thirty seconds in which to discharge
his torpedo. His clothing perforated by bullets, the young lieutenant stood calmly in the bow of the launch with four lines
attached to his person: two to direct the movements of the
launch, one running from his wrist to the engineer's ankle, and
the fourth a trigger line to explode the torpedo. The slightest
mistake, a pull on the wrong line, would have spelled disaster.
As Cushing hoped, the momentum of the launch carried it clear
over the logs, and with stern down and bow up it came along-

side the ram. Cushing could see a big rifled gun pointed directly at him ten feet from where he was standing. As the forward motion of the launch carried it under the "overhang" of the *Albemarle*, he gave the signal to lower the boom. Then with his left hand he pulled on the trigger line and the torpedo tore a hole in the hull of the ram, as her captain later said, "big enough to drive a wagon through." The dreaded *Albemarle*, which an entire Union fleet had been unable to destroy, sank to the bottom.

At the moment the torpedo exploded, a hundred-pounder on the *Albemarle* hurled its mass of grapeshot into the launch. At the same time the geyser of water created by the torpedo came pouring down on Cushing and his crew. Twice refusing a call to surrender, he told his men to save themselves and, throwing off his sword, revolver, shoes, and coat, leaped into the dark river. Boats from the *Albemarle* had put out to pick up the crew, and Cushing heard his name called twice, but escaped capture. Far down the river, he was struggling to reach the bank when he heard a cry behind him and turned back. The man whose cry he had heard was Acting Master's Mate Woodman. Supporting him with his right arm, and telling him to strike out as best he could, Cushing kept him afloat for ten minutes, when the mate's strength gave out and he sank like a stone.

Half a mile down the river, his own strength almost gone, Cushing pulled himself up the bank, where he sank down exhausted, half in the river and half in the mud, and lay there till dawn. Unable even to crawl on his hands and knees, nearly frozen and with his brain in a whirl, he still felt one compulsion: a "fixed determination to escape." The same inflexible purpose which had sunk the *Albemarle* now saved his life.

When the sun appeared, his spirits rose and a degree of his strength returned. From his hiding place in a swamp he could see the excited movements of the Southern soldiers and sailors at Plymouth; it gave him considerable satisfaction to know that he had pulled the line which had stirred all this commotion. In

trying to reach a dry spot in the swamp he narrowly avoided a
sentinel, and four soldiers passed so near to him that they could
have trodden on his arm. For a period of five hours, lying on his
belly and sinking his elbows and feet into the mud, he made his
way through the swamp to an open space, his hands and feet
raw and bleeding from their desperate labor. There he encountered a Negro, to whom he gave twenty dollars and a few texts
of Scripture and entrusted him to go and bring him news of the
ram. The Negro returned with the tidings that the *Albemarle*
was under the water, only her smokestack visible. Heartened by
this word, Cushing set out again through the swamp and came
at length to a place by the river from which he could see a
Confederate picket of seven soldiers with a skiff tied to the roots
of a cypress tree by the opposite bank. Watching his chance,
when the soldiers went off to eat he swam the stream, cast the
skiff loose, and floated down behind it until the boat rounded a
bend, when he got in and paddled for his life. All the rest of that
day and far into the night he paddled until he reached the mouth
of the Roanoke and the open sound which, fortunately, was
calm. Steering by a star for what he thought was the flotilla's
location, he paddled his craft for ten hours more, all but his
arms and his brain asleep, until he saw a picket vessel, the
Valley City. With the last of his strength he shouted, "Ship
ahoy!" and fell helpless into the water in the bottom of the
skiff. The *Valley City* lowered boats; but they were afraid at
first to pick him up, fearing that he was a rebel with an infernal
machine, and certain that Cushing had perished the night before.

Safe now on the deck of the *Valley City* and soon revived
with water and brandy, Cushing announced that he had sunk the
Albemarle. This was greeted by cheers, and rockets shot into
the sky to let the other ships of the fleet know of the success of
the great exploit. A few days later the *Valley City* took him to
Hampton Roads, where he said to Admiral Porter, "I have the
honor to report that the rebel ironclad is at the bottom of the

Roanoke River." When the Secretary of the Navy received Cushing's report, he wrote him a fatherly letter of praise, in which he said:

On four previous occasions the Department had the gratification of expressing its approbation of your conduct in the face of the enemy, and in each instance there was manifested by you the same heroic daring and innate love of adventure; a mind determined to succeed and not to be deterred by any apprehension of defeat. It gives me pleasure to recall the assurance you gave me at the commencement of your active professional career, that you would prove yourself worthy of the confidence reposed in you and of the service to which you were appointed. I trust you may be preserved through further trials; and it is for yourself to determine whether, after entering upon so auspicious a career, you shall, by careful study, and self discipline, be prepared for a wider sphere of usefulness, on the call of your country.

Just before leaving New York on his perilous expedition, Cushing wrote to one of his relatives: "Cousin George, I am going to have a vote of thanks from Congress, or six feet of pine box by the next time you hear from me." He received the thanks of Congress. On the 5th of December, 1864, President Lincoln sent this message to Congress:

I most cordially recommend that Lieutenant William B. Cushing, United States Navy, receive a vote of thanks from Congress for his important, gallant, and perilous achievement in destroying the rebel iron-clad steamer *Albemarle*, on the night of the 27th of October, 1864, at Plymouth, North Carolina. The destruction of so formidable a vessel which had resisted the continued attacks of a number of our vessels on former occasions, is an important event, touching our future naval and military operations, and would reflect honor on any officer, and redounds to the credit of this young officer and the few brave comrades who assisted in this successful and daring undertaking.

More than that of any officer of the army or navy in the great four-year conflict on land and sea, the portrait of Cushing shows a face of rare and classic beauty and refinement; a face which reveals tender affection, deep moral earnestness, high resolve, great daring and invincible determination, the determination of a man who said and proved that "impossibilities are for the timid." He was just a few days under twenty-two when he sank the *Albemarle*. At the age of thirty he was promoted to commander, the youngest officer of that rank in the navy. He had all the qualities of a great admiral, and undoubtedly would have attained that rank, had not death, which had so long withheld his shaft and let him pass unharmed through a thousand perils, struck him down at the age of thirty-two in a government hospital for the insane.

VIII

WINSLOW

UNTIL THE END of a bright June Sabbath in 1864, the name of Captain John A. Winslow was, outside of limited naval circles, altogether unknown. But the one-hour battle fought that day off the harbor of Cherbourg in which Winslow's ship, the *Kearsarge*, sent the Confederate raider and cruiser *Alabama* to the bottom of the ocean, made his name echo throughout Europe and America. That victory had no influence whatever upon the issue of the Civil War, for when it was won the Confederacy itself was a sinking ship. Nor, if the result of the sea duel had been otherwise and the *Alabama* had sunk the *Kearsarge*, would it have made any difference in the outcome of the war. Yet the victory over the *Alabama* and Raphael Semmes, her commander, won for Winslow tremendous acclaim. One reason for this was the fact that for two years United States warships had been searching the seven seas for the *Alabama*, which had destroyed much of the seaborne commerce of the nation, leaving behind her a smoky trail of burning ships across the oceans. Another reason the people of the North exulted so greatly over the destruction of the *Alabama* was the resentment felt toward England for the favors she had shown to Confederate raiders, permitting them to be built in her yards and winking at neutrality laws. The *Alabama* was built in the Birkenhead Yard, near Liverpool, was armed with English-made cannon, flew the English colors when approaching her prey, and carried a number of British gunners. The nation looked upon the battle as a victory over England, as well as over the Confederacy. It carried the thought of the nation back to the great sea duels between American and British frigates in the War of 1812. When Gideon Welles received Winslow's dispatches telling of the sinking of the *Alabama*, he wrote in his diary: "There is great rejoicing throughout the country over this success, which is universally and justly conceded a triumph over England as well as over the rebels."

John Ancrum Winslow was born November 19th, 1811, at Wilmington, North Carolina. Through his father, a Bostonian who had gone to North Carolina to establish a commercial business, he traced his lineage back to the *Mayflower*. At Wilmington his father married Sarah Ancrum, twice married before, the mother of six children, and related to the well-known Rhett family of South Carolina. After a brief schooling in Massachusetts, young Winslow showed a strong liking for the sea, and at the age of sixteen received a midshipman's warrant. Sixteen was an early age, but many other midshipmen of that era had entered the service when even younger. His appointment came through the influence of Daniel Webster, on whose lands at Marshfield some of Winslow's Puritan ancestors had settled.

Winslow's youthful enthusiasm for the sea and the navy began to ebb as the years went by and he became a husband and a father. The poor remuneration, the monotony of the long cruises, and the separation from his family caused him to make an effort to enter another calling. He invented a steam tug for carrying vessels over bars and procured a patent for it; but the lack of capital made it impossible to produce it and he never reaped any financial benefit from the invention. His letters at this time reveal a deep discontent with the navy. At Honolulu, in September, 1852, he wrote: "Few people know the trials of the Navy life, this continued surveillance of the worst set of scoundrels under the sun. Formerly orders were promptly obeyed; now you have to go after a man and enforce your orders. We have now four men confined for attempt at murder."

Two years later, when his ship, the *St. Lawrence,* was at Valparaiso, and the Crimean War had broken out in Europe, Winslow showed his deeply religious nature and his careful following of the world drama by this comment: "A fearful crisis seems to be upon the world. Look at China, an empire standing 2,200 years without change, now deluged with blood, and the revolutionists [the Tai-ping rebels] carrying a cross upon their banners, with Protestant principles,—what but God's power could effect this! Our own country is not secure either; corruption in morals, in the Government; the people everywhere forgetting the great Author of their happiness, forgetting blessings far greater than those promised the chosen people of God. Everywhere ingratitude is manifest to Him. In Congress men rise up in hopes of getting the presidency and renew the negro or slavery war. I know not where the question will end, but it seems to me one of uncommon magnitude. Everything looks gloomy."

The same year, when his ship was lying at Callao, Peru, Winslow wrote to his wife: "Your letter with accounts of home made me homesick. It requires great self-denial to be away from you all. I have missed my profession, I am not fit to remain away. There are many who like this life, but I cannot believe that anyone who is of a domestic turn of mind can receive pleasure away from those he loves." This was after twenty-seven years in the navy!

In the six years before the outbreak of the Civil War Winslow was on shore duty, first in charge of recruiting at Boston and then as inspector of lighthouses. At the beginning of the war, Flag Officer Foote, who was building up a river squadron on the Mississippi, and who esteemed Winslow highly, asked the Navy Department to assign him as his chief assistant in preparing the ships. In moral character and religious faith Foote and Winslow were much alike. While taking the flagship *Benton* down the river from St. Louis to Cairo the ship grounded. In directing the work of getting her afloat again Winslow received a severe injury to his left arm through the snapping of a hawser and was invalided home. He rejoined the flotilla in May of 1862 in command of the *Baron de Kalb*,[1] too late to participate in Foote's attacks on Fort Henry, Fort Donelson, and Island No. 10.

The day before Winslow returned to the fleet, Foote, still not recovered from a wound received at Fort Donelson, struck his flag and was temporarily succeeded by Captain Charles H. Davis. For a few weeks Winslow saw service on the Mississippi as far south as Memphis, but did not participate in any notable engagement. At Memphis he wrote to his wife: "I see the news —it is very rebellious. Until the slaves are manumitted we shall do nothing; then we shall go forward to fight God's battles and relieve thousands of His praying Christians."

When Davis was succeeded by David D. Porter the following October, Winslow was in poor health, was displeased with the government, and resented the fact that Porter, his junior in rank, had been promoted over him; consequently, he asked to be assigned to some other duty. In his letter to Secretary Welles, Winslow referred to the "conditions" under which he had accepted service with Foote. In forwarding his letter to the Secretary, Davis wrote: "The application contained in this letter, which, if unqualified, would be regarded as an act of insubordination, is forwarded with the following remark: 'The language of Captain Winslow implies that there is a special understanding with the Department; otherwise, I should recommend that the request be not complied with.' " This makes it plain that Winslow was unhappy in his relationship with Davis. In response to his application for a new field of service, Welles sent a curt message, saying, "You are hereby detached from the Mississippi Squadron and placed on furlough."

Sensing the Secretary's displeasure, Winslow replied that he had not meant to reflect on the Department for placing Porter, his junior, in command of the river flotilla, and that he "did not

[1] The *Baron de Kalb*, one of the seven original Eads ironclads, was at first known as the *St. Louis*.

know a better officer than Porter." He added that his relations with Foote were such that it was a pleasure to be with him, and that Porter's appointment now warranted his request for a better command. He also enclosed for the perusal of the Secretary a testimonial from the officers of the *Baron de Kalb*.

Shortly before he applied for new duty, Winslow had written a letter to Fox, in which he referred to an article written by a Baltimore newspaper correspondent on the *Baron de Kalb*. The article launched two charges against Winslow which, if believed by the Navy Department, would have injured his standing and perhaps put an end to his career in the navy. One was that he had treated a prisoner on his ship with unseemly courtesy, and had showed him all the weak points of his ship. This Winslow answered by saying that the officer in question had fought the *de Kalb* at Donelson and was well-acquainted with her weak points, and that it was to remove this impression of inferiority that he had invited his prisoner to inspect the vessel. The other allegation was that after the Second Battle of Bull Run in the summer of 1862, when Pope's army was driven back on Washington, Winslow had exclaimed: "I was glad of it. I wish they would bag Old Abe!" He admitted this utterance, but contended that the "eavesdropping" reporter was silent as to the context which followed, "for until something is done to arouse the Government we shall have no fixed policy." This reminds one of what Stanton, not yet Secretary of War, wrote to ex-President James Buchanan at the time of the first disaster which befell the Union army at Bull Run in 1861: "The capture of Washington seems now to be inevitable. The dreadful disaster of Sunday can scarcely be imagined. The imbecility of this administration culminated in that catastrophe; an irretrievable misfortune, and national disgrace, never to be forgotten, are to be added to the ruin of all peaceful pursuits, and national bankruptcy is the result of Lincoln's running the machine for five months." Stanton went on to say that he had no hope of improvement in the administration of the Government "until Jeff Davis turns out the whole concern." If such criticisms of Lincoln and expressions of disgust with the management of the war as uttered by Winslow and Stanton had been regarded as treasonable, many an officer in the army and navy would have lost his commission.

In July, 1862 Winslow was made a captain, but it was not until the following December that he received orders to sail from New York in the U.S.S. *Vanderbilt* for Fayal in the Azores to take command of the *Kearsarge*, then undergoing repairs at Cadiz, Spain. Winslow reached Fayal the day before Christmas, and settled down to a long, dismal, and lonely wait for his new ship. During that period he was suffering from affliction of the left eye, the sight of which he later lost completely. In low spirits, he wrote his wife: "It is literally an exile—nothing to do and nothing to relieve the ennui. I am utterly dispirited."

The *Kearsarge*, a steam sloop of 1030 tons, was launched at Portsmouth, New Hampshire in October, 1861, and commissioned in January, 1862. Her name was derived from one of New Hampshire's rugged mountains. Under her first skipper, Charles H. Pickering, the *Kearsarge* had hunted the *Sumter*, Raphael Semmes' first raider. After the *Kearsarge* and other Federal cruisers had hemmed in the *Sumter* at Gibraltar, she was sold, and Semmes was given the *Alabama*. Now the *Kearsarge* was once again on his trail. Four months after Winslow arrived in the Azores, the *Kearsarge* reported to him at Fayal. Thence, with Winslow finally in command, she sailed in April, 1863. It was the beginning of a quest which was to last for more than a year and at length bring fame to her commander and joy to the nation.

The sea is wide, as well as deep. The *Kearsarge's* only chance of catching the *Alabama*, save by accident, was to intercept her when she was entering a port or leaving one to which she had gone for repairs or supplies. Winslow searched up and down the sea lanes between the Azores and Britain and through the waters off the west coast of Spain. Even when, as frequently happened, a United States warship found a Confederate raider in a neutral harbor, the chances were all on the side of the raider, for, if it put to sea first, the United States ship could not pursue her until after the lapse of twenty-four hours.

While Winslow, led on by false rumors and reports, was scouring European waters in a vain hunt for the *Alabama*, Semmes was capturing and burning United States vessels near the South American coast. Meanwhile, the *Florida*, another Confederate raider second only to the *Alabama* in injury inflicted on American shipping, was roaming the seas, capturing and burning merchant ships. Winslow at length caught up with the *Florida* at Brest, where she was undergoing repairs. The two ships lay near each other in the harbor, and there were several clashes between seamen from the two vessels when they encountered one another on land. Another Confederate cruiser, the *Georgia*, had taken refuge at Cherbourg. Winslow asked the Navy Department in vain for more ships with which to watch and pursue these raiders.

The *Florida* made her escape from Brest on a dark February night while Winslow was at Cadiz, where he had taken the *Kearsarge* for repairs. Learning that the *Rappahannock*, another Confederate raider, was lying in the harbor of Calais, Winslow took his station in the waters off that port, hoping to catch the *Rappahannock* if she ventured out.[2] But a far more important prize was awaiting him. On the 12th of June, 1864, when the *Kearsarge* was at anchor in the River Scheldt, near Flushing, in the Netherlands, Winslow received a telegram from William L. Dayton, United States Minister to France, telling him that the long-sought *Alabama* had dropped her anchor in the harbor of Cherbourg. He immediately got under way for that port, stopping only briefly at Dover to take on new sails. Before starting he dispatched a message to Commander George Preble, on the *St. Louis*, to sail "with all possible haste" and join the *Kearsarge*

[2] The French government had given the *Rappahannock* permission to leave Calais, but with no increase in her already inadequate crew. Since she also lacked sufficient cruising range and speed, she was partly dismantled and put to barracks use for Confederate naval men in Europe.

off Cherbourg. As he started for Cherbourg Winslow mustered
the ship's company and gave them the news, which they greeted
with wild cheering, that the ship was sailing to fight the *Alabama*.

On the afternoon of the 14th of June the *Kearsarge* sailed
into the port of Cherbourg, and came to a stop near the *Alabama*. Without anchoring, Winslow sent an officer ashore to
visit the Port Admiral and ask permission to take on board mariners whom Semmes had captured and landed at Cherbourg; the
request was refused. The *Kearsarge* then steamed out of the
harbor and took up a position from which she could intercept
the *Alabama* if she ventured out. Winslow's great chance had
come and he and his ship were ready for it.

He had not long to wait to learn the intentions of the *Alabama*. Soon after the *Kearsarge* appeared in port, Semmes wrote
to the Confederate Agent at Cherbourg, A. Bonfils, telling him
that he had heard that the Union cruiser's sole purpose in coming to Cherbourg was to take aboard the prisoners who had
been landed, and then depart. He asked Bonfils to notify the
United States Consul and, of course, through him Winslow, that
it was his intention to fight the *Kearsarge* as soon as he had
made necessary repairs. He hoped that these repairs would not
detain him after the next day's morning at the latest. "I beg,"
he said, "that she will not depart before I am ready to go out."
To this impudent defiance Winslow made no reply. There was
no need for Semmes to "beg" Winslow to wait until the *Alabama* appeared; that was now his only objective.

When Semmes took the raider into Cherbourg, he immediately called on the Port Admiral and obtained permission to
land the prisoners he had taken from the last two ships captured. This request was granted. The next day Semmes called
again on the Port Admiral and asked permission to dock and repair his ship. The Admiral expressed regret that Semmes had
not gone into some commercial port where there were private
docks, for those at Cherbourg belonged to the Government.

He could not grant permission to make use of them until he had communicated with the Emperor, Napoleon III, then vacationing at Biarritz, and not expected back in Paris for several days. If permission to dock and repair the ship had come from the Emperor, which, from his past attitude, was quite likely, it was Semmes' intention to lay the *Alabama* up for two months and give his crew leave of absence. "They would have been discharged," he wrote, "and dispersed in the first twenty-four hours after my arrival but for this temporary absence of the Emperor. The combat, therefore, which ensued may be said to be due to temporary absence from Paris."

Save in the case of his battle off Galveston with the *Hatteras*, a much inferior vessel which had once been a river excursion boat, Semmes had always avoided an encounter with a United States warship. Why, then, did he, after two years of "alternate arson and evasion," now resolve to fight the *Kearsarge?* Undoubtedly, one reason was that all Europe had heard about the arrival of the two ships at Cherbourg and awaited a battle. What would Europe (especially England, where the *Alabama* had been built, and many of whose seamen were on board) think if he now declined to fight? He did not dread the wrath of the Confederacy, should he choose to avoid battle, for his purpose was only to sink merchant ships. Bonfils had sent a message to John Slidell, the Confederate representative at Paris, asking him to forbid Semmes to do battle with the *Kearsarge*, for he was fearful as to the outcome. Slidell received the message just as he was starting for the race course at Fontainebleau, but declined to interfere, saying: "I have the most entire confidence in his judgment, his skill and his cool courage. I believe he would not proceed to the encounter of the *Kearsarge* unless he thought he had a reasonable chance of capturing her."

Another consideration in the mind of Semmes was his certain realization that the end of the Confederacy was not far off. The Mississippi River had been won by the Federal army and navy from its source to its mouth; Grant had won a great victory at Chattanooga and now, in command of all the National armies, had fought his way from the Wilderness to the James River. Farragut was preparing his blow at Mobile. The English and French governments were finally beginning to make it difficult for the Confederate raiders to coal and effect repairs in their ports. If he declined to fight now, Semmes' last chance to gain fame and glory through a victory over a Federal warship might disappear. Some months after his battle with the *Kearsarge,* Semmes passed through the Confederate States on his way to Richmond and noted the "heart-sickening" depression and indifference:

> Men generally seemed to have given up the cause as lost, and to have set themselves to work, like wreckers, to save as much as possible from the sinking ship . . . The *Alabama* had gone to her grave none too soon. If she had not been buried with the honors of war, with the howling winds of the British Channel to sing her requiem, she might soon have been handed over to the exultant Yankee, to be exhibited at Boston as a trophy of the war.

While, at the time of the battle, he may not have realized completely the desperate state of the Confederacy, he must have known that his days of capturing, burning, and escaping on the trackless oceans were numbered. Why not take the chance of winning a victory over the *Kearsarge* and thus endow the *Alabama* and himself with everlasting fame?

The two ships were equally matched. The *Kearsarge* was three years old; the *Alabama* two. The tonnage of the *Kearsarge* was 1,031, that of her adversary 1,016. The *Kearsarge* mounted seven guns, with a total broadside of 430 pounds; the *Alabama* carried eight guns of the latest English make, with a broadside of 360 pounds. The length of the Union ship was 201 feet; that of the Southerner 212 feet. The crew of the *Kearsarge* numbered 163, and of her opponent 149, including officers. No two ships to meet in combat were ever so evenly matched. Semmes realized fully that his men had had little real practice in gunnery; he knew, too, that the foul bottom of the *Alabama* would cut down her speed; but, despite these disadvantages, he felt he had a good chance to defeat the *Kearsarge* "in a fair fight."

In preparation for the battle Semmes had sent ashore the ship's papers, a large sum in specie, and some sixty chronometers taken from the ships he had captured. Thursday, Friday, and Saturday passed, but the *Kearsarge*, cruising up and down off the harbor, saw no sign of the foe. There had been rumors of a possible night attack, and Winslow maintained a close watch. Saturday night, French sympathizers gave a banquet for the *Alabama's* officers and wished them godspeed. Answering the toasts, the officers declared that they would either sink the Federal vessel or make "another Corsair," implying that they would convert her into another raider if they captured her.

Sunday, June 19th, dawned fair and bright; there was a slight haze, with a soft wind blowing. The news of the impending battle had been flashed over Europe and thousands of people, attracted to Cherbourg, stood along the mole, on the cliffs by the sea, and on every vantage point. An excursion train had brought hundreds down from Paris alone to witness the battle. Hawkers circulated through the crowds selling spyglasses and camp stools to enable them to view the spectacle in comfort. Semmes was not sorry it was Sunday; he considered the Sabbath his "lucky day," for it was on an August Sunday, almost two years before in the waters off the island of Terceira in the Azores that the *Alabama* had been commissioned and his flag raised to the stirring strains of "Dixie." But this Sunday his luck was to fail him.

At 9:30 the *Alabama* weighed anchor and started for the open sea, the Stars and the Bars floating at her peak. As she passed the harbor entrance she was greeted by the cheers and shouts of the throngs standing on the mole. On the *Kearsarge*, three miles off the harbor, a bell was calling the crew to Divine Worship. Semmes was a Catholic; on Saturday he had sent word to the Confederate Agent Bonfils that he would not be able to attend church on Sunday and asked him to go in his

stead to have mass celebrated for him. As was his custom, the
Puritan Winslow was beginning to read the Scriptures and make
comment on the lesson, when he was interrupted by a shout
from the lookout, "She's coming out, and she's heading straight
for us!" Winslow put the sacred book aside and, as the drums
beat to quarters, took his station. On the *Alabama*, Semmes assembled his crew aft and addressed them thus:

> You have at length another opportunity of meeting the enemy.
> . . . The name of your ship has become a household word, wherever
> civilization extends! Shall that name be tarnished by defeat? The thing
> is impossible! Remember that you are in the English Channel, the
> theatre of so much of the naval glory of our race, and that the eyes of
> all Europe are at this moment upon you. The flag that floats over you
> is that of a young Republic, which bids defiance to her enemies when-
> ever and wherever found! Show the world that you know how to up-
> hold it! Go to your quarters.

As soon as the *Alabama* was sighted, the *Kearsarge* turned
her head to the northeast. To the spectators it looked as if she
were running away from the conflict; but that was far from
Winslow's purpose. Some days before the battle, the French
Minister of Marine at Paris had informed the American Minister
that France objected to having a battle fought within gunshot
of her shores. He contended that the old rule forbidding fighting
within the three-mile limit had been adopted long before, when
three miles was greater than the range of cannon. Dayton replied that he could not accept such a revision of the neutrality
law, but he would suggest to Captain Winslow that, if nothing
were lost by it, he open the battle well beyond the three-mile
limit. Then he sent a message to Winslow informing him that
he had the right to fight three miles off the coast, but advised
him to go out as far as six or seven miles, provided he suffered
no disadvantage thereby. This suited Winslow's plan of action;
he had already told his officers that he would engage the Confederate cruiser well beyond the three-mile limit because, if
Semmes saw that he was getting the worst of it, he would cer-

tainly try to get the *Alabama* back into neutral waters. If he did this, it would be easier for the *Kearsarge* to intercept her over a course of seven miles rather than one of three.

At a distance of seven miles to the northeast of Cherbourg, at 10:50 A.M., Winslow wheeled the *Kearsarge* about and headed her straight for the oncoming *Alabama*. It was his purpose to ram and sink the foe and, if he failed in that, to engage her at close quarters. When the two ships were a mile apart, the *Alabama* opened the battle with a broadside from her starboard batteries. Because the English guns on the raider had a longer range than those of her opponent, Semmes hoped to disable the Union ship before his own vessel was hurt. A little later there came a second broadside from the *Alabama*, and then a third. Still no answer from the *Kearsarge*.

At nine hundred yards the *Kearsarge* shook with the roar of her first broadside. As the ships drew still closer, Winslow tried to put the *Kearsarge* astern of the *Alabama* and rake her. The *Alabama* nullified this move by sheering off to port. Thus it came about that, with both ships using their starboard battery, the battle was fought in seven circles, each ship discharging its broadside as it passed the other. A few minutes after the battle opened, a shot from the *Kearsarge* cut down the *Alabama*'s ensign. About the same time, one of the raiders' shots flung open a spare American flag on the *Kearsarge* which had been furled in a position where it could be hoisted if the other ensign were shot down. The crew of the *Kearsarge* regarded these two incidents as good omens and greeted them with loud cheers.

The firing of the *Alabama* was rapid, wild, and inaccurate; most of her shots passed harmlessly through the rigging of her adversary. The *Kearsarge* fired more slowly, but with great accuracy. Winslow had charged his gunners to aim at the water line; before the battle was long in process, the Confederate ship was badly hulled. As the two ships made their seven smoky circles about each other, it soon became evident to those on the *Kearsarge* that the *Alabama* was in trouble. A light wind car-

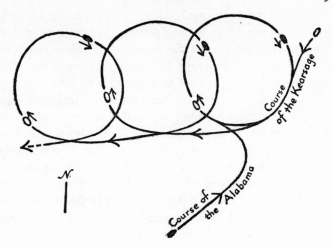

ried off the smoke, enabling the gunners on the United States ship to see every hit, and every one was greeted with jubilation.

The battle had not lasted long when the *Alabama* listed badly to starboard. The voice of Admiral John Dahlgren spoke loudly in the uproar, for it was the two eleven-inch Dahlgren pivot guns which were tearing the *Alabama* to pieces. Shots from the big guns swept away the crew of one of the *Alabama's* guns three times; the corpses were such an encumbrance to those remaining at the guns that Lieutenant Commander John Kell, the executive officer, ordered the mangled bodies to be cast overboard. On the *Kearsarge*, a shell burst near the quarter deck, wounding three men, one of whom later died. Another hundred-pound shell imbedded itself in the stern-post of the *Kearsarge* without exploding.[3]

[3] The section of the stern-post with the Confederate shell lodged in it was cut away after the fight and deposited in the museum of the Bureau of Ordnance at Washington. It was also exhibited at the World's Columbian Exposition at Chicago in 1893. The explosion of this shell would not have sunk the *Kearsarge*, as Semmes afterwards asserted, for it struck twenty feet from the stern-post and had it exploded there the damage would have been slight. But the shell bounded over the planking and found its resting place in the stern-post, again without exploding. The only damage done was the binding

When the two antagonists had completed the seventh circle, Semmes, seeing that he was getting the worst of it, ordered
Kell to steer for the French shore, just as Winslow had foreseen.
This the *Kearsarge* prevented by passing between the *Alabama*
and the shore, putting herself in a position to rake the Confederate ship. Then the chief engineer came on deck and reported
to Semmes that the fires were out and that he could no longer
work the engines. Semmes turned to Kell, who was at his side,
and said to him, "Go below, sir, and see how long the ship can
float." As Kell went below he passed through the wardroom and
saw a terrible sight. One of the big Dahlgren shells had passed
through the ship, opening a huge hole in her side through which
the sea was rushing. The assistant surgeon, a young English
doctor, stood at his post, but the operating table and the unfortunate seaman on it had been swept away.

When Kell returned to the deck he reported to his commander that the *Alabama* could not float ten minutes. Hearing
that, Semmes said: "Then, sir, cease firing, shorten sail and haul
down the colors; it will never do in this nineteenth century for
us to go down, and the decks covered with our gallant
wounded." Kell executed the order immediately, and the *Alabama's* colors came down. In a few minutes, however, the two
port-side guns of the *Alabama* once more opened fire on the
Kearsarge. This was the work of a pair of mutinous young officers who had rushed to the guns, swearing they would never
surrender. When he saw the two guns fired, Winslow gave the
order, "He is playing us a trick; give him another broadside," and
one more storm of iron hail swept through the *Alabama*. This
time the white flag went up, and the battle was over.

Semmes now sent off an officer to the *Kearsarge* announcing the surrender, and asked for help to remove the wounded.
As the famous raider was settling low in the water, the wounded

---

of the rudder, making it difficult to steer the ship. See Frank M. Bennett's
The Steam Navy of the United States, 435. The *Kearsarge* herself survived
until 1894 when she was wrecked in the Caribbean.

were taken off barely in time. Kell now gave the order for every man to jump overboard with a spar and save himself, if he could. When the decks were cleared of all except the dead, Kell joined his commander at the taffrail. Throwing off most of their clothing, the two officers leaped into the sea, Semmes with a life preserver, and Kell with a crate. Before he jumped, Semmes drew his sword and flung it before him into the sea.

Semmes thus records his feelings when he saw the *Alabama*, "like a living thing in agony," toss her bow high out of water and go down: "A noble Roman once stabbed his daughter, rather than she should be polluted by the foul embrace of a tyrant. It was with similar feelings that Kell and I saw the *Alabama* go down. We had buried her as we had christened her, and she was safe from the polluting touch of the hated Yankees."

Semmes and Kell were picked up by boats from the English yacht *Deerhound*, together with thirty-eight crewmen. The remaining survivors were saved by boats from the *Kearsarge* and two French pilot-vessels. The *Deerhound*, owned by a Mr. John Lancaster, had come close to the *Kearsarge* after the battle, and Winslow, as most of his own boats had been smashed, hailed her saying, "For God's sake, do what you can to save them!" When an officer later reported to Winslow that the *Deerhound* was making off with the prisoners and suggested that he bring her to with a warning shot, Winslow could not credit it, saying that the yacht was simply coming round, and that no Englishman who carried the flag of the Royal Yacht Club would act so. The *Deerhound's* flight to Southampton with Semmes and his men occasioned great anger in the United States. It was contrary to the traditions of the sea for a beaten commander to escape his conquerors in such a manner. It must be remembered, however, that Winslow himself had requested the *Deerhound* to engage in the rescue. Once the Confederate seamen stood on the deck of the *Deerhound*, they were on English soil.

When the battle was over, Winslow cleared the decks, assembled his crew, and held a service of thanksgiving to God for the victory. Then, with flags flying from every mast, about three in the afternoon the triumphant *Kearsarge* steamed into the harbor of Cherbourg. She was at once surrounded by swarms of boats filled with people who had come down to Cherbourg to see the *Alabama* conquer the Yankee cruiser, but who were now curious to see the vessel which had sunk the raider. The three wounded seamen were carried to the Marine Hospital and tenderly cared for. One of them, William Gouin, of Michigan, died of his injuries. Gouin was the real hero of the battle. He was stationed at the after pivot gun, when a shell from the *Alabama* burst near him, shattering one of his legs. He dragged himself to the forward hatch, trying, unsuccessfully, to conceal the extent of his injury, so that his comrades would not leave their posts to assist him. When he was carried below, he said to the surgeon, "I can fight no more, and so come to you. But it is all right; I am satisfied, for we are whipping the *Alabama*. I will willingly lose my leg or my life if it is necessary." As he lay on his mattress and heard from time to time the cheers of his shipmates on the deck above whenever the guns of the *Kearsarge* scored a hit on the *Alabama*, he lifted a feeble hand and tried to join in the cheering.

On the day of Gouin's death, Captain Winslow and two of his officers were at a victory banquet tendered them by patriotic Americans at Paris. When the telegram announcing Gouin's passing arrived, there was a period of silence; then a toast was drunk to his memory.

Winslow was now a famous man. From admirals down to fishermen, throngs came to visit his ship in such numbers that Commander Thornton, the executive officer, said that handling the crowds and seeing them safely on and off the *Kearsarge* was more onerous than the fight had been. To see what could be done for his eye, still ailing and worse than ever, Winslow consulted a noted doctor in Paris. Previously unwilling to leave his blockading station, he now learned that he had come too late, for the specialist told him that the sight of the right eye was "irretrievably gone."

When the Navy Department received Winslow's report of the victory on July 6th, the Secretary wrote him a fine letter of congratulation, in which he notified him that he would be promoted to Commodore, dating from June 19th, the day of the battle, and said: "I congratulate you on your good fortune in meeting the *Alabama,* which has so long avoided the fastest ships and some of the most vigilant and intelligent officers of the service—The battle was brief, the victory so decisive, and the comparative results so striking that the country will be reminded of the brilliant actions of our infant Navy, which have been repeated and illustrated in the engagement." By contrast, when Welles learned that Winslow had paroled his prisoners, he sent him an unwarranted rebuke, saying: "In paroling the prisoners, however, you committed a grave error . . . Extreme caution must be exercised that we in no way change the character of this English-built and English-manned, if not English-owned, vessel, or relieve those who may be implicated in sending forth this robber upon the seas from any responsibility to which they may be liable for the outrages she has committed."

On December 5th, 1864 President Lincoln sent the following message to the Senate and the House of Representatives: "I most cordially recommend that Captain John A. Winslow, United States Navy, receive a vote of thanks from Congress for the skill and gallantry exhibited by him in the brilliant action whilst in command of the United States steamer *Kearsarge,* which led to the total destruction of the piratical craft *Alabama,* on the 19th of June, 1864, a vessel superior in tonnage, in the number of guns, and superior in number of crew."

Captain Semmes and his officers were received with extraordinary honors in Engand, as if they had won one of history's greatest naval victories. Invitations to country homes poured in upon him, together with a flood of letters offering such financial aid as he or his men might need. One of the letters came from a sister of the Chancellor of the Exchequer, William E. Gladstone, who, after the early reverses of the Union armies, had said in the House of Commons: "We may have our own opinions about slavery; but there is no doubt that Jefferson Davis and the other leaders have made an army. They are making, it appears, a navy; and they have made what is more than either, they have made a nation." The echo of the Dahlgren guns on the *Kearsarge* as she sent the *Alabama* to the bottom of the English Channel, soon augmented by the echo of Farragut's guns at Mobile Bay, announced to England and the world the end of the Confederate Navy. The end of the Confederate Army and nation was not far in the future.

In his official report of the battle Captain Winslow pays high tribute to his executive officer, Lieutenant-Commander James S. Thornton: "It would seem almost invidious to particularize the conduct of any one man or officer, in which all had done their duty with a fortitude and coolness which cannot be too highly praised; but I feel it due to my executive officer, Lieutenant-Commander Thornton, who superintended the working of the battery, to particularly mention him for an example of coolness and encouragement of the men while fighting which contributed much toward the success of the action." It was Thornton who suggested to Winslow, when the *Kearsarge* was at the Azores almost a year before, that he protect her midship section with chain-cable. When serving with Farragut at New Orleans he had discovered how effective that kind of armor was.

The high praise which Winslow bestowed upon Thornton is the bright end to a story of misfortune and adversity nobly overcome and "captivity taken captive." Thornton had served as a lieutenant on the *Hartford*, Farragut's flagship at the battle of New Orleans. Later, when in command of the *Winona* on blockade duty off Mobile, he showed great recklessness and disregard for her welfare and that of his men by taking his ship in toward one of the forts whose guns outranged those of his vessel. Officers on the ship complained to the next in command, Lieutenant Winfield Scott Schley. When Schley went to speak to Thornton about the matter, he found him in a state of delirium tremens, altogether unfit for command. Painful though it was for him, Schley felt it his duty to report Thornton's condition to Captain Alden, senior officer in the blockading force. Alden ordered Schley to take command of the *Winona* and, if necessary, put Thornton under restraint. Brought before a court martial, Thornton was found guilty and dismissed from the service. When he was leaving the squadron he commended Schley for doing his duty. Despite this lapse, Thornton was restored to his rank and given a second chance. How nobly he made use of that second chance is part of the story of the victory of the *Kearsarge*.

The commander of the *Alabama* took his defeat with ill grace. He advanced excuses and hypothetical alternatives to explain that the issue of the battle would have been different if this or that had, or had not, happened. In an extraordinary statement he claimed that he had a good chance to defeat the *Kearsarge* in a "fair fight." "But he did not give me a fair fight, for as it afterwards turned out, his ship was iron-clad. It was the same thing as if two men were to go out to fight a duel, and one of them, unknown to the other, were to put a shirt of mail under his outer garment. The days of chivalry being past, perhaps it would be unfair to charge Captain Winslow with deceit in withholding from me the fact that he meant to wear armor in the fight. He may have reasoned that it was my duty to find it out for myself. Besides, if he had disclosed this fact to me, and so prevented the engagement, the Federal Secretary of the Navy would have cut off his head to a certainty."

The "shirt of mail" which Semmes referred to was composed of the anchor chains which Winslow had hung over the mid-section of the *Kearsarge* to protect her boilers in the battle. Farragut used the same arrangement on the *Hartford* when he ran past the forts below New Orleans. It had become a common practice, of which Semmes was cognizant, and he would have been wise had he made the same use of the abundant anchor chains which were stowed on the *Alabama*.

Confederate naval officers, apparently without exception, regarded as absurd Semmes' claim that the *Kearsarge* had not given the *Alabama* a "fair fight" because she had thus protected her boilers. The *Alabama's* splendid executive officer, John M. Kell, says that Semmes felt more keenly "the delusion to which he fell a victim" [not knowing that the *Kearsarge* was chainclad] "because he was exceeding his instructions in seeking action with a United States warship" and, still more, "to seek a fight with an iron-clad. . . . At the same time it must be admitted that Captain Winslow had the right unquestionably to protect his ship and crew." Commodore J. D. Bulloch, the Confederate Agent in England and under whose directions the *Alabama* was built at Liverpool, said: "Captain Winslow was quite right in doing whatever he could to increase the defensive power of his ship, and was not bound to inform his adversary that he had encased her most vulnerable parts with chain-cables. It has never been considered an unworthy ruse for a commander, whether afloat or ashore, to disguise his strength and to entice his weaker opponent within his reach."

Semmes claimed also that if the 100-pounder Blakeley shell which embedded itself in the stern-post of the *Kearsarge* had exploded, the victory would have been his: "In spite of the armor of the *Kearsarge*, I had mortally wounded that ship in the first thirty minutes of the engagement. I lodged a rifle percussion shell near her stern post—where there were no chains —which failed to explode because of the defects of the cap. If the cap had performed its duty and exploded the shell, I should have been called upon to save Captain Winslow's crew from drowning, instead of his being called upon to save mine. On so slight an incident—the defect of a percussion cap—did the battle hinge."

If the *Kearsarge* had not been protected with her anchor

chains—if the shell in the stern-post had exploded—if the *Alabama's* powder had not deteriorated—if the *Alabama's* bottom had not been foul—but history is not written nor are battles won with an If.

IX

NAPOLEON
COLLINS

SOME FOUR HUNDRED MILES below Pernambuco and the most easterly projection of South America's great hump, a picturesque promontory, rising in some places to a height of two hundred and fifty feet, juts into the sea to form a beautiful and spacious bay, twenty-five miles long and twenty miles wide. This great arm of the sea is called All Saints' Bay because it was on All Saints' day in 1501 that Amerigo Vespucci sailed into it. Eastward of this promontory rolls the Atlantic Ocean, and on the hills west of All Saints' Bay rises the town of Salvador, also called Bahia after the province of which it has been the capital for two hundred and fifty years. It is the oldest city of Brazil, and in 1816 it was one of the cities associated with the Philadelphia-Brazil plot to rescue Napoleon from St. Helena. A notorious privateer, the *True-Blooded Yankee*, had put in at Bahia, where the crew disclosed their intention to take part in the rescue. On the ground of this information, sent to London from Bahia, a British admiral was ordered to occupy immediately the tiny volcanic island of Tristan da Cunha, a lonely rock far to the south of St. Helena, lest the American schooner should seize it and use it as one of the bases for the expedition to deliver Napoleon from his prison.

The emperor's escape was quite possible, and was often discussed by Napoleon and his companions at St. Helena. He

240

himself finally vetoed the Philadelphia-Brazil plot and other proposals for his deliverance, for he had the long view of history and saw that a Napoleon living in New Jersey with his brother Joseph, or as a planter in Louisiana, or sitting on a tawdry throne in Mexico would be a far less imposing figure than a Napoleon ending his days on his lonely wave-washed rock in the South Atlantic.

Napoleon never reached Bahia; but on an October day in 1864 the United States sloop-of-war *Wachusett*, sister ship to the *Kearsarge* which four months before had sunk the *Alabama*, cast anchor in All Saints' Bay. On her quarter deck stood her captain, Napoleon Collins, U.S. Navy. Napoleon was his name, and Napoleonic he certainly was, in daring, courage, quickness of decision, and in contempt for the niceties of international law. The *Wachusett* had been at Bahia but a short time when a trim, low-lying, handsome ship came up the bay on October 5th, 1864 and saucily cast anchor between the *Wachusett* and a Brazilian warship. She was identified at once as the long-sought Confederate cruiser and commerce destroyer, *Florida*, the very ship Collins was searching for. The *Florida* had no fear of the Federal warship, for she was protected by the laws of neutrality which forbade belligerent ships to take hostile action within three miles of the shore of a neutral country. Yet the *Florida* was doomed; for when Napoleon Collins, standing on his quarter deck, saw her cast anchor he vowed that, international law or no international law, she would never destroy another American ship.

Like the *Alabama*, to which she was second in her record of destruction of American merchant ships, the *Florida* was built in the yards at Liverpool under the direction of the Confederate agent in England, James D. Bulloch. Everyone except the British authorities seemed to know that the *Florida* (then known as the *Oreto*) was being built as a commerce raider for the Confederate States. On March 22nd, 1862, the *Florida* cleared without a cargo "for Palermo, Sicily, and Jamaica." She had no intention, however, of going to Palermo, and steered for Nassau in the Bahamas where, despite the protests of the United States Consul, she took on supplies. She then sailed to Green Cay, an uninhabited isle, where her armament was installed. Her first skipper was Lieutenant John N. Maffit, an officer of the old Navy who had spent many years in the Coast Survey charting the New England and South Atlantic coasts. When the batteries were placed on the *Florida*, it was discovered that, through some oversight, sights and rammers and sponges had not been furnished, in consequence of which the guns were useless. Unable to obtain what he required at Cardenas or Havana, and himself and many of his crew stricken with yellow fever, Maffit resolved on a bold stroke and in broad daylight ran the *Florida* through the blockading fleet and took refuge in Mobile, Alabama. Four months later, while Northern newspapers were boasting that she was "hermetically sealed up," the *Florida*, choosing a dark and stormy night, again penetrated the blockading fleet, reached the open sea, and commenced her career of capture and destruction. Maffit in his report to President Davis tells of the ruse by which he escaped the Federal cruisers: "The canvas was secured in long neat bunts to the yards, and the engines were stopped. Between high toppling seas, clear daylight was necessary to distinguish her low hull. In eager pursuit, the Federals simply passed us, and we jubilantly bade the enemy goodnight and steered northward." Admiral David D. Porter, commenting on the *Florida*'s exploit in twice running through the blockading squadron, said: "His being permitted to escape into Mobile Bay, and then to get out again, was the greatest example of blundering committed throughout the war. Every officer who knew Maffit was certain that he would attempt to get out of Mobile, and we are forced to say that those who permitted his escape are responsible for the terrible consequences of their want of vigilance and energy."

The senior officer of the blockading squadron was Captain George Preble, who bore one of the most honored names in the history of the navy. His uncle, Captain Edward Preble, commanded the *Constitution* on the occasion of the first assault on that stronghold of the Mediterranean corsairs, Tripoli. Secretary Welles was greatly distressed and not a little angry at the escape of the *Florida*. In his *Diary* he wrote: "Am troubled by Preble's conduct. There must be a stop to the timid, hesitating, and, I fear, sometimes traitorous course of some of our officers. Preble is not a traitor, but loyal. An educated, gentlemanly officer of a distinguished family and more than ordinary acquirements, but wants promptitude, energy, audacity, perhaps courage. I am inclined to believe, however, an excess of reading, and a fear that he might violate etiquette, some point of international law, or that he should give offense to Great Britain, whose insolence the State Department fears and deprecates, and submits to with all humility, had its influence."

Determined to make Preble a lesson and warning to other naval commanders, Welles wrote out an order for his dismissal. Realizing the delicate nature of so severe a sentence on an officer of Preble's connections, Welles first consulted Lincoln. After he had read to him Preble's report which had been forwarded by Farragut, telling of the *Florida*'s escape, the President said: "Dismiss him. If that is your opinion, it is mine. I will do it."

The punishment dealt Preble for a fault which, at worst, was one of too great caution, was unusually severe. Addressing Preble as "Late Commander, U.S. Navy, West Gulf Blockading Squadron," Welles told him that he had submitted to the President his report which he had made to Admiral Farragut of the escape of the *Florida*, and "received from him prompt directions to announce to you your dismissal from the service. You will from this date [September 20, 1862] cease to be regarded as an officer of the Navy of the United States." Welles was not long in hearing from the friends of Preble, among them the influential and highly esteemed Senator William Pitt Fessenden of Maine. When Welles read to Lincoln a memorial asking for Preble's reinstatement, the President remarked that no one could be dismissed without bringing up a host of sympathizing friends to resist the unpleasant but necessary action of the government and make the victim a martyr. The President stated that he would do nothing in the matter unless Welles advised it. Fessenden asked that Welles first reinstate Preble, and then bring him before a court martial; but Welles pointed out that, since he had been dismissed from the service, the only way to restore him was by reappointment.

After Preble made a personal appeal to Welles, telling him that he had been trying to keep the peace and had refrained from firing on the *Florida* because she was flying English colors, Welles consented to appoint a board to consider the reports Preble had sent in and promised to abide by their decision. The board, which consisted of Admiral Andrew Foote, Commodore C. H. Davis, and Lieutenant Commander T. S. Phelps, brought in a verdict to the effect that Preble had failed to do his "whole duty." Nevertheless, at Lincoln's request, Preble was restored to his former rank as commander; Welles, however, humiliated him by assigning him to the command of the *St. Louis*, a venerable sailing sloop-of-war on the European station off Portugal.

Untutored by his experience at Mobile, Preble again let the *Florida* escape him when he encountered her some time later in the harbor of Funchal, Madeira, once more because of his over-scrupulous regard for neutrality and international law. When the *Florida* anchored near him at midnight in Funchal Harbor, Preble ordered the shots removed from all the guns on the *St. Louis*, lest his crew fire on the raider without orders. For this he was reprimanded by the Secretary of the Navy, who told him that he had "humiliated" himself by this act. In defense of his action, Preble cited the Ordnance Instructions to Captains: "Before entering any friendly port he will cause every species of projectile to be drawn from the guns." Here certainly was the case of a high-minded naval officer whose chief thought seems to have been, not to capture and sink the hostile cruiser which was harassing the shipping of his government, but to avoid "the very appearance" of violating international law.

After running the blockade at Mobile in January, 1863, the *Florida* roamed the seas for fifteen months, destroying thirty merchant vessels. She left behind her a trail of burning ships from New York to the West Indies, and from the West Indies to Brest, where she was refitted. After a six-months' stay in the French port, the *Florida* sallied forth again, crossing and re-crossing the Atlantic, successfully evading the Federal cruisers. At Madeira she narrowly escaped from the *St. Louis* and Captain Preble. Now, on the 5th of October, 1864, she cast anchor in the harbor of Bahia, where she was to meet her fate at the hands of Commander Napoleon Collins.

Napoleon Collins, born in Pennsylvania on March 4th, 1814, was appointed a midshipman when he was twenty years of age, much older than most midshipmen of that day were when they received their appointment. In the Mexican War he served as a lieutenant on the *Decatur* and saw action in the attacks on Tuxpan and Tabasco. In Du Pont's great victory at Port Royal he commanded the gunboat *Unadilla*. In July, 1862, Collins was promoted to commander. His new ship, the *Octarara*, seized a British vessel, the *Mont Blanc*, at the uninhabited isle of Sand Key in the Bahamas, over which the British claimed jurisdiction. The British government at once protested. In an interview with the Secretary of State, Lord Lyons, the British minister, stated that Commander Collins had been guilty of "inconsiderate conduct" in seizing the *Mont Blanc* when at anchor in British waters, and that "compensation ought to be made for the wrong done." After this incident President Lincoln directed that all officers of the navy be reminded of their instructions. He also directed the Secretary of the Navy to notify Commander Collins that by seizing the *Mont Blanc* in British waters and at anchor, he had incurred the displeasure of the President, and that any repetition would be visited with a more severe and effective censure.

Feeling that he had been unjustly censured for the honorable discharge of his duty, Collins forwarded to Welles a copy of the decree of the Prize Court which met at Key West. The court ordered that the *Mont Blanc* be restored to her claimants, but added that there was probable cause for the capture and detention of the vessel, and that each party pay its own costs. In a letter to the Secretary of State, Welles wrote that the judgment of the Court was "an exculpation of Commander Collins, who nevertheless stands reproved and censured for doing that which the Court declares he had probable cause for doing." He added that "it is a simple act of justice to Commander Collins that the censure upon him should be removed and that his record should remain unstained by the capture of the *Mont Blanc*."

In his reply to the Secretary of the Navy, Seward related that, according to the report of the British Consul at Key West to the British Consul at New York, Collins had seized the *Mont Blanc* when at anchor at Sand Key, Bahama and within a marine league of British territory. He held that no prize court of the United States could adjudicate a claim made by another nation that its sovereignty and dignity had been violated. Seward reported that the President was of the opinion that, although he was glad to learn that Commander Collins was "actuated by loyal and patriotic motives" in making the capture, he could not now withdraw or retract the satisfaction which he had awarded and which the British Government had accepted. Welles replied that the Navy Department had "conveyed to the Commander of the *Octarara* the Executive censure for doing what the Court had decided he was excusable in doing." The *Mont Blanc* and her cargo were restored to the ship's owners. The *Octarara* belonged to the West Indies Squadron, at that time commanded by Charles Wilkes, an acting rear admiral. In the seizure of the Confederate commissioners Mason and Slidell on the British ship *Trent* in November, 1861, Wilkes had not been too scrupulous in dealing with neutrals, and it is not strange that he commended Collins for what he had done. Collins did not deny that he had seized the *Mont Blanc* within a marine league of the coast of a neutral power, but claimed he did so under cover of Wilkes' instructions, which said not to regard bare rocks and uninhabited sand patches as neutral territory. Wilkes had logic and common sense on his side, but he was not supported by custom and international law. It is not likely that Commander Collins was greatly distressed over a censure for an action which the court had refused to condemn and which it declared he had "probable cause for doing." Welles and Seward were constantly at loggerheads over such matters. Welles considered that Seward was too anxious to avoid offending neutral nations, and that in the case of Great Britain, which permitted the Confederate raiders to be built in her ports and depart on their destructive course, his attitude had humiliated the United States.

The difficulties into which Collins fell through his seizure of the *Mont Blanc* did not deter him from seizing a far more important ship. When the *Florida* sailed into Bahia, the Brazilian admiral commanding the port granted her a stay of forty-eight hours for repairs. He instructed her commander, Lieutenant C. M. Morris, who had succeeded Maffit, to anchor between the Brazilian flagship and the *Wachusett*, thus seeming to promise that the *Wachusett* would not be permitted to molest the newcomer. Thus assured, Morris and several of his officers left the ship and went into the city to attend the opera, and thereby missed the more realistic drama in which the *Florida* became involved. Half of the crew were given shore leave and went into town, presumably in search of entertainment less expensive than grand opera.

Commander Collins had first thought to provoke the *Florida* to do battle with him outside the port. To this end, he sent a communication through the United States Consul to her commander, challenging him to come out and fight. With this he coupled the ironic promise that, if the challenge were accepted, the American Consul would use his influence to expedite such repairs as were necessary on the *Florida* to put her in fighting condition. To this Morris answered that, while he would depart from Bahia when it pleased him, he would also be pleased to engage the *Wachusett* should he meet her on the open sea.

Meanwhile, the American Consul at Bahia had protested to the President of the Province against the courtesies shown the *Florida*, saying that "in association with the pirate *Alabama* the *Florida* had violated the sovereignty of Brazil by destroying ships of the United States near the island of Fernando de Noronha."

When Collins learned that the American Consul's protest had been rejected, he at once prepared for hostile action against the *Florida*, regardless of international law. A number of considerations motivated Commander Collins when, in the deep silence of the night, he turned the prow of his ship toward the *Florida*. In the first place, he regarded the *Florida* as a pirate, and he knew that his Government shared this opinion. He was aware, too, of the fact that the Brazilian Government had not recognized the Confederacy as a belligerent nation. Had the *Florida* been a French or English ship, and had the United States been at war with either nation, he would not have considered attacking her in Brazilian waters. Collins likewise realized that, although the *Florida* had been given the right to stay in the harbor for forty-eight hours, she would be permitted to remain much longer if she so desired.

Moreover, Collins was aware that Brazil had permitted Captain Semmes to violate her neutrality without protest when the *Alabama* seized an American ship, the *Louisa Hatch*, loaded with coal which the raider badly needed. Correctly foreseeing that Brazil would not be too strict in enforcing its neutrality,

Semmes had towed his capture to Fernando de Noronha, a remote penal colony, 125 miles off the coast of Brazil, and there
filled his almost empty bunkers with coal taken from his prize,
all in plain violation of the laws of neutrality. Semmes had also
sallied forth from Fernando de Noronha and seized two other
ships, one of which he burned and the other of which he
towed into the Brazilian harbor. Thus to use a neutral port as
a base for seizing ships of a friendly nation was an equal in-
fringement of neutrality.[1] Although his proposed action against
the *Florida* involved a much more flagrant violation of neutrality, Collins felt that Brazil had created such precedents that it
could hardly take offense at further actions of the same nature.
Furthermore, he was motivated by the dissatisfaction of his own
government over the fact that United States ships had been
unable to capture and destroy more Confederate raiders and
cruisers. Southern papers, too, had frequently sneered at the
Union cruisers' failure to catch the raiders, implying that their
commanders lacked both ability and courage. Collins determined
to show them that there was at least one officer who lacked
neither courage nor aggressiveness.

If Collins was bold in action, he was also careful in preparation. After dark, and some hours before he made his attack, he
sent a whaleboat to reconnoiter and report to him conditions
on the *Florida*. When the whaleboat returned, he cut it loose so
that those on the *Florida* would not hear the noise of hoisting
the boat on board. At three in the morning, when all was still
on land and sea, the *Wachusett* slipped her cables and under a
full head of steam bore straight down on the *Florida*. It was
Collins' intention to sink her without firing a shot and then
immediately proceed to sea. But the blow which the *Wachusett*
struck the unsuspecting *Florida* proved to be but a glancing one
on the starboard quarter, carrying away her mizzen mast and

[1] In his *Memoirs Afloat*, Semmes says that he seized these ships and burned
them "outside the charmed marine league."

main yard and cutting down her bulwarks. Collins thought he had given the *Florida* a mortal blow, and was backing out to let her sink, when there was a discharge of small arms from the Confederate ship. This was answered in kind by the Yankee warship and, contrary to Collins' orders, her two great guns were fired by command of Lieutenant Commander Beardsley, who also issued an order to "stand by to repel boarders" when there were no boarders to repel.

The firing of the guns on the *Wachusett* awakened the crew on the Brazilian corvette in the harbor and the soldiers in the fort. In answer to a demand for surrender, Lieutenant T. K. Porter, the ranking officer left on the *Florida,* boarded the *Wachusett* to surrender his ship, although protesting against this hostile act in a neutral port. Collins immediately ordered a hawser attached to the *Florida* and proceeded to tow her to sea. The Brazilian naval commander had seen the Federal ship nearing the *Florida* and had sent an officer to warn her to keep off; however, by the time the officer reached the *Wachusett,* she had already rammed the raider. Collins humorously promised the Brazilian officer that he would do "nothing further." The captain of the corvette apparently saw the *Wachusett* returning to her anchorage, followed by the *Florida.* When it was finally discovered that the *Wachusett* had the other ship in tow and was proceeding to sea, three shots were fired from the fort and three Brazilian ships set out in pursuit. The faster American sloop of war, however, soon outdistanced her pursuers. Collins took with him on his own ship fifty-eight men and seven officers of the *Florida.*

After accomplishing this daring feat, Collins affected to be concerned only with the loss of the whaleboat and a cutter he had cut loose as he was about to ram the *Florida.* In his report to the Navy Department he slyly observed that the two boats could probably be recovered for the United States "upon payment of salvage"! Collins' homeward voyage with his captive was not altogether a happy one. At St. Thomas, in the Danish West Indies, he connived at the escape of eighteen of his prisoners while the *Wachusett* was coaling. He excused this action on the grounds that his ship was crowded, that there was a case of smallpox on board, and that the prisoners were mostly "Dutch, Spaniards and Italians." The Danish Government at once made a protest to Washington against his liberation of the prisoners on neutral territory.

Collins likewise had difficulties with Lieutenant Commander Beardsley, whom he had put in command of the *Florida* after her capture. In one of the charges Collins later preferred against his subordinate, he accused Beardsley of failing to obey orders to keep the *Florida* always in sight of the *Wachusett*. Beardsley denied that he had ever been out of sight; he added that he had been informed that Collins had contemplated firing on the *Florida* and had warned his commander that if he should fire on the *Florida*, he, Beardsley, would conclude that the *Wachusett* had been seized by the prisoners aboard her, and that duty to his flag and country "called him to destroy her. If I shall have made a mistake, none of us probably will live to rectify it, as I shall sink this ship if I cannot the *Wachusett*."

When the captain of the *Florida* awoke from sleep early that October morning at Bahia and learned that his ship had been seized and towed out to sea, he filed an indignant protest with the Brazilian authorities against such "a barbarous and piratical act." The Brazilian government thereupon complained to Washington against the violation of its waters and demanded reparation. Lincoln at once disavowed Collins' action. In his statement to the Brazilian minister, Secretary of State Seward said: "You have, therefore, justly expected that the President would disavow and regret the proceedings at Bahia. He will suspend Captain Collins and direct him to appear before a court martial. The consul at Bahia admits that he advised and incited the captain, and was active in the proceedings; he will therefore be dismissed. The flag of Brazil will receive from the United States navy the honors customary in the intercourse of friendly maritime powers."

Having thus soothed the feelings of Brazil, Seward went on to deliver her government a lecture, saying:

This Government disallows your assumption that the insurgents of this country are a lawful, naval belligerent; on the contrary, it maintains that ascription of that character by the Government of Brazil to insurgent citizens of the United States, who have hitherto been, and still are, destitute of naval forces, ports, and courts, is an act of intervention in derogation of the law of nations, and unfriendly and wrongful, as it is manifestly injurious to the United States. So also this Government disallows your assumption that the *Florida* belonged to the aforementioned insurgents, and maintains, on the contrary, that that vessel, like the *Alabama* was a pirate, belonging to no nation or lawful belligerent, and therefore that the harboring and supplying of these piratical ships and their crews in Brazilian ports were wrong and injurious, for which Brazil justly owes reparation to the United States.

Collins brought his two ships into Hampton Roads on the 12th of November. Admiral David D. Porter, then commanding the North Atlantic Blockading Squadron, ordered her to be stripped, and then had her moored at Newport News at the very place where the *Cumberland* had been rammed and sunk by the *Merrimac* more than two years before. As she was being moved, the *Florida* collided with a transport, apparently the result of an accident. It was not realized that she had been seriously damaged until she suddenly foundered while anchored at her new mooring off Newport News.

Thus ingloriously ended the saga of the *Florida*. Her demise was undoubtedly a matter of relief to all concerned, especially to Captain Collins, who might very well have been ordered to take her back to Bahia. When Admiral Porter heard of the sinking of the *Florida*, he commented, "Better so." "This," he later wrote, "was about the best thing that could have happened to the *Florida*, for the Northern people would not have been satisfied to see her sent back to Brazil." Though a naval court rendered a verdict to the contrary, there was a strong suspicion that the collision was not altogether accidental. But, as Admiral Porter said, "The Secretary of State and the Secretary of the Navy never asked any questions about the sinking. Seward's disavowal of the act of Collins was enough to make Welles defend him. There was no doubt that Welles would have been glad if all the Confederate cruisers could have been disposed of in the same manner." The American public, with whom Collins was now a hero, entertained the same sentiment.

The Confederate authorities were convinced that the *Florida* had been deliberately sunk to avoid the humiliation of returning her to Brazil. "Mr. Seward," wrote Jefferson Davis, "with his usual diplomatic insincerity and Machiavellianism, characteristically prevaricated, while he plotted with a distinguished admiral [meaning Porter] as to the most adroit method of disposing of the 'elephant.' The result of these plottings was that an engineer was placed in charge of the stolen steamer, with positive orders to 'open her sea-cock at midnight, and not to leave the engine room until the water was up to his chin, as at sunrise *the* Florida *must be at the bottom.*'"

Although suspended as an officer and, at the request of the Secretary of State, ordered before a court martial to satisfy the wounded pride of Brazil, Collins was honored by many naval officers for his daring act. Among these was Wilkes. In acknowledging Wilkes' commendatory letter Collins said: "In taking the *Florida* in port, I felt that I was only doing what you would have done with pleasure, had such an opportunity presented itself." He recalled that when serving under the command of Wilkes in the West Indies against the Confederate commerce destroyers, he was instructed to "Take the *Alabama* wherever we found her, unless under the guns of a fort strong enough to protect her." "If I have made mistakes," he wrote, "I am sure greater men made greater ones during the war."

The Secretary of the Navy had sent Captain Wilkes a congratulatory letter when he seized Mason and Slidell on the

British ship. It is no surprise, therefore, that, although he perforce ordered Collins to appear before a court martial, Welles sympathized with the officer and was pleased with his bold deed. He agreed that the act of Collins had "disturbed the peace of Brazil," and that some kind of an apology was due; yet he opposed any restitution. "What Brazil will require or demand I know not. Although she has done wrong to us in giving comfort and assistance to these robbers, I would make amends for her offended sovereignty by any proper acknowledgments. I do not believe she will have the impudence to ask restitution. If she did, it would be under British promptings and I would not give it. . . . If we have injured Brazil, let us make reparation full and ample. If she has injured us, let her do her duty also, in this respect. So far as her majesty is disturbed by our taking a sneaking thief, whom she was entertaining, by the throat,—an outlaw with some of his robberies upon him,—let all proper atonement be made."

The court martial before which Collins was summoned to appear, and which convened on the U.S.S. *Baltimore* on April 7th, 1865, was composed of distinguished officers. The president and senior member of the Court, Rear Admiral Goldsborough, who commanded the North Atlantic Blockading Squadron and, in cooperation with General Burnside, had captured Roanoke Island in February of 1862; Captain H. H. Bell, who commanded one of the three divisions under Farragut at New Orleans; Captain Melancthon Smith, who had seen service as captain of the *Mississippi* at New Orleans and Port Hudson; and Captain Percival Drayton, who had served under Du Pont at Port Royal and was captain of Farragut's flagship *Hartford* at Mobile Bay.

The charge made against Collins was that he had attacked the *Florida* within a marine league of the port of Bahia, thus violating the territory of Brazil. To this charge Collins pled guilty, for there was no disputing the facts. Asked to testify, he said: "I respectfully request that it may be entered on the records of the Court as my defense that the capture of the *Florida* was for the public good."

This is one of the shortest court-martial trials on record; since Collins pled guilty, the Court could not do otherwise than to find the charges against him proved. The sentence, however, was very severe. He was to be "dismissed from the Navy of the United States of America." Secretary Welles set aside the verdict. On September 17th, 1866, he notified Collins, then at Burlington, New Jersey, that the sentence had not been approved and that he might expect further orders. Restored to the Navy, he was captain of the *Sacramento* when she was wrecked in the Bay of Bengal in June of 1867. For this he was once more suspended, but again quickly reinstated by Welles. He was a rear admiral in command of the South Pacific Squadron when he met the "last enemy" at Callao, Peru, on August 9th, 1875.

Napoleon Collins was cast in a mold different from that of Captain Preble who twice let the *Florida* escape him lest he offend a neutral nation. He belongs in that by no means undistinguished company of army and navy officers of many nations who, although disobeying instructions or violating laws of neutrality, have nevertheless served well the cause and the nation for which they fought. His ruling passion was the destruction of his country's enemies. His epitaph might well be his statement to the court before the sentence of dismissal was pronounced upon him: "My defense is that the capture of the *Florida* was for the public good."

On July 27th, 1866, almost two years after Collins rammed and captured the *Florida*, the harbor and cliffs of All Saints Bay at Bahia echoed once again with the thunder of United States naval guns; but this time there was no midnight attack, no violation of the international law of neutrality. It was the salute of twenty-one guns fired by the United States Ship *Nipsic* by direction of the United States Government as the *amende honorable* for the offense of Collins to the dignity of Brazil. Lieutenant Commander Frank B. Blake, commander of the *Nipsic,* having fired the salute, sent a message to the governor of the Province of Bahia, expressing for the United States its "sincere hopes that with the dying echoes of the last gun will also expire any unkind feeling that may exist in Brazil from the cause which has given rise to it."

X

PORTER

NOT OFTEN has preeminent military ability been handed down from father to son. But there have been exceptions. Alexander the Great was the son of Philip of Macedon, creator of the Macedonian Phalanx; Hannibal was the son of Hamilcar, one of the ablest of the Carthaginian generals. David Dixon Porter was the son of one of the chief heroes of the War of 1812, Commodore David Porter. General Grant, who was inclined to be somewhat extravagant in his praise of his favorite generals and admirals, ranked Sheridan with Wellington and Napoleon. He was equally immoderate, according to John Russell Young, in lauding Porter: "I have always placed Porter in the highest rank. I believe Porter to be as great an admiral as Lord Nelson. Some of his achievements during the war were wonderful. He was always ready for every emergency and for every responsibility." Like Farragut, Porter was denied the opportunity of leading a great fleet against another squadron. His battles were waged against rivers, swamps, bayous, and forts. In nobility of character he was by no means first among our admirals; but in genius for battle, in power of organization, in dash, daring, fighting spirit, in courage and resolution in desperate situations, and in leadership of men he was without a peer.

Porter was born at Chester, Pennsylvania, on June 3rd, 1813, three months after his father, the Commodore, fought and lost the bloody battle with the two British ships *Phoebe* and *Cherub* off Valparaiso, Chile. Not long after young David's birth, his

257

father purchased an estate, "Meridian," just north of the White House at Washington, and there the future admiral spent part of his childhood. Embittered by the reprimand of a court martial for what he considered a patriotic act in a disturbance at Puerto Rico, Commodore Porter in 1825 resigned from the navy on which he had shed great renown, and entered the naval service of Mexico, then in revolt against Spain. Both the younger David Porter and his brother Thomas, then only ten years of age, were appointed midshipmen in the Mexican navy. David first tasted powder in a fight between the Mexican ship *Guerrero* and a Spanish frigate. The Spaniards boarded the *Guerrero*, threw overboard her captain (a cousin of Porter), and took David prisoner. After languishing for a season behind the walls of grim Morro Castle at Havana, he was released and sent home. At the age of sixteen, somewhat older than most of the naval cadets of that day, he received his warrant as a midshipman in the United States Navy.

His first cruise was made in 1829 on the famous *Constellation*, the frigate on which his father had served during the brief undeclared war with France. His next cruise, four years later, was on the *United States*, commanded by Commodore Daniel T. Patterson. Following the pleasant, peacetime custom of that day, the Commodore took his family with him on a cruise through the Mediterranean. On this two years' voyage a romance sprang up between the young midshipman and George Ann, the daughter of the Commodore. They were married in 1839, and the romance which began on the deck of the *United States* lasted through life.

In the Mexican War Porter served as first lieutenant on the *Spitfire*, commanded by Josiah Tattnall, one of the navy's most distinguished officers. In 1849, after twenty years of service, Porter, dissatisfied with his pay and rank, obtained leave and took command of a merchant ship, the *Panama*, which sailed for the Orient by way of the Straits of Magellan. His next ship was the *Georgia*, which made regular trips between New Orleans, Ha-

vana, and New York. These frequent trips to New Orleans gave
him a familiarity with the Gulf of Mexico and the Mississippi
which later was to serve him in good stead when he was with
Farragut in the attack on New Orleans. His service on commercial ships was climaxed by a record-making voyage from England to Australia on the *Golden Age*.

After Porter returned to the navy, Jefferson Davis, then
Secretary of War, twice dispatched him in 1855 and 1856 to the
Near East to purchase camels for use as pack animals in army
transportation over the trails of the Southwest. On these voyages he visited Tunis, Smyrna, Constantinople, and Alexandria.
On the first of these two voyages he sailed into the Black Sea
and saw something of the Crimean War. The seventy-six camels
he brought over were landed at Indianola, Texas. The camel experiment was not successful, for the sight and smell of these
ships of the desert stampeded the horses and mules which encountered them on the desert trails.

Early in 1861, Porter, then forty-eight years of age and
still a lieutenant after thirty-two years of service, resolved to
quit the national service and obtain command of one of the
Pacific Mail Company's ships. As a preliminary step he secured an
appointment to undertake Coast Survey work on the Pacific
Coast. At that critical time, when men's feelings were so deeply
stirred and when such army officers as James B. McPherson and
James H. Wilson were asking the War Department to recall
them from the Pacific Coast so that they might participate
in the nation's defense, Porter's course seemed strange, indeed.
Although he rendered outstanding service during the war, he
certainly revealed little of that burning zeal for the Union
which characterized Du Pont, Foote, and even Southern-born
officers like Farragut and Drayton who remained loyal to the
flag.

In his later account of his actions at this time Porter said:

During the Presidency of James Buchanan, and just previous to
the inauguration of Mr. Lincoln, I was ordered to take the command of

the Coast Survey Steamer *Active* on the Pacific Coast. I could not conceive why I was thus ordered, except that ships and officers were at
that period being sent out of the way. This, too, at a time when the
Southern States were threatening to secede, and it seemed probable
the Government would require the services of all its officers to maintain the integrity of the Union. At this moment I was in a despondent
frame of mind and troubled with the most gloomy forebodings. I felt
that a crisis was impending that might influence all my prospects of
life and cast me upon the world without resources and with a large
dependent family.

This exposition of Porter's state of mind when the nation
was on the verge of a great struggle for its existence has a strange
sound when compared with the ringing declarations of Du Pont,
Foote, Farragut, and others who were ready to lay down life itself to maintain the Union. Although Porter says that he "could
not conceive why" he was ordered to take command of a Coast
Survey ship on the Pacific Coast, in the most positive way the
Secretary of the Navy declares that Porter himself sought this
appointment:

He sought and obtained duty for Coast Survey service in the Pacific, which indicated an intention to avoid active participation in the
approaching controversy. That class of officers who at such time
sought duties in the Pacific and on foreign stations were considered,
prima facie, as in sympathy with the Secessionists, but not yet prepared
to give up their commissions and abandon the Government. No men
were more fully aware that a conflict was impending, and that, if
hostilities commenced and they were within call of the Department,
they would be required to participate. Hence a disposition to evade
an unpleasant dilemma by going away was not misunderstood.

One thing is certain: Porter's close friendships at Washington were chiefly with Southern men, both civil and military. "I
sought consolation," he says, "by visiting the houses of Southern
members of Congress in Washington whom I knew." He tells us
about the kind of "consolation" he received on one of these
visits. On a December night in 1860 he was on his way home from
a session of Congress where he had "listened to a great deal of

incendiary language from Southern members and plenty of vituperation from Northern ones," when a man on the street told him that South Carolina had seceded. As he was passing a mansion where a "distinguished Southern gentleman" lived, he saw carriages about the door and the house ablaze with light. Being on familiar terms with its occupants, who were, incidentally, Jefferson Davis and his wife, Varina Davis, he turned aside and entered just as the lady of the house was descending the stairs in bonnet and shawl. When she saw Porter, she exclaimed, "Ah, Captain, I am so glad to see you. I want you to escort me to the White House. The horses are sick, and I am going to walk over." As they drove to the executive mansion in a hack which Porter had called, he remarked that he had entered her home uninvited when he saw the lights, assuming a party was in progress. "No, indeed," she said, "but we have received glorious news from the South, and my husband's friends are calling to congratulate him. South Carolina has seceded; and Captain, we will have a glorious monarchy, and you must join us." "Yes," replied Porter, "and be made Duke of Benedict Arnold!" "Nonsense," rejoined the lady, "we will make you Admiral of the Blue." After he left her at the White House, he returned to the mansion, where everybody was celebrating the secession of South Carolina, and where all except the master of the house were heated with drink. Seeing Porter, the host greeted him and said, "You will join us, and we will make you an admiral." "Thank you," replied Porter, "but I am going to the California gold mines, and when the South and the North have done quarreling, and all you seceders have come back and taken your seats in Congress, I will join the Navy again." This conversation makes it clear that Porter then entertained no strong Union sentiments and regarded the whole matter as a foolish quarrel, which he planned to avoid by taking service on the Pacific Coast. It seems incredible that, writing almost a quarter of a century after the conflict, Porter expressed the view that the capital and its surroundings seemed stupid "to these vivacious Southerners," and that "an opera house or two, half a dozen fine theatres and a court, or the semblance of one, at the White House, might have prevented the catastrophe which overwhelmed both North and South."

The national forts and shipyards located in the territory of the Southern states presented Lincoln with one of his most difficult problems immediately after his inauguration. The two government shipyards in the South were the Gosport Yard at Norfolk, Virginia and the yard at Pensacola, Florida, guarded by Fort Pickens with a very small garrison. At the distance of ninety-five years it is difficult fully to understand the government's reluctance to strengthen its forts and shipyards in the South. Postmaster-General Montgomery Blair advocated strong measures to hold all the forts and shipyards; he was convinced that this was the only honorable course for the administration to follow, whether or not it precipitated a conflict. The leaders of the secession movement had little dread of war, confident that they could seize and hold the forts and shipyards and that the South would emerge victorious should a struggle ensue. On the part of Buchanan and then of Lincoln and of their administrations, it was not so much the fear of defeat in war which made them hesitate to take strong defensive measures, but an honorable dread of the woe and bloodshed of civil strife.

Lincoln, loath to give up Sumter, to the very end hoped that South Carolina would refrain from taking hostile action against the Union. To satisfy himself as to the sentiment prevailing in South Carolina, he sent three emissaries to Charleston: Stephen A. Hurlbut, an Illinois friend; Ward H. Lamon, a former law associate and now his bodyguard; and Gustavus V. Fox, a former lieutenant in the navy, and soon to be its Assistant Secretary. Hurlbut and Lamon both reported that the flame of national patriotism had been extinguished in South Carolina. The governor of the state, Francis W. Pickens, informed Lamon that if Lincoln attempted to reinforce Sumter, the "tocsin of war would be sounded from every hilltop and valley of the South."

Fox's mission was undertaken more to advise Lincoln as to the wisest course to follow to reinforce Sumter. He reported that it would be hazardous to attempt to relieve Sumter by sea without simultaneously dispatching troops. In his view the best plan would be to send troops to Charleston with navy protection, transfer them off Charleston to light-draft vessels, and run the batteries by night. The President authorized this expedition and Fox was given the heavily gunned *Powhatan* for his flagship. The Secretary of State, however, resolutely opposed any effort to reinforce Sumter, convinced that it would lead to war; he correctly believed that, with regard to slavery and secession, Charleston was the most sensitive spot in the South. If war came, he wished it to commence anywhere but at Charleston. He therefore suggested to the President that an expedition be sent to the Gulf to strengthen Fort Pickens. This would be rendered easier of accomplishment since the attention of the people, North and South, was then centered on Fort Sumter.

It was this plan of Seward's, kept secret from both the War and Navy Departments, which launched Porter on the stage of great events. He was having his last meal with his family before leaving for New York to take the steamer for California and assume his duties with the Coast Survey, when a carriage drove up to his door with a message from the Secretary of State requesting his immediate presence. He jumped into the carriage and was driven to Seward's office. There he found the Secretary lying on a couch with a document in his hand. Without rising, Seward said to him, "Can you tell me how we can save Fort Pickens from falling into the hands of the rebels?" Porter's quick and ready answer was, "I can, sir." "Then," said Seward, getting up from his couch, "you are the man I want." Porter then outlined his plan, which was to send six or seven companies of infantry on a steamer and land them at the fort under the guns of a warship. To this end he asked Seward to give him the *Powhatan*.

It may be asked how it came about that Seward sent for Porter, then only a lieutenant in the navy, to consult him on so grave a matter. The fact is that Colonel M. C. Meigs, an army officer and friend of Porter, had talked with him about the possibility of relieving Fort Pickens. It was Meigs who had suggested Porter as a good officer to command the naval part of the expedition.[1] As Porter was talking with Seward, Meigs happened to come in, and Seward asked both of them to accompany him to the White House. When they reached the White House, Lincoln, who was aware of their errand, opened the conversation by saying, "Tell me how we can prevent Fort Pickens from falling into the hands of the rebels." Porter stated his plan and suggested that all orders for the expedition should come direct from the President, on the ground that there were so many disloyal clerks and officers in the Navy Department that word of the plan would quickly be flashed to Pensacola if the orders emanated from the Secretary of the Navy. When Lincoln asked if that would not be an irregular proceeding, Porter agreed, but argued that the exigencies of the matter warranted it and that the President, as the commander in chief of the army and the navy, had only to exercise his undoubted powers. "But what will Uncle Gideon [Welles] say?" asked Lincoln. "Oh, I will make it all right with Mr. Welles," Porter replied. Two orders were then written out by Porter and signed by the President. The first of these gave Porter command of the *Powhatan* and directed him to proceed to Fort Pickens and establish himself within the harbor. The second was directed to the Commandant of the New York Navy Yard, ordering him to prepare the *Powhatan* with all speed and in no case to inform the Navy Department until the expedition had sailed.

[1] Meigs was afterward the indispensable Quartermaster General of the Union armies. Had he been at the head of an army in the field, his abilities undoubtedly would have won him great distinction.

At nine o'clock the next morning Porter appeared at the office of the New York Navy Yard and showed his order for fitting out the *Powhatan* to the Commandant, Captain Andrew Hull Foote, later the great leader of the Mississippi flotilla. Not unnaturally, Foote immediately suspected that some disloyal scheme was under way. He said to Porter: "How do I know that you are not a traitor? Who ever heard of such orders as these emanating from the President? I must telegraph Mr. Welles before I do anything, and ask instructions." Foote's perplexity was increased by the fact that he had received orders from the Navy Department to recall the crew of the *Powhatan*, which had been laid up, and recondition her for the expedition to Sumter under Captain Fox. After a long and heated discussion, Foote was finally prevailed upon to accept the order signed by the President, and gave directions to fit out the *Powhatan*.

Meanwhile Meigs had telegraphed Seward with reference to difficulties in getting the expedition ready. When Seward received this message, he went with his son and assistant, Frederick, between eleven and twelve at night to see Welles in his rooms at the Willard Hotel, telling him that the movements at the New York Navy Yard were being retarded and embarrassed by conflicting orders from the Secretary of the Navy. Welles asked him to clarify his meaning. Seward said he "supposed" the message from Meigs had to do with the *Powhatan* and Porter's command. Welles told him he must be mistaken, for Porter had no command, and that the *Powhatan* was to be Fox's flagship for the expedition for the relief of Sumter. Welles was greatly excited, and Seward, apparently unwilling to reveal anything about the other expedition under Porter, suggested that they go over to see the President.

Although it was nearly midnight, the President was still up. He manifested considerable surprise when he learned their errand; looking from one to the other, he said there must be some mistake in regard to the *Powhatan*. When Welles reminded him that he had read to him the confidential instructions sent to the captain of the *Powhatan*, Mercer, Lincoln recalled them, but did not remember that the *Powhatan* was to be employed by Fox at Fort Sumter. To remove all doubt from his mind, Welles went to his office in the Navy Department and returned with the instructions. When he had read them, Lincoln turned to Seward and said that on no account must the Sumter expedition be interfered with and that the *Powhatan* must be restored to Captain Mercer. Seward demurred, saying that the Pickens expedition was quite as important as that to Sumter and might fail if the *Powhatan* were detached at that late hour. The President nevertheless peremptorily ordered him to dispatch a message to have the *Powhatan* returned to Mercer.

Meanwhile the *Powhatan*, with Porter hid in Captain Mercer's cabin, so that none should know he was to command the expedition until the *Powhatan* was well out to sea, had proceeded as far down New York bay as Staten Island, where Captain Mercer, who had agreed to submit to the President's order, was landed. The ship had hardly gotten under way again before a fast tug dispatched by Captain Foote came alongside with a telegram which read: "Deliver up the *Powhatan* at once to Captain Mercer. Seward." Porter telegraphed back: "Have received confidential orders from the President, and shall obey them. Porter." Had Lincoln signed the message, Porter would have had no excuse for not relinquishing the ship; but the propriety of his refusal to subordinate a Presidential order to that of a Cabinet member cannot be questioned. Additionally, he doubtless felt that the State Department had no authority over a naval officer on active duty. Going on deck, he gave orders for full steam ahead; but, in order to throw any further pursuing telegrams off his track, he first steered due east, and then at sundown set a course for Fort Pickens. Thus it was that an important naval and army expedition was sent out, and the Secretary of the Navy and the Secretary of War were as ignorant of it as if they had been members of the Confederate cabinet instead of Lincoln's.

Never dreaming that the ship had been taken from him, Fox proceeded to Charleston, where he vainly awaited the appearance of the *Powhatan,* then well on her way to Fort Pickens. Now he could do no more than impotently suffer the humiliation of witnessing the surrender of Sumter and take its garrison north on his ship.

The transport *Atlantic* with the troops on board arrived off Pensacola on April 16th. The next day Porter arrived with the *Powhatan,* flying English colors. In obedience to Porter's orders to establish himself in the harbor, the *Powhatan* was standing in toward Fort Pickens and the harbor when signals were made from the *Wyandotte* to stop. Porter had crossed the bar when Colonel Meigs, who was then on the *Wyandotte,* asked her captain to lay his ship directly in the path of the *Powhatan.* This compelled Porter to stop. Acting upon authority given him by Lincoln, Meigs protested against Porter's entering the harbor, on the ground that since Fort Pickens was unprepared for an attack, the *Powhatan's* entry would draw the fire of the Confederate batteries on the shore. Porter was tempted to run over the little *Wyandotte* but had no alternative other than to turn about and cast anchor near the transport. That night six hundred soldiers were safely landed at Pickens under the guns of the *Powhatan.* Thus the fort and, ere long, the navy yard too, were saved to the Union.

For the fiasco of the Sumter expedition and Fox's humiliation, Lincoln quite properly accepted the entire blame, for he had promised both Porter and Fox that each might have the *Powhatan* for different and simultaneous expeditions. The President did what he could to soothe the feelings of Welles and of Simon Cameron, then Secretary of War, both of whom had been passed over in the entire affair. To the chagrined Fox he wrote as follows:

> I sincerely regret that the failure of the late attempt to provision Fort Sumter should be the source of any annoyance to you. The practicability of your plan was not, in fact, brought to a test. By reason of

a gale, well known in advance to be possible, and not improbable, the tugs, an essential part of the plan, never reached the ground; while, by accident, for which you were in no wise responsible, and possibly I to some extent was, you were deprived of a war vessel with her men which you deemed of great importance to the enterprise. I must cheerfully assure you, and truly declare that the failure of the undertaking has not lowered you a particle, while the qualities you developed in the effort have greatly heightened you in my estimation. For a daring and dangerous enterprise, of a similar character, you would today be the man, of all my acquaintances, whom I would select.

After the Fort Pickens expedition Porter received a long overdue promotion to Commander, to date from April 22nd, 1861. His first regular assignment in the war, for the Fort Pickens assignment had been decidedly irregular, was blockade duty on the *Powhatan,* first off Mobile, and then off the Southwest Pass of the Mississippi. On June 30th the *Sumter,* one of the first Confederate raiders, under the command of Raphael Semmes ran the Mississippi blockade and began a brief but colorful career as a commerce destroyer. On August 13th Porter learned from documents found on a recaptured American schooner that the *Sumter,* short of coal, was at Puerto Cabello, a Venezuelan port. The next day he received orders from Flag Officer Mervine, commanding the Gulf squadron, to go in pursuit of the *Sumter.* It was a chase which lasted till the end of October and took him clear down to Brazil and back to St. Thomas. He never once sighted the *Sumter,* and in one whole month saw only one ship of any description. The *Powhatan* was now in bad shape and needed overhauling. He therefore sailed for home, reaching New York on November 9th. Three days later he reported at Washington, where he urged upon the Department and President Lincoln an attack on New Orleans. The part he played in initiating that expedition and in having Farragut chosen as its commander, and the work of his mortar schooners in the attack are related in the chapter on Farragut.

While Porter was assembling and outfitting his mortar schooners, the Navy Department ordered him to make a careful inspection of the *Monitor,* then under construction at Greenpoint, near Brooklyn, New York. Ericsson was one of the greatest geniuses in the field of engineering, a brilliant intellect, and intensely devoted to the cause of the Union; but he was arrogant and conceited beyond measure. When Porter called on him at New York, Ericsson treated him with contempt and ridicule. After reading Porter's orders, he said: "Well, you are no doubt a great mathematician, and know all about the calculations which enter into the construction of my vessel." Porter replied that he was no great mathematician, but that he was a "practical man," and thought he could find out whether or not the *Monitor* would do what was promised for her. "A practical man!" snorted Ericsson. "Well, I've had a dozen of those fellows here already. I don't want practical men here, sir. I want men who understand the higher mathematics that are used in the construction of my vessel—men who can work out the displacements, horse-power, impregnability, endurance at sea in a gale, capacity to stow men, the motion of the vessel according to the waves, her stability for guns, her speed, actual weight,— in short, everything pertaining to the subject. Now, young man, if you can't fathom these things you had better go back where you came from. If the Department wants to understand the principles of my vessel, they should send a mathematician."

In reply Porter told the haughty inventor that he at least knew the rule of three and that twice two are four. This made Ericsson so angry that for a moment Porter feared he was about to be ejected from the office. "My God!" exclaimed Ericsson, "do they take me for a fool!" To mollify him, Porter added that he did know a little of "simple equations." "Worse and worse," said Ericsson. "This beats the devil; it would be better if you knew nothing. Here's a man who tells me he knows a little of equations, and they send him to examine John Ericsson!" When Porter asked for a look at the plans, Ericsson showed him a drawing of the turret on the *Monitor* and asked him to tell him what it represented. Porter took a careful look at it, and then said, "It looks like a coffee mill." This did not soothe the feelings of the angry engineer, but he yielded to Porter's request to see the ship and took him over to Greenpoint where it was building. After a half hour's examination Porter emerged from the depths of the vessel, saying, "I know all about your machine." "Yes," replied the scornful Ericsson, "and you know twice two are four, and a little of simple equations!" Abandoning the somewhat casual tone in which he had been speaking, Porter told him that the report he was going to make to the Department would have much to do with the acceptance or rejection of the vessel. "I will say that Mr. Ericsson has constructed a vessel, —a very little iron vessel—which, in the opinion of our best naval architect [John Lenthall], is in violation of well-known principles and will sink the moment she touches the water." "Oh," exclaimed Ericsson, "he's a fool!" "But," went on Porter, "I shall say also that Mr. Ericsson has constructed the most remarkable vessel the world has ever seen—one that, if properly handled, can destroy any ship now afloat, and whip a dozen ships together, if they were where they could not maneuver so as to run her down." At that Ericsson seized him by the hand and exclaimed, "And all this time I took you for a fool, and you're not a fool after all!" That day Porter telegraphed the Navy Department, "Mr. Ericsson's vessel is the best fighting machine ever invented, and can destroy any ship of war afloat." Despite this favorable report by Porter there were still some high up in navy counsels, among them John Lenthall, Chief of the Bureau of Construction, who held the *Monitor* in very low esteem. But within a few weeks the unorthodox vessel proved her capacities.

On leave for a time after he returned from the victory at New Orleans in the spring of 1862, Porter was with his family at Newport, Rhode Island, whither the Naval Academy had been transferred for the duration of the war. There he was perturbed to learn that unfavorable rumors had been set afloat concerning him, among others that he was the brother-in-law of Raphael Semmes and had connived at his escape from New Orleans when the *Sumter* ran the blockade. Summoned to Washington, he was informed by the Assistant Secretary that he was to go to St. Louis to superintend the construction of river ironclads. Angry at such an appointment after the part he had taken in the New Orleans expedition, Porter said to Fox, "This is ostracizing me. Certainly my services deserve something better. You can't send me there." "Do you mean," asked Fox, "that you will refuse to obey the order?" "Not exactly," replied Porter, "but I look upon such orders as an indignity. I will cheerfully obey any order where I can be of service against the enemies of my country; but treat me in that way, and I will resign, and get the merchants of New York to give me a suitable vessel, and then I will go out and show you how to catch the *Alabama*."

Porter left Fox with the definite impression that Newport scandalmongers had sown seeds of distrust in his mind. He was not able to see Welles, but wrote him saying that he was ready for active duty at any time, but that until his services were required he would like to rejoin his family at Newport. Welles, who probably never knew that Fox had sent for Porter, gave him permission. Porter was greatly downcast, feeling sure that the Navy Department was hostile to him, and that his chances for further distinction were at an end. "But," he says, "I forgot, for the moment that 'there's a divinity that shapes our ends, rough hew them how we will.' The very wind that I thought was blowing me to destruction was, in fact, wafting me to fortune."

Before returning to Newport, Porter called at the White House to pay his respects to the President, and found him in conversation with the Secretary of State. Both gave him a very friendly reception. Lincoln asked what he could do for him. "Sir," said Porter, "I am thinking of resigning from the navy and getting the merchants of New York to give me a suitable steamer, so that I may show the Navy Department how to catch the *Alabama*.[2] That would suit my disposition better than superintending ironclads at St. Louis. That's what the Navy Department proposes doing with me."

Jumping to his feet, Seward exclaimed, "They shall not do it. I have not forgotten how you helped me to save Fort Pickens to the Union." "Yes," interposed Lincoln, "and got me into hot water with Mr. Welles, for which I think he has never forgiven me." Lincoln then went on to say that he was disappointed that Vicksburg had "slipped through our fingers," referring to the unsuccessful attacks of Farragut in May and June of 1862, but added that if he lived, Porter would be in at the taking of the fortress. The President then asked Porter to tell him about the passage of the forts and the taking of New Orleans. When Porter had finished his recital, Lincoln said he had read all about it: "how the mortars pitched into the forts; how the forts pitched into the ships; and the ships into the rams, and the rams into the gunboats, and the gunboats into the fire rafts, and the fire rafts into the ships." It reminded him, he said, of a fight in a Natchez barroom; but, no doubt to the great satisfaction of Seward, added, "I won't tell that now." At the end of the interview Lincoln called a messenger and said to him, "Go tell the Assistant Secretary of the Navy that I wish to see him at once." As Porter was leaving to catch his train for Newport, the President said, "Good-by; you shan't go to St. Louis, you shan't resign, and you shall be at Vicksburg when it falls."

At Newport Porter found awaiting him a telegram from the Secretary of the Navy: "Proceed to Washington without delay, and report in person to the Department." When he reported back at Washington the Secretary handed him a sealed document. Opening it, Porter read, "You have been appointed to command the Mississippi Squadron, and you will proceed at once to Mound City [Illinois] and relieve Flag Officer Davis." The

[2] In view of Porter's futile three months' chase of the *Sumter* this remark to Lincoln would seem somewhat boastful.

Napoleon Collins
1814—1875

David Dixon Porter
1813—1891

order was dated October 9th, 1862. As he finished reading the order, Porter repeated aloud his favorite quotation, "There's a divinity that shapes our ends, rough-hew them how we will." It is plain from this conversation that the divinity which was shaping Porter's destiny was working through human agents and instrumentalities, and that here its chief agent was Abraham Lincoln.[3]

The scientifically minded Charles Henry Davis, who had succeeded Foote as acting commander of the Mississippi Squadron, had made a good record at Fort Pillow and Memphis; but the Secretary of the Navy wanted a fighting commander on the upper Mississippi, and knew that Porter had the fighting spirit. At the time he was appointed Welles had this to say of Porter:

> Relieved Davis and appointed D. D. Porter. . . . Porter is but a Commander. He has, however, stirring and positive qualities, is fertile in resources, has great energy, excessive and sometimes not overscrupulous ambition; is impressed with and boastful of his own powers, given to exaggeration in relation to himself,—a Porter infirmity,—is not generous to older and superior living officers, whom he is too ready to traduce; but is kind and patronizing to favorites who are juniors. Is given to cliquism, but is brave and daring like all his family. He has not the conscientious and high moral qualities of Foote to organize the flotilla, and is not considered by some of our best naval men a fortunate officer. His selection will be unsatisfactory to many, but his field of operation is peculiar, and a young and active officer is required for the duty to which he is assigned.

So Porter overslaughed more than eighty senior officers; but a more fortunate naval appointment was not made during the war. On the vast stretches of the Mississippi and its tributaries, Porter's gunboats wrote a great record. Army commanders freely acknowledged that the army's victories would not have been possible without the help of the navy.

[3] Secretary Welles in his *Diary* for October 1st, 1862, says that Lincoln favored Dahlgren for the Mississippi squadron, and, at that time, did not hold Porter in high esteem.

Before starting west to take command of the Mississippi squadron, Porter called on the President, who inquired about his plans for taking Vicksburg. Porter replied that at one time the stronghold could have been easily captured, but now it was a "second Gibraltar" and the navy alone could not take it without the help of a large body of troops.

"Well," said Lincoln, "who do you think is the general for such an occasion?" Porter answered, "General Grant, sir. Vicksburg is within his department; but I presume he will send Sherman there, who is equal to any occasion."

To Porter's surprise, Lincoln replied: "Well, Admiral, I have in mind a better general than either of them; that is McClernand, an old and intimate friend of mine." [4]

"I don't know him, Mr. President," Porter said.

"What," exclaimed Lincoln, "don't know McClernand? Why, he saved the battle of Shiloh, when the case seemed hopeless!"

To this Porter replied that it was the general opinion that Grant had won the battle of Shiloh, and that he was entitled to the credit since he was in command of the army there. "No," said Lincoln, "McClernand did it; he is a natural-born general."

Porter answered that he had little faith in "natural-born" generals unless they had had some degree of military training; he felt that Vicksburg was too great an undertaking to be committed to any except a professional military man and that any troops taken from Grant would weaken his army. Lincoln denied that he had any such intention. McClernand was to proceed to Indiana, Illinois, and Iowa to raise troops for the capture of Vicksburg; in the interim Porter could prepare to cooperate with him.

As Porter was leaving the White House Lincoln gave him

[4] Lincoln's opinion of Grant at this time must not be judged by his later estimate of him. Incredible as it now seems, when General Ben Butler was relieved at New Orleans, Lincoln offered him Grant's command in the Mississippi Valley.

a note of introduction to McClernand, with whom it was suggested he might talk over the Vicksburg project. Porter then called on McClernand at his hotel. Two hours later he was on his way to Cairo to see Grant and inform him of what was in the air. Thus did Grant learn that Lincoln had commissioned McClernand to take Vicksburg.

At Cairo, Illinois, on October 15th, 1862, Porter assumed command of the Mississippi Squadron. His command consisted of one hundred and twenty-five vessels of all kinds and thirteen hundred officers, of whom only twenty-five had been in the old navy. The ironclad gunboats, most of which had been designed and built by James B. Eads in the brief period of three months, were the backbone of his squadron. They had already made their mark at Fort Henry, Fort Donelson, at Island No. 10 under Foote, and at Fort Pillow and Memphis under Charles H. Davis.

Soon after he reached Cairo, Porter sent word to Grant, then at Holly Springs, Mississippi, notifying him that he was to command the Mississippi flotilla. Since the information had not been given him in confidence, he also informed Grant that McClernand was raising troops for an attack on Vicksburg. A few weeks later, while Porter was still at Cairo, he was the guest at a supper for the officers of the station. The repast was under way when a "travel-worn person dressed in citizen's clothes" came in and was introduced as General Grant. Thus did the two great leaders meet. When the naval officer and the general were seated at a table by themselves, Grant opened the conversation by saying, "Admiral, what is all this you have been writing me?" When Porter told him of his interview with Lincoln, Grant said, "When can you move with your gunboats, and what force have you?" "I can move tomorrow," said Porter. "Well, then," Grant replied, "I will leave you now and write at once to Sherman to have thirty thousand infantry and artillery embarked in transports ready to start for Vicksburg the moment you get to Memphis."

Thus Grant and Porter planned to forestall McClernand in the capture of Vicksburg. Grant's action was warranted, not only because of his own, Sherman's, and the army's lack of confidence in McClernand, but because he had not yet received official notification from Washington of the part Lincoln wished McClernand to take in the expedition.[5] Grant planned to have Sherman make an assault from a landing on the Yazoo River while he himself held General Joseph E. Johnston at bay, should he attempt to reinforce the Vicksburg garrison commanded by the Pennsylvania general who had "gone South," John Pemberton. After he had outlined his plan to Porter, Grant started back for his headquarters at Holly Springs without tasting the supper laid out before him.

Three days later, Porter's gunboats pulled into the wharf at Memphis, where he went at once to Sherman's headquarters to meet him for the first time. Thinking that Sherman would be dressed in full regalia, Porter arrayed himself in his dress uniform coat, "the splendor of which rivalled that of a drum major," only to find Sherman, who had heard that Porter was as careless in dress as Grant, wearing a plain blue flannel suit. The next day the transports and the gunboats started up the Yazoo River and into the Chickasaw Bayou where, on December 29th, 1862, Sherman attacked the Confederate position at Haynes' Bluff and met with a bloody repulse. In the meantime, General Earl Van Dorn had captured Grant's base at Holly Springs and cut his communications with the north for a week. Thus the first assault on Vicksburg ended in complete failure.

The night after the battle at Haynes' Bluff, Sherman came on board Porter's flagship, the *Black Hawk*, in a state of dejection over his repulse. Porter inquired why he was so downcast. "I have lost seventeen hundred men," answered Sherman, "and those infernal reporters will publish all over the country their ridiculous stories about Sherman being whipped." "Only

[5] Official notification reached him December 18, 1862.

seventeen hundred!" said Porter. "That is nothing; simply an episode in the war. You'll lose seventeen thousand before the war is
over, and will think nothing of it. We'll have Vicksburg yet
before we die." "That's good sense," responded Sherman, "and I
am glad to see you are not disheartened; but what shall we do
now? I must take the boys somewhere and wipe this out."

Then and there Porter suggested an attack on Arkansas
Post, fifty miles up the Arkansas River. When they were about
ready to start, McClernand, armed with his commission from
Lincoln, appeared on the scene. Sherman at once went to call
on McClernand, who outranked him, and then accompanied him
to talk with Porter on the flagship. Porter asked McClernand if
he had brought with him an army and siege tools to insure the
fall of Vicksburg. "No," said McClernand, "but I find this army
in a most demoralized state, and I must do something to raise their
spirits." "Then, sir," asked Porter, "you take command of this
army?" "Certainly," replied McClernand; "and if you will let me
have some of your gunboats, I propose to proceed immediately
and capture Arkansas Post." At this point, in answer to a remark by Sherman, McClernand made what Porter considered a
discourteous reply, whereupon Sherman walked away to another
cabin.

Porter then informed McClernand that he and Sherman
had discussed an attack on Arkansas Post the previous evening;
that he would never let his gunboats go on such an expedition
without him; and that, unless Sherman were in command of the
army, he himself would have nothing to do with the expedition.
Just then Sherman beckoned to Porter from the cabin to which
he had retired. When Porter went to him, Sherman exclaimed,
"Porter, you will ruin yourself if you talk that way to McClernand. He is very intimate with the President, and has powerful
influence." "I don't care who or what he is, he shall not be rude
to you in my cabin," answered Porter. When Porter returned
to join McClernand, he asked him if he understood his proposi-

tion. "Yes," said McClernand, "and agree to it. There is no objection, I suppose, to my going along?" "None in the world," replied Porter; "only be it understood that Sherman is to command this army." [6]

On January 11th, 1863, a combined army force of thirty thousand men and seven gunboats overpowered the garrison at Arkansas Post, taking five thousand prisoners. McClernand, assuming the credit for the victory, exclaimed to Sherman, "Glorious! Glorious! My star is ever in the ascendancy!" Following this victory, McClernand established his headquarters at Young's Point, a little distance above Vicksburg. Porter accompanied him, but sent word to Grant that McClernand was unjust to Sherman; that he could never cooperate with him; and that Grant must come down to take command of the army in person. After an acrimonious exchange of letters between McClernand and himself, Grant cut the Gordian Knot by joining the army at Young's Point, above Vicksburg, where he assumed command in person.

The capture of the Confederate stronghold at Vicksburg was an objective of the first importance in the campaign against the Confederate armies. "The fate of the Confederacy was sealed when Vicksburg fell." That was General Grant's comment on the significance of his campaign against the river fortress. The first attempt by the army to take Vicksburg ended, as we have seen, in the repulse of Sherman at Haynes' Bluff, nine miles up the Yazoo River from Vicksburg on December 29th, 1862. From then until Grant threw his army across the Mississippi south of the city and attacked it from the rear in April of 1863, the history of the campaign was a succession of always baffled efforts to capture the city. To take Vicksburg was indeed a formidable undertaking, for the Mississippi washed the high bluffs of the city and the batteries of artillery were so located that boats attempting to run up or down the river would be

[6] One gets the impression from the account of this interview that McClernand was rudely and shabbily treated.

under fire for a distance of several miles.[7] Two efforts were made to get into the Yazoo River above the defenses at Haynes' Bluff to find a landing place from which the army might attack the city in the rear; two additional attempts were undertaken to get the army in a position where it could be transported across the river south of the city and attack from that point. These undertakings were titanic in their proportions, feats of digging and engineering far beyond those of the Medes and Persians when they diverted the Euphrates from its course into the canals which had been built by Nebuchadnezzar, and so marched by the empty river bed into the city.

Porter played a leading part in one of the attempts to get at the city from the north and east and strike the enemy on his right flank. Near Milliken's Bend, where the army was encamped, an opening leading from the Mississippi into Steele's Bayou was discovered. From Steele's Bayou there was a passage into Black Bayou, thence into Deer Creek, from Deer Creek into the Sunflower, and from the Sunflower into the Yazoo not far from its mouth, where an army could be landed. Porter explored this waterway as far as Deer Creek and reported it as navigable. On the strength of this report Grant authorized the expedition.

On March 15th Porter started up Steele's Bayou with five gunboats and four mortar boats. Grant went along for some distance, and then returned to hurry forward Sherman, who was to accompany the fleet with a division of infantry. Never was a stranger campaign made by any army, and especially by any navy. Sherman's transports with their lofty smokestacks made much slower progress than the gunboats, and the fleet was soon

---

[7] The battery half a mile below the city was called the "Hospital Battery." It was commanded by David Todd, Mary Todd Lincoln's brother. Mrs. Lincoln's four brothers were in the Confederate army. Three of them were killed: David at Vicksburg, Alexander at Baton Rouge, and Samuel at Shiloh. Only one brother, George, survived the war. A brother-in-law, Ben Hardin Helm, husband of Mrs. Lincoln's favorite sister, Emilie, was killed at Chickamauga. None drank a deeper cup of sorrow during the war than Mrs. Lincoln.

far in advance of the army. In ordinary waters and under normal circumstances, the journey on which Porter embarked with his gunboats could have been accomplished in forty-eight hours; however, these were not ordinary waters, and both man and nature combined to make the expedition end in failure. Porter had some of his best ships with him. If only a Porter would have risked his ships in such gloomy swamps and bayous, no commander could have shown greater courage, intrepidity, and resourcefulness in saving those ships from disaster.

As the flotilla pushed its way through the bayous, it began to encounter huge trees, giants of the forest, which had reigned for centuries in the unsunned solitudes. Instead of attacking forts as he had done so successfully heretofore, Porter had now to attack huge trees to clear a way for his ships. His method was to ram them with one of the gunboats going at a speed of three knots. This first shock bent the tree down and loosened it, for the soil about the roots was softened by the waters which encompassed them. A second ramming brought the tree almost down to horizontal. The next gunboat astern then dragged the tree out of the way with heavy chains. As the fleet slowly proceeded, the sailors could see the smoke and flames of burning cotton, for wherever there was open country, there were plantations. The gunboats were fifty feet in width; in some places the bayous were hardly wider. Whenever a ship struck a tree, flocks of startled birds flew from their perches and a shower of rats, lizards and snakes came down on the decks, whence the sailors swept them overboard with brooms.

As the fleet penetrated deeper into the bayous the obstacles became more difficult to overcome. When struck by the ships, heavy logs which had been floating in the waters for years would sink to the bottom, but often with one end protruding above the surface, over which it was not possible to pass. Working parties with block and tackle were out day and night to clear the way. Here and there, too, they encountered sunken rafts which had been imbedded in the mud for years. Frequently the ironclads were caught between two great trees which could not be rammed down; to clear a passage, men with axes chopped down the sides of the trees. As the ships passed, the Briarean arms of the gigantic trees caught and swept away everything on the decks. Sometimes, where the country was more open, the fleet passed through pleasant and well-cultivated fields, and now and then came to bridges, which the ironclads knocked over like ninepins. Again they would find themselves in the midst of a vast solitude, passing through bayous, the dark waters of which had never been parted by the prow of a boat, unless by the rude canoe of the savage.

Along these western rivers, the Tennessee, Cumberland, and Mississippi, wherever Union soldiers or sailors appeared, the friendly "contrabands" [8] communicated with them and furnished useful information as to the positions and purposes of the enemy. Passing through these bayous, Porter marvelled at their absence. He was soon to learn the reason for it. One evening when the ships had stopped for a short rest, Porter and his officers heard the sound of wood-chopping in the distance ahead of them. To ascertain what this meant, Porter sent on a small tug armed with a twelve-pounder howitzer. When the tug returned, her commander reported that he had come upon a large company of Negroes, in charge of white men carrying lanterns, felling the trees ahead of the gunboats. Porter then sent the tug ahead again with instructions to fire, if necessary, on the Negroes who were felling the trees. "Contrabands" brought on the ships said that officers who had come up from Vicksburg had compelled the Negroes to do this work by putting pistols to their heads or plying them with whiskey.

After several days of the hardest kind of work, the ships had covered a distance of only seventy-five miles. Only six hundred yards, however, remained to be traversed to reach the Rolling Fork where it would be clear sailing into the Sunflower and thence into the Yazoo. But for these six hundred yards the bayou

* The name the Union soldiers gave the Negroes.

was filled with willow withes which fouled the paddlewheels and, clinging to the bottoms and sides of the ships, stopped their progress more effectually than the great trees had done. By this time, too, Confederate soldiers had come up, and artillery and sharpshooters began to fire on the gunboats.

A tug which had been sent back over the course which the ships had followed reported that Negroes were now felling trees in the rear of the fleet. Porter was like an animal caught in a net. But where was Sherman? A trustworthy "contraband" volunteered to get a message through to him. This was the dispatch Porter sent: "Dear Sherman: Hurry up, for heaven's sake. I never knew how helpless an ironclad could be steaming around through the woods without an army to back her."

As night came on Porter tied up the ships and landed several hundred men with howitzers to protect them from an attacking party. It was not now possible to proceed, and even the prospect for a safe withdrawal was dim. Since the bayou was too narrow to allow the ships to turn, the rudders were unshipped and, when day dawned, the gunboats began to back down the tortuous course they had come. To keep off boarders Porter had the sides of the boats covered with slime; for protection from sharpshooters the officers and crew sought what shelter they could find. Porter shielded himself with a section of an iron smokestack.

Pushing forward as rapidly as he could, Sherman heard the booming of the navy guns. As the sound of firing became heavier, he grew anxious. That night the faithful contraband, carrying Porter's message in a piece of tobacco, got through to Sherman. In response to the call for help Sherman at once sent General Giles Smith ahead in the blackness of the night with eight hundred men; he himself followed, traveling part of the way in a canoe. On Sunday morning a picket came in with the news that Porter had turned back, but that, although there was a Confederate force beyond the flotilla, there was nothing between the ships and Sherman's army. Weary with his all-night journey, Sherman sat down on the doorsill of a cabin to rest. He had been there but a few minutes when he heard heavy firing. A colonel came in to report that the Confederates were felling the trees in front of Porter's now retreating squadron, but that he had dispersed them with his guns. Seeing a major with a horse he had picked up in a field, Sherman leaped to the back of the horse and, riding bareback, galloped toward the vessels caught in the narrow passes of Deer Creek. Soon he came in sight of the gunboats. When the sailors saw him, they came out of their hiding places and cheered wildly, for they knew that the army was at hand and that they were now safe.

Just before Sherman appeared with the relief column, things looked so dark for Porter that he had made up his mind, if worst came to worst, to blow up the ships and try to get his crews through the swamps to the Mississippi. At that moment Sherman came riding up to the bank of the bayou. "I soon found Admiral Porter," wrote Sherman long after, "who was on the deck of one of his ironclads with a shield made of the section of a smokestack, and I doubt if he was ever more glad to meet a friend than he was to see me." Greeting Porter, Sherman exclaimed: "Haloo, Porter, what did you get into such an ugly scrape for? So much for you navy fellows getting out of your element; better send for the soldiers always. . . . This is the most infernal expedition I was ever on. Who in thunder proposed such a mad scheme? But I'm all ready to go on with you again. Your gunboats are enough to scare the crows; they look as if they had got a terrible hammering. However, I'll start at once and go back with you; my boys will clean those fellows out." "Thank you, no," said Porter; "I have had enough of this adventure. It is too late now; the enemy are forewarned; and all the energies of the Confederacy will be put forth to stop us."

From the 29th of December, 1862, when Sherman met his bloody repulse in the attack at Haynes' Bluff, until the 16th of April, 1863, when Porter ran the Vicksburg batteries with his gunboats and the transports, every effort of the army under

Grant to take the river stronghold had been frustrated. Long after the Vicksburg campaign, Grant said in his *Memoirs* that the plan which ultimately brought success had been in his mind from the beginning. "I had in contemplation the whole winter the movement by land to a point below Vicksburg from which to operate, subject only to the possible, but not expected, success of some one of the expedients resorted to for the purpose of giving us a different base." Through the winter months, however, he was singularly silent about the joint project by river and land, speaking of it to none of his generals. The failure of the Steele's Bayou expedition under Sherman and Porter, together with the fact that the receding waters made a land march along the west bank of the Mississippi possible, finally determined Grant to march his army to a point south of Vicksburg, cross the river, and so get at Vicksburg from the rear. This could not be accomplished without the cooperation of the navy under Porter. The transports and barges were indispensable, not only to carry down the river the supplies necessary for a great army, but to ferry the troops across the river at the place chosen for a landing; the gunboats were needed to guard the supply ships and protect the crossing of the troops. Grant had no authority to command Porter, but the admiral gave him full and enthusiastic support. Voluntary cooperation between the army and the navy in some campaigns, notably in the attacks on Charleston and Fort Sumter, was a dismal failure; this was not true at Vicksburg. Throughout the Vicksburg campaign there was not a single disagreement or dispute between Grant and Porter.

In order to disrupt the transportation of Confederate supplies below Vicksburg, Porter sent down the ram *Queen of the West* under command of twenty-year-old Colonel Charles Ellet, son of the noted engineer who built the army's ram fleet. The *Queen of the West* ran the batteries successfully on February 2nd and went down the Mississippi as far as the Red River, which she ascended for fifteen miles, capturing three steamers laden with provisions for the Confederate armies. At the end of three days Ellet was back again at a point just below Vicksburg. Returning down the river with a coal barge in tow, the *Queen of the West* again ascended the Red River, making several captures. Unfortunately, while attempting to pass Fort Taylor, she ran aground under the guns of the fort. The unwounded officers and men abandoned the vessel and made their escape by drifting down the river on the bales of cotton which had been used to protect the sides of the *Queen*.

Before Porter had learned of this misfortune, he had sent down the river one of his strongest ships, the *Indianola*, to assist and protect the *Queen of the West*. The *Indianola* went down as far as the Red River, where her captain learned the fate of the *Queen of the West* and also that the Confederates had repaired her. On her way up the Mississippi with a pair of coal barges in tow, the *Indianola* encountered two Confederate ships, the *Webb* and the captured *Queen of the West*. Commander Brown made the mistake of attempting to fight the battle while encumbered with the barges. The result was that, although the *Indianola* was more powerful than the Confederate ships, a hole was smashed in her stern and she was run aground and surrendered to the enemy. This was a grievous disappointment to Porter. With characteristic exaggeration, he said in his report to the Navy Department: "There is no use to conceal the fact, but this has, in my opinion, been the most humiliating affair that has occurred during the rebellion." The loss of the *Indianola*, however, was cancelled to a degree by a remarkable and shrewd bit of horseplay on the part of Porter. On a raft of logs three hundred feet long he had built a log casemate, pierced with portholes through which wooden guns thrust their muzzles. At both ends of the raft were canvas frames set up in the shape of a monitor's turret. Towering smokestacks built of empty barrels were erected, and in each smokestack a pot of tar was placed. On the night of February 24th, the tar pots in the smoke stacks were lighted and the fake ironclad was set afloat. As soon as the smoke announced her presence, all the

Vicksburg batteries opened fire. Still intact, the log-cabin war-ship got by the batteries and drifted on down the river until she grounded a short distance above New Carthage, where the Confederates were attempting to repair the captured *Indianola.* Warned by a telegram from Vicksburg that a dangerous ironclad was descending the river, the *Queen of the West,* which had been lying at Warrenton, fled at first sight of the sham monitor. When she passed the point where mechanics were at work on the *Indianola,* she warned them of the approach of the supposed ironclad, whereupon the workmen, after throwing some of the heavy guns overboard and firing the ship, abandoned her. It was not until some days had passed that the Confederates learned of the hoax which Porter had perpetrated upon them, and that the guns which protruded so grimly from the portholes of the dummy monitor were made of wood. Thus the Confederates were deprived of a powerful acquisition to their river navy; at the same time, Porter, through the bombardment which was given the sham ironclad, gained valuable knowledge about the location of the Vicksburg batteries.[9]

In view of the success of Foote's gunboats in running the formidable batteries at Island No. 10 the previous year, which proved that gunboats could run batteries planted on river bluffs without suffering serious injury, it seems strange that sending Porter's fleet past the batteries at Vicksburg should have been regarded so hazardous an undertaking. It is true that the bat-teries at Vicksburg were posted on much higher ground than at Island No. 10, and therefore harder to reach with the ships' guns. On the other hand, batteries only slightly above the water were in a better position for firing on the ships. Two of Grant's officers, John Rawlins, his adjutant general, and James H. Wilson, chief engineer of the army, claimed an important part in Grant's final decision to march his troops down the river and run the

---

[9] The Confederate Army had frequently resorted to similar ruses with wooden artillery, notably before Washington, at Yorktown, Virginia, and at Corinth, Mississippi.

batteries with the gunboats, transports, and barges. Shortly after Grant had personally taken command of the army near Vicksburg and established his headquarters at Milliken's Bend, a number of his generals, McPherson, Sherman, McClernand, and others, were taking a look at Vicksburg from the western shore. Rawlins and Wilson left the group and crawled out on the butt of a cottonwood tree which had fallen into the river, and there talked over the different plans that had been discussed for the capture of the river fortress. It was then that Wilson proposed running the batteries. He was convinced that if ships had successfully passed forts and batteries at New Orleans, Port Royal, and Island No. 10, the same thing could be done at Vicksburg. Rawlins was much interested in the idea and soon after brought it up at a dinner at Grant's headquarters when the generals present discussed ways of attacking Vicksburg. As the dinner was about to break up, Rawlins said, "Wilson and I have a plan for taking Vicksburg none of you have referred to yet."

"What is it? What is it?" Sherman asked in his quick, incisive way.

"Oh," replied Rawlins, "you will condemn it as too dangerous."

"Never mind that; let us have it," said Sherman.

Rawlins then outlined the plan to run the batteries with the transports and gunboats and march the troops by land to a crossing south of the city. With characteristic emphasis Sherman denounced the project: "It can't be done. It is impracticable. The transports will be destroyed. The enemy's guns will sink them or set them afire."

Of the officers present, only Rawlins and Wilson favored the plan. Grant kept silent. So strong was Sherman's opposition that, when it became evident that Grant was favoring the project, he wrote a letter to Rawlins suggesting that Grant first consult all his corps commanders. If this were not done, and the plan failed, the corps commanders might say that the failure was due to Grant's refusal to ask the advice of his generals. At the very last, just before Grant gave the word for the river movement, Sherman sought him out and pled with him not to make the attempt, on the ground that, by entering the enemy's country with a large river behind him and while the enemy held strong points above and below, he would voluntarily be putting himself into a position for the creation of which the Confederates would be glad to wait and maneuver for a whole year. Instead, he urged Grant to send the army back to Memphis and start all over again from the north. To this Grant answered that the nation was becoming discouraged at the lack of success on the part of its armies; volunteering was on the wane; and if the army were taken back to Memphis, the people would be still more discouraged. Hence bold measures to achieve a quick and decisive victory were imperative.

There was another and very important adviser to whose counsel Grant had listened, Admiral Farragut. Just a month before Grant and Porter made their movement against Vicksburg, Farragut had attacked the batteries at Port Hudson, three hundred miles down the Mississippi. He succeeded in bringing only his flagship and a consort past them, and then went up the river to Vicksburg to consult with Grant and Porter. Porter was away at the time on the unsuccessful Steele's Bayou expedition, but Grant met with Farragut on the *Hartford* a few miles below the city. At this meeting Farragut urged Grant to have Porter run the batteries with the gunboats and transports. This might not have been known had not a young gunner on the *Hartford*, Bartholomew Diggins, been stationed near the place where the admiral and the general were sitting and overheard Farragut's earnest exhortation. If Grant's mind was fully made up by that time, the advice of the admiral who had passed the forts at New Orleans must nevertheless have strengthened him in his resolution.

The army having started on its march for New Carthage, the night of April 16th was chosen for the passing of the batteries. Porter's fleet lay some distance above Vicksburg, completely screened from view by a dense intervening forest. The civilian captains and crews of some of the transport steamers refused to risk their lives in the dangerous adventure; but men from the army—engineers, pilots, firemen, deck hands—all experienced and in numbers sufficient to have manned scores of steamers, came forward as volunteers. The ships were protected by bales of cotton, wet hay, and sacks of grain which later would feed the army. Barges laden with coal and other supplies for the army and the fleet were lashed to the transports on the side away from the Confederate batteries on the cliffs.

The ships were to follow one another at intervals of two hundred yards. The gunboats were to take the lead, followed by the transports and barges, which were to hug the Louisiana shore in the hope that in the smoke and confusion of battle they could run by unobserved. The night was dark and moonless. At 10 o'clock the signal was given and the fleet got under way, Admiral Porter leading in the *Benton*. Except for the guiding lantern at the stern of each vessel, not a light showed on any ship. Absolute silence was observed. One by one, like dark, phantom ships, the gunboats and transports came round the great bend which the volatile river makes just north of Vicksburg.

As the minutes passed and not a hostile shot was fired, the men on the ships began to hope that they might succeed in running the batteries unobserved. Standing on the bridge of the *Benton*, Porter remarked to the ship's captain, Lieutenant Commander Greer, "We will no doubt slip by unnoticed; the rebels seem to keep a very poor watch." The words were hardly out of his mouth when a bright beacon and warning light sprang up on the levee, illuminating river, bluffs, city, and forts. Immediately there was a burst of flame as the heavy guns of the first battery opened on the *Benton*. But her forty inches of oak shield and four inches of iron plating repelled the hostile shots as if they had been hailstones. As there was no longer any advantage in silence, the *Benton* and the following gunboats hurled answering broadsides as each came in range of the batteries, which extended for several miles along the river. Soon every bluff and battery was vomiting forth shot and shell. Across the river on the Louisiana side the Confederates fired an old railroad station, and the onrushing fleet became plainly visible. Thousands of the citizens of Vicksburg and soldiers of Pemberton's army watched the fiery spectacle.

The river itself was almost as great a hazard for the fleet as the miles of batteries; several of the ships were caught in powerful eddies and whirled around as many as three times in full view of the gunners on the bluffs. Charles A. Dana, the War Department's special representative assigned to the army to report on its movements (and on Grant, who was standing on the deck of a river steamer during this action), claimed to have counted as many as twenty-five hundred discharges of artillery. General Grant, knowing that the great turning movement which he had just started depended on the fleet's success in getting by the batteries, watched anxiously from the deck of his headquarters steamer as the hills reverberated with the thunder of the cannonade and the sky flamed with the flashing of the great guns and the bursting shells. He remembered the sight as "magnificent, but terrible."

At the end of two hours the uproar ceased. The lights which had been flashing from the gun-studded bluffs one by one went out. Darkness once more enveloped river, forest, and hill. Silence reigned, broken only by the sound of the rushing waters as they washed the banks of the river. With the loss of only one transport, and without a single man killed, the fleet passed in safety, and early in the morning came to anchor above New Carthage, where the advance unit of Grant's army, McClernand's corps, had already arrived. General McClernand's headquarters were on a beautiful Louisiana plantation. When the plantation owner saw the burning fragments of the *Henry Clay* floating by in advance of the gunboats, he exclaimed to some of McClernand's officers, "Where are your gunboats now? Vicksburg has put an end to them all!" But the gunboats soon made their appearance off his plantation and his rejoicing was turned into anger and despair; rather than allow his mansion to shelter the enemy, he put the torch to it with his own hand.

Before the army could cross the river to the eastern shore and begin operations to capture Vicksburg, it was necessary to seize Grand Gulf. There a Gibraltar-like hill, Bald Head, rose above the river to a height of a hundred and eighty feet. Under this hill, at Point of Rocks, where the Mississippi forms a bay, the Confederates had posted their batteries on an escarpment fifty feet above the river. It was a strong position. Porter, who had gone down to make a reconnaissance, reported to Grant that his gunboats might not be able to silence the batteries. He suggested that the troops march down the shore to a point south of Grand Gulf and there be ferried across or, alternatively, that they be embarked on the transports and barges and pass the batteries in the night. After making his own reconnaissance, however, Grant thought Grand Gulf not as formidable as Porter considered it to be and resolved to attack it with his troops as soon as the gunboats silenced the batteries. For this purpose ten thousand troops were embarked on the transports.

From eight in the morning till one in the afternoon the Confederate positions were bombarded by the eight gunboats, which at times ventured almost within pistol shot of the shore. After five hours' bombardment had failed to silence a single one of the high batteries, Porter considered further attack futile and withdrew his ships. As soon as the firing ceased, General Grant boarded the *Benton*, where, he says, the sight of the mangled and dying men on the deck "sickened" him. In conference, the two commanders decided to disembark the troops from the transports and march them to a point opposite Bruinsburg, some miles below Grand Gulf, while the gunboats and transports ran the batteries in the night, as at Vicksburg. This was accomplished without loss. Early on the morning of April 30th the transports ferried McClernand's corps and one division of McPherson's across the river to Bruinsburg. The first serious obstacle had been overcome and the great turning movement was well underway. Grant said he experienced a feeling of great relief when this had been accomplished. "I was now in the enemy's country, with a vast river between me and my base of supplies. But I was on dry ground, on the same side of the river with the enemy." That was Grant at his best—"on the same side of the river with the enemy."

As soon as Porter had seen Grant's army safely across the Mississippi and in a position to begin the advance against Vicksburg, he started with his flagship and three other vessels for the Red River, where the next year he was to have a narrow escape from disaster. Farragut, who had been blockading the Red River since he ran the batteries at Port Hudson in April with the *Hartford* and the *Albatross,* had "implored" Porter to send down some of his gunboats to assist on the Red River. In a quick nine days' operation Porter compelled the evacuation of Fort de Russy, some distance up the Red, and then ascended the river as far as Alexandria, which he captured on May 7th. He turned the city over to General Banks' army which reached Alexandria the same day, and at once set out on the return journey to Grand Gulf to be ready to aid Grant in the event of a reverse in his campaign. From then on until the surrender of Vicksburg Porter's gunboats and mortars periodically bombarded the city, driving its inhabitants into the caves and shelters which they had dug in the soft soil.

Two months later, on the 4th of July, a soldier of General John Logan's division, which was in the advance, climbed the ladder to the cupola of the noble old Court House at Vicksburg. The banner of the Confederacy which had so long flaunted its defiance to the Union army and navy came fluttering down like a wounded bird, and the national flag was raised in its place. As soon as the ensign was observed by the men on Porter's ships lying in the river, it was greeted by salvos of artillery and the deep long-drawn-out roar of the whistles of the steamers and the gunboats. At that same hour on that memorable 4th of July, the passes of the South Mountain at Monterey and Fairfield were crowded with the wagons, artillery, ambulances, infantry, and cavalry of Lee's army retreating from the bloody repulse at Gettysburg, Pennsylvania. The war was to continue for almost two years, but after Gettysburg and Vicksburg it was for the South the energy and valor of a lost cause. In Lincoln's splendid sentence, "The Father of Waters goes unvexed to the sea." [10] Without the help of the gunboats under Foote, Davis, Farragut, Porter, and the brave men who fought and died on them, Lincoln could never have written that sentence.

General Sherman, who had met Porter on the wharf the morning of the surrender of Vicksburg but was not present at the actual surrender, having joined his command on the Black River, wrote Porter a warm letter of congratulation upon the part his fleet had played in the downfall of the Confederate stronghold:

Dear Admiral: No event in my life could have given me more personal pride or pleasure than to have met you to-day on the wharf at Vicksburg—a Fourth of July so eloquent in events as to need no words or stimulants to elevate its importance. I can appreciate the intense satisfaction you must feel in lying before the very monster which has defied us with such deep and malignant hate and seeing your once disunited fleet again a unit; and, better still, the chain that made an enclosed sea of a link in the great river broken forever. In so magnificent a result I stop not to count who did it. It is done, and the day of our nation's birth is consecrated and baptized anew in a victory won by the united army and navy of our country. God grant that the harmony and mutual respect that exists between our respective commanders, and shared by all the true men of the joint service, may continue forever, and serve to elevate our national character, threatened with shipwreck.

The next episode in Porter's Civil War adventures was the ill-fated Red River expedition. Twice during his command on the Mississippi he almost lost his gunboats; the first time, as we

[10] Lincoln, Letter to James C. Conkling, August 26, 1863.

have seen, in the Steele's Bayou expedition in the Vicksburg campaign; the second time on the Red River expedition. On both of these occasions we see Porter at his poorest in judgment, but at his best in courage, daring, self-reliance, and leadership of men in a desperate situation. Porter and Sherman had talked of a joint campaign up the Red River. That plan failed of fruition, however, when the command of the army was given to Nathaniel Banks, a former Congressman and Governor of Massachusetts. Banks was an ardent patriot who had left Congress for the field, but he proved to be a poor general. Had Sherman been in command of the troops, the story of the campaign would very probably have been different. Grant thoroughly disapproved of the expedition: "I had opposed the movement strenuously, but acquiesced because it was the order of my superior at that time. By the direction of General Halleck, I reinforced Banks with a corps of ten thousand men from Sherman's command." The campaign was conceived at and ordered by Washington. One of its purposes was to restore the authority of the Government in Louisiana and Texas, and also to put a damper upon any designs Napoleon III (whose troops were then in Mexico upholding the regime of Maximilian) might have to establish himself in that land or to intervene on the side of the Confederacy.

The Red River is fickle and treacherous. To take warships up the stream at any season of the year was a hazardous undertaking because of the sudden changes in the depth of the water. Porter's fleet entered the Red River on March 12th, 1864. The annual spring rise of the river as a rule came in March; but this year the river was slow in rising and quick in falling. Sherman, who had been superintendent of a military academy at Alexandria almost up to the outbreak of the war, and who was familiar with the river, considered twelve feet of water necessary for the ascent of the river; but when the flotilla reached the falls, or rapids, at Alexandria on March 15th, the river was so low that it was necessary to leave the heavier ironclads behind.

At Alexandria the fleet met the troops under General A. J. Smith, a part of the reinforcements sent by Sherman. On the 27th of March General Banks also reached Alexandria. Porter informed him that because of the state of the river and the delay at Alexandria, the gunboats would run the risk of getting stranded above the falls were he to take them further. This very thing later occurred. The admiral advised Banks to press on with the army to Shreveport, almost three hundred miles further up the river. However, since Banks was reluctant to advance without naval support, Porter selected gunboats and transports of lighter draft, got them beyond the falls, and steamed up the river for two hundred miles, slowly searching out a channel through shoals and snags and constantly fired on by sharp-shooters hidden in the dense forests along the high banks of the river.

Meanwhile, Banks and his men had met a reverse in a battle with the Confederate army at Sabine Cross Roads on April 8th. This defeat, however, was compensated for by a Union victory the next day at Pleasant Hill. General Kirby Smith, the Confederate commander in that region, said that his troops were so broken up by the second battle that Banks would have found few obstacles in his way had he decided to march on to Shreveport. Unfortunately, Banks decided to take his whole army back to Alexandria. It was not until the 10th that Porter learned that the army was withdrawing. Realizing his perilous situation, he began the descent of the river that very night. Well on his way toward Alexandria, his further prog-ress was threatened by the Confederate forces which had rallied after Banks began his retreat. With the well-directed fire of his veteran gunners Porter scattered these troops and reached Grand Encore, where he found Banks and the army. He coun-seled Banks to establish himself at Grand Encore and then pro-ceed up the river when the rains of the next spring had raised the level of the water. Banks, however, continued his retreat to Alexandria, and Porter was obliged to follow. On his way down to Alexandria, he lost just one ship, which grounded and had to be blown up.

The problem now was to get the gunboats over the falls below Alexandria. The spiritless Banks and General David Hunter, courageous veteran of many battles in the East, called on Porter on his ship, the *Cricket*, and asked him which of his vessels above the falls he could best afford to blow up. Jumping up from the sickbed on which he was lying, Porter exclaimed, "Not one of them, sir; not even the smallest. If I can't get over the falls, and the army leaves me, I can take care of myself and get out at the first rise. I'll wait here for high water if I have to wait two years." One of his captains, Thomas A. Selfridge, said to him, "A bad fix we're in, sir." "I don't think so," replied Porter. "We will get out of it all right." "What do you propose to do?" Captain Selfridge asked. Falling back on the lines which he quoted at every crisis Porter said, "There's a Divinity that shapes our ends." "But," replied Selfridge, "that won't hold water, which is what we want just now."

Porter's confidence in a higher wisdom was not misplaced. General Franklin, the ablest general in Banks' army, told the admiral that there was a Colonel Joseph Bailey of the 41st Wisconsin Regiment in his corps, who was quite familiar with rivers, rafts, and dams. Porter asked Franklin to bring Bailey to see him. When he proposed damming the river, Porter, as much of a jester as Lincoln, said that if "damning the river would do any good" they would have been out of their trouble long ago. The thoughtful and earnest Bailey gave no sign that he understood the joke. When Porter submitted Bailey's plans to General Banks he at once approved them, and several thousand soldiers were set to work.

The falls, or rapids, stretch for a mile below Alexandria and are choked with rugged rocks. Bailey's plan was to build wing dams between the upper and lower falls, causing the river to rise and thus make a channel for the ships. First of all, what was called a "tree dam" was built out from the left bank of the river for a distance of three hundred feet. The dam consisted of the trunks of great trees which had been felled, with brush, bricks, and stones packed in between them. At the end of this three-hundred-foot dam Bailey sank four large coal barges filled with bricks. From the other side of the river cribs filled with stones were then run out to meet the barges. This work, which Porter declared would have taken a construction company a year to build, was finished in eight days in spite of a rapid nine-mile-an-hour current.

Meanwhile, there had been a rise in the river sufficient to permit three of the gunboats to get over the upper falls and descend the river as far as the dam. But just when the three vessels were ready to attempt the passage through the second falls at Bailey's dam, the swollen river swept away two of the barges which swung round and lodged below the dam. The moment Porter saw this mishap, fearing that the dam might break before he could get the ships through, he leaped on a horse and galloped up the shore to where the ships lay and ordered the captain of the *Lexington,* a veteran of many river battles, to pass the upper falls and then go through the dam. The *Lexington,* which started just in the nick of time, for the river was beginning to fall again, passed the upper falls and steered straight down for the opening at the dam through which the waters were frantically rushing. As the ship drew near the opening, where thousands of Banks' soldiers were anxiously watching, there was deep silence, broken only by the noise of the waters. With a full head of steam, the *Lexington* plunged into the gap, rolled frighteningly several times, hung for a moment on the rocks, and then was swept into deep water and rounded to at the shore. As she did so, a great roar of cheering, drowning the noise of the waters, went up from the thousands of soldiers and sailors who had been watching on the shore and on the ships. The other vessels soon followed. Porter's flotilla was saved. Bailey received the thanks of Congress and was presented with a sword by Porter. He became a brigadier general and was breveted a major general for gallant service at Mobile. Survivor of the perils of many battles, he was shot to death in peacetime by bushwhackers in 1866 when he was serving as sheriff of Vernon County, Missouri.

On the 21st of May the flotilla floated out upon the broad Mississippi. In his letter to the Secretary of the Navy Porter said: "If this expedition has not been so successful as the country hoped for, it has exhibited the indomitable spirit of Eastern and Western men to overcome obstacles deemed by most people unsurmountable. It has presented a new feature in the war, nothing like which has ever been accomplished before." Writing a quarter of a century after the passage of his fleet over the falls, Porter said: "No one ever knew who started the expedition generally called the Banks Expedition up the Red River, or what its object was. No one cared to father it after it was over, for it was one of the most disastrous affairs that occurred during the war. It was undertaken at a season of the year when it could not possibly succeed, if it was the intention that any number of transports should accompany it, as well as gunboats." Why, then, it may be asked, did Porter commit his gunboats and his reputation as an admiral [11] to such a hazardous undertaking? The answer is found in his never-failing courage, his love of adventure, and his consistent readiness to afford the army all possible help in the common effort to bring down the Confederacy and preserve the Union. In view of his narrow escape from disaster, one must inevitably conclude that his judgment, at least on this occasion, as well as in the Steele's Bayou expedition at Vicksburg, was not equal to his courage and determination.

On October 9th, 1864, Admiral Porter was transferred from the Mississippi flotilla to the command of the North Atlantic Squadron, with orders to bombard and reduce Fort Fisher, the

---

[11] In August, 1863, Porter was promoted rear admiral, to date from July 4th, the day Vicksburg surrendered. He never held the rank of captain. Two years earlier he had been a lieutenant.

chief defense of Wilmington, North Carolina. Because of the
two entrances to Cape Fear River and the location of the forts
guarding these entrances, Wilmington, twenty-eight miles up
the river from the sea, was the favorite port for the blockade
runners. After the fall of New Orleans, early in 1862, and the
close blockade of the harbor at Charleston by Dahlgren's fleet in
the following year, it was the Confederacy's last important
port of communication with the outside world. The blockade
runners brought in war material and other articles desperately
needed by the Confederate armies, and carried out cotton, which
sold for only eight cents a pound in the South, but brought two
shillings a pound in England. This meant profits for the blockade
runners so enormous that even one successful trip would pay
for the vessel. Although many of the blockade runners were
captured and the shores strewn with the wreckage of others, almost four hundred ships are known to have run the blockade
during the war. Some of these ships came and went almost with
the regularity of scheduled ocean liners. Unimpeded by modern
methods of detection, these swift, low-cut ships, passing in or
out at night or hidden in mist and fog, stood a fair chance of
eluding the warships on guard. To maintain at the entrance of
the Cape Fear River, as was done toward the end of the war,
three cordons of vessels, one near the port, another farther out,
and a third still farther out to sea, involved tremendous expense.
For all these reasons the Navy Department, the War Department, and President Lincoln all greatly desired the capture of
Fort Fisher and Wilmington.

Porter was enthusiastic and eager to make the attack; but
Grant was long in making up his mind to allow the army to
cooperate, for all his energies were centered upon his chief
objective, the defeat of Lee's army which was then confronting
him before Richmond. When eventually he decided to detach
troops to join with the navy in the expedition, he selected for
command General Godfrey Weitzel, who had been with General
Ben Butler at New Orleans and was now again serving under

him in the Army of the James. Grant's orders for Weitzel and the part he was to take in the attack were necessarily transmitted through General Butler because he commanded the department within which Fort Fisher was situated. Grant had not thought that Butler would choose to accompany the troops; but this Butler decided to do. Weitzel never saw Grant's orders which designated the place where the troops were to land, and specified that they were to intrench themselves after landing. When Grant learned that Butler intended to take active command of the troops, he made no move to prevent this, for he still hesitated to offend Butler who, up to the time of the repulse of this first assault on Fort Fisher, had some mysterious hold upon him. That Butler was to command the troops was unfortunate, not only because of his military record, but because on a previous occasion, at New Orleans, he had clashed with Admiral Porter, who was to command the fleet.

General Butler had heard of a gunpowder explosion near the Thames River in England which had blasted houses within a wide radius and broken windows in the suburbs of London, fifty miles away. He was convinced that if a sufficiently heavy charge of powder were exploded at the right place, Fort Fisher could be breached and the troops could easily seize it. On his way to New York, whither he had been sent to keep order on election day in 1864, a task for which he was obviously and eminently fitted, Butler stopped in Washington and laid his gunpowder plan before Fox, the Assistant Secretary of the Navy. Both Fox and Admiral Porter gave their support to the idea; but General Richard Delafield, chief of engineers in the army, reported adversely to a council of army and navy officers, and presented the history of many powder explosions to back up his conviction that Butler's plan was impracticable. Notwithstanding this opinion, the council of officers favored the attempt. Grant had no confidence in the plan and doubted that the effect of the explosion would be sufficient even to waken the garrison at the fort. However, since an old ship was to be used and the experiment would be relatively inexpensive, he gave his consent. It seems strange that, having experienced the bloody fiasco of the gunpowder explosion under the Confederate lines at Petersburg the previous July, Grant should have given his consent to the effort at Fort Fisher. As for Lincoln, the President gave his consent with the remark, "We might as well explode the idea with gunpowder as anything else."

An old steamer, the *Louisiana*, worth only a thousand dollars, was prepared and loaded with powder. Butler had asked for one hundred and fifty tons of powder; but, in his enthusiasm for the idea, Porter sent a telegram to the Chief of the Bureau of Ordnance of the Navy Department asking for fifteen thousand tons! Captain Wise, Chief of the Bureau, telegraphed back, "Why don't you make a requisition for Niagara Falls and Mount Vesuvius? They will do the job for you." Porter confirms his enthusiasm for the gunpowder plot by saying: "This little mistake of two ciphers would indicate that I was not so phlegmatic as usual; so I really think I must have believed in the scheme."

The powder ship was anchored two hundred yards off the north salient of the fort. In the cabin of the ship a clock device was set to fire the fuse and explode the powder at 12 o'clock on the morning of December 24th. Somewhat skeptical of the clock device, Porter ordered that half a cord of pine knots be heaped up in the cabin and ignited by the last man to leave the ship. In the end it was the pine knots, and not the clock device, which exploded the powder. After the pine knots had been fired, the men on the *Louisiana* quit the ship and rowed twelve miles out to sea.

At 1:45 in the morning there was a blaze on the distant horizon, then a dull rumble, followed by silence. A few panes of glass were broken on some of Porter's vessels. The Confederate lookouts on the fort thought no more than that a boiler had exploded on one of the Federal ships. When day dawned, Porter moved in to bombard the forts, expecting Butler to appear with the transports and land the troops. But the transports did not arrive until evening, too late to begin the operation. The next day, Christmas, a portion of the troops were landed some five miles north of the fort. After a reconnaissance, General Weitzel advised Butler against an assault. Despite Grant's orders to Butler that, once landed, the troops were to intrench themselves, the men were reembarked on the transports and returned to Fortress Monroe. Grant was partly to blame for both gunpowder failures, that at Fort Fisher and that at Petersburg the previous July. At Petersburg he erred in permitting Meade at the last moment to compel Burnside to substitute a white contingent for the colored division which he had carefully trained for the assault after the explosion; at Fort Fisher he made the mistake of permitting Butler, in whom he had no confidence, to take personal command of the troops. Annoyed and chagrined at the failure, Grant telegraphed to Lincoln: "The Wilmington Expedition has proved a gross and culpable failure . . . Who is to blame, will, I hope, be made known."

Admiral Porter was furious and wrote to Grant, "Send me the same soldiers with another general, and we will have the fort." Deeply disappointed, Lincoln ordered Porter to remain off Fort Fisher and directed the Secretary of the Navy to send a message to Grant inviting him to offer renewed cooperation in a second attack. Grant sent the same troops, this time under command of General Alfred H. Terry. Terry landed his troops on the 13th of January, 1865, two weeks after the previous failure, and quickly made his position secure with intrenchments.

Both the general and the admiral were determined that this time there would be no withdrawal of either land or naval forces until the fort had fallen. Porter's determination echoes in the final sentences of his landing orders to the fleet: "If when our men get into the fort, the enemy commence firing on Fort Fisher from the Mound [a high position at one end of the fort] every three men will seize a prisoner, pitch him over the walls, and get behind the fort for protection, or into the bomb proofs."

When Porter had decided to assist the army by an amphibious assault on the sea face of Fort Fisher, he called for volunteers for this dangerous duty. More than two thousand officers and seamen responded to his call. On the morning of January 15th the fleet subjected the fort to a heavy bombardment. During the forenoon the four hundred marines and sixteen hundred sailors landed and dug in near the beach. There was no little confusion among the men of the naval contingent, for not only had the sailors never drilled together, but the officers at the head of the different quotas from the ships did not know to whom to report or who was to lead them. The one designated by Porter, Fleet Captain K. R. Breeze, was in conference with General Terry and did not arrive on the scene until shortly before the attack was made. The sailors were armed with cutlasses and pistols; a few had carbines; the four hundred marines were to cover with their fire the assaulting sailors.

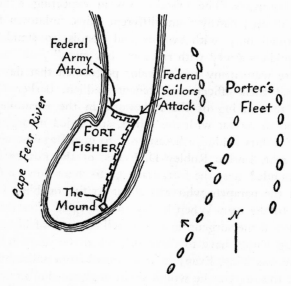

At three in the afternoon the guns of the fleet lifted their fire from the lower defenses of the fort to the upper works to make way for the assault and, to the roar of the whistles of fifty ships, the sailors sprang forward to the attack. They had nearly half a mile to traverse before they got close to the fort. Soon they were under heavy fire, and were falling by the score. Those in the rear, seeing what was happening to those in front of them, broke and fled back to the beach. "The rush of the sailors was over; they were packed like sheep in a pen," writes a participant, "while the enemy were crowding the ramparts not forty yards away, and shooting into them as fast as they could fire. There was nothing to reply with but pistols."

Porter laid the blame for the bloody repulse on the failure of the marines to cover the charging sailors with their fire and sweep the parapets clear of the defenders. Captain Selfridge, on the other hand, points out that the marines "were only four hundred against twelve hundred of the garrison: the former on the open plain, and with no cover; the latter under the shelter of their ramparts. The mistake was in expecting a body of sailors, collected hastily from different ships, unknown to each other, armed only with swords and pistols, to stand against veteran soldiers armed with rifles and bayonets."

There were many acts of valor performed that day by the sailors and their officers. Lieutenant William Barker Cushing, hero of the sinking of the *Albemarle* in the Roanoke River, compelled to retreat with the others, succeeded in organizing a group of sailors behind a breastwork to guard against an attack in their rear. Ensign Robley D. Evans, of the *Powhatan*, four times wounded, near the fort, managed to shoot down a Confederate on the parapets who was about to fire on him, and then crawled to the rear. When he lay in a hospital after the battle, he overheard the surgeon in charge telling some of his staff that Evans' leg would have to come off; when the surgeon came to where he was lying, Evans drew his pistol from under his pillow and told the surgeon he would shoot anyone who attempted to amputate his leg. The leg was not amputated and Evans recovered from his wound. Thirty-three years afterward, known everywhere as "Fighting Bob" Evans, in command of the *Iowa*

A steam sloop: U.S.S. Brooklyn (1858—1891). One of the Hartford class, she is a typical ocean-going cruiser of the Civil War period. Winslow's Kearsarge and Collins' Wachusett were similar but smaller. In this view Brooklyn's funnel has been telescoped, but the top can be seen just before the mainmast.

A Confederate ram: C.S.S. Atlanta. Converted from blockade-runner Fingal in 1862, she was captured by U. S. monitor Weehawken in 1863. The picture shows her in Federal service on the James. C.S.S. Merrimac, Tennessee, and Albemarle were similar.

A river ironclad: U.S.S. Benton (1862—1865). The most powerful of nine warships built or converted by James B. Eads, she served as flagship at one time or another for both Foote and Porter.

A monitor: U.S.S. Mahopac (1864—1904), in the Appomattox River. Ships of this type served under Du Pont, Dahlgren, and Porter on the East Coast. Others were with Farragut in the Gulf. These four photographs were taken in the last two years of the war.

he fired the first shot in the battle with the Spanish fleet off Santiago, Cuba.

Although the land attack by the naval contingent was a complete and bloody repulse, due chiefly to lack of preparation and training, and also to confusion as to orders and leadership, it was the heavy bombardment by the fleet which prepared the way for the soldiers' success and the capture of the fort. Fighting in the darkness, as the heavy guns of the *New Ironsides* and the monitors hurled their shells into the fort ahead of them, Terry's soldiers drove out the defenders, and by 10 o'clock that night, January 15th, Fort Fisher fell. On Washington's Birthday, February 22nd, General John M. Schofield's Twenty-third Corps, which had been detached from the army of General Thomas in Tennessee and brought east, entered Wilmington, and the blockade runners had lost their last haven of refuge.

Butler's failure to take the fort on the first attack in December, together with the powder-ship fiasco, gave Grant the opportunity and the courage to relieve him of his command and order him to his home at Lowell, Massachusetts. In a bombastic farewell address to the Army of the James, Butler said: "I have refused to order the useless sacrifice of the lives of such soldiers, and I am relieved from your command. The wasted blood of my men does not stain my garment." The powerful Congressional Committee on the Conduct of the War heard the testimony of Grant, Porter, and Butler concerning the first attack on Fort Fisher, and by a unanimous verdict exonerated Butler of all blame, declaring that his refusal to make an assault after the troops were landed on Christmas day was justified by the facts then known. The committee was sitting at the time Fort Fisher fell to the second attack. Butler was in the course of a demonstration to prove that the fort could not be carried without stronger forces when the shrill voice of a newsboy was heard in the corridors shouting "Extra! Extra!" The committee chairman, Ben Wade of Ohio, called the boy in and asked him what event he was announcing. When the boy answered, "Fort

Fisher done took!" everyone laughed, and none more heartily than Ben Butler.

In the last week of March, 1865, as the war was drawing to a close, Lincoln responded to Grant's invitation to visit army headquarters at City Point, Virginia, on the James River. There he was the guest of Admiral Porter on his flagship, the *Malvern*. During his stay, the President asked Porter to attend him. The admiral took him about on the *Malvern*'s barge and in the buggy of General Ingalls, Quartermaster General of the Army of the Potomac. Because of this association, we owe to Admiral Porter the best account we have of Lincoln and the clearest portrayal of his personality during these days which were near the end of his life. There is no question as to the trustworthiness of this narrative, for Porter made it his rule every night before retiring to write down what had occurred each day; when the President was with him, he did this with particular care.

Earlier in the war Lincoln had not entertained a very high opinion of Porter, regarding him as a good deal of a showman and boaster; but after Porter's achievements as commander of the Mississippi flotilla and then his capture of Fort Fisher, the President came to hold him in high regard. As Porter's guest on the *Malvern*, Lincoln refused to take the admiral's cabin which was offered him, but occupied that of Porter's secretary, a little room six feet by four-and-a-half. The first night Lincoln put his boots and socks outside the door of his cabin. During the night his boots were cleaned and his socks washed and mended. When the President came in to breakfast he remarked to Porter: "When I went to bed I had two large holes in my socks, and this morning there are no holes in them." Asked how he slept, the President replied: "I slept well; but you can't put a long blade in a short scabbard. I was too long for that berth." Lincoln was six feet four inches in height; the berth was only six feet in length. The next day, while Porter and Lincoln were ashore, a squad of carpenters went to work and enlarged the cabin to eight feet. The following morning Lincoln said to Porter: "A greater miracle than ever happened last night: I shrank six inches in length and about a foot sideways."

During his visit to the army at City Point, Lincoln was determined to be free for a time from his cabinet and the other Washington advisers. One day he received a telegram from the Secretary of State which read, "Shall I come down and join you?" "No," Lincoln said to Porter, "I don't want him. Telegraph him that the berths are too small, and there's not room for another passenger." "But," said Porter, "I can provide for him if you desire his presence." "Tell him then," replied Lincoln, "I don't want him; he'd talk to me all day about Vattel and Pufendorf.[12] The war will be over in a week, and I don't want to hear any more of that."

Porter and Lincoln frequented a little hut which had been set up as telegraph headquarters, where the President liked to read the latest reports from the front. When a telegram came in about Sheridan's movements, Lincoln unfolded his map and pointed out to Porter the position of Sheridan's troops, saying: "Sheridan is just starting off up this road. That will bring about a crisis." As Lincoln laid aside the telegram, he picked up three kittens which had been playing on the floor of the hut, and placed them on the map which lay on the desk. "There, you poor, little miserable creatures," he said, "what brought you into this camp of warriors? Where is your mother?" "The mother is dead," Colonel Bowers of Grant's staff informed him. "Then," said Lincoln, "she can't grieve for them as many a poor mother is grieving for the sons who have fallen in battle, and who will still grieve if this surrender does not take place without bloodshed. Ah, kitties, thank God you are cats, and can't understand this terrible strife that is going on. There now," he went on, wiping the dirt from their eyes with his handkerchief, "that is all I can do for you. Colonel, get them some milk, and don't

[12] Vattel was an eighteenth-century Swiss jurist and author; Pufendorf a seventeenth-century German jurist and author.

let them starve; there is too much starvation going on in this land anyhow; mitigate it when you can."

Just as Lincoln was concluding his apostrophe to the kittens, a midshipman appeared with a message saying that Vice President Johnson and the influential ex-Senator Preston King of New York were on the *Malvern* and desired to see the President. In great agitation, Lincoln jumped up, exclaiming: "Don't let those men come into my presence. I won't see either of them; send them away. They have no business here anyway; no right to come down here without my permission. I won't see them now, and never want to lay eyes on them again." [13]

On March 27th General Sherman, whose victorious army had reached Goldsborough, North Carolina, arrived at City Point to see General Grant and plan with him the final steps in their campaigns. The next day there took place the memorable meeting of Lincoln, Grant, Sherman, and Porter on the *River Queen*, the vessel which had brought Lincoln to City Point. The President expressed anxiety lest Lee should unite his army with that of Joseph E. Johnston, which had been retreating before Sherman's advance, and thus prolong the war. Sherman assured him that this was impossible. "Mr. President, the Confederacy has gone up, or will go up . . . We could flood the South with troops and provisions without hindrance. We hold the situation, and General Johnston can surrender to me on my own terms." Lincoln made it clear to Sherman and Grant that the main thing was to obtain the surrender of the armies of Lee and Johnston without being too particular about the terms, for he was convinced that once these armies surrendered there would be no more fighting. "Let them once surrender," he said, "and reach their homes, they won't take up arms again. Let them all go, officers and all. I want no submission, and no more blood-

[13] The reason for Lincoln's displeasure is not clear. Porter says he had his own opinion but did not care to put it on paper. The incident, however, reveals Lincoln's distaste for his new Vice President, in office less than a month.

shed. Let them have their horses to plough with, and, if you like, their guns to shoot crows with. I want no one punished; treat them liberally all around. We want these people to return to their allegiance to the Union and submit to the laws. Again I say, give them the most liberal and honorable terms."

It was on the ground of this interview that Sherman in the terms of surrender he offered General Johnston gave the unwise permission for the Confederate soldiers to stack their arms in the state capitals. These terms, which were at once repudiated by the government, brought a storm of popular wrath down upon the head of Sherman, who was up to that time the second hero among the Union generals. Admiral Porter, who took careful notes on this interview, felt that if the terms of surrender granted Johnston embodied matters which could be settled only by the government, it was because Sherman thought he was carrying out the President's wishes.

When the news came that Richmond had been evacuated, Lincoln and Porter started up the James to visit the fallen capital of the Confederacy, the one on the *River Queen*, the other on the *Malvern*. Some distance below the city the *Malvern* grounded and Porter, taking the President with him in the *Malvern*'s barge, continued on to Richmond. At the landing an aged Negro fell on his knees and kissed the President's feet. "Don't kneel to me," Lincoln said to him. "That is not right. You must kneel to God only, and thank Him for the liberty you will hereafter enjoy. I am but God's humble instrument; but you may rest assured that as long as I live no one shall put a shackle on your limbs." The Negro and others with him then sang a hymn to which the President listened with reverence. On his way into the city Lincoln paused for a moment to look at Libby Prison, the huge tobacco warehouse where thousands of Union soldiers had suffered a dismal captivity. The crowd which stood about began to shout, "We will pull it down!" "No," said Lincoln, "leave it as a monument." After a visit to the State House and the mansion of Jefferson Davis, Lincoln returned to the *Malvern* at Porter's urging, for the admiral had become uneasy for the President's safety.

That night, after Lincoln's tour of Richmond, the strangest and humblest visit a conqueror ever made to a fallen capital, a man on the shore hailed the *Malvern,* saying he had dispatches for the President. Porter sent off a boat with an officer to bring back the dispatches. Soon the boat returned without either the dispatches or the bearer. Asked to describe the man with whom he talked, the officer said: "He was a tall man with a black moustache, wore a slouch hat and a long coat, a regular theatrical villain." After the tragic event at Washington, so soon to occur, Porter was convinced that the strange man was John Wilkes Booth. That same night there came another hail from the shore, saying that a sailor wished to report on board. Porter sent off an officer and four men with orders to bring the man aboard and put him in irons. When the boat landed, however, no man was to be found. These two incidents made Porter uneasy, and that night he stationed a marine to keep watch at the door of Lincoln's cabin.

The next day former Associate Justice of the Supreme Court John A. Campbell, accompanied by General Weitzel, the Union commander at Richmond, came on board to talk with Lincoln. Campbell was one of the Southern commissioners who came to Washington on an errand of peace before the flag was fired on at Sumter; he was also one of the three Confederate commissioners who had met with Lincoln and Seward on a peace mission at Hampton Roads in the previous January. After Campbell had left the ship, Lincoln said to Porter: "I am sorry you were not here when Mr. Campbell was on board. He has gone on shore happy. I gave him written permission to allow the Virginia legislature to convene in the Capitol in the absence of all other government."

Campbell had persuaded Lincoln that, if the legislature could meet at Richmond, it would vote Virginia back into the

Union. Astounded at this, Porter, never a backward man, took the liberty to point out to the President that Richmond was under military jurisdiction, that no court or legislature could meet without the sanction of General Grant, and that he was sure Grant would not consent to such a proposal. Lincoln acknowledged his mistake and asked Porter to send a messenger to overtake Campbell and recall the permission he had given. Porter then wrote out an order which the President signed, telling General Weitzel to withdraw the permission for the legislature to meet. When Lincoln had signed the order, Porter gave it to an officer to deliver to Weitzel. Seeing a one-horse ambulance at the landing, Porter said to the officer, "Jump into that wagon and kill the horse if necessary, but catch the carriage which carried General Weitzel and Mr. Campbell, and deliver this order to the general." Campbell's carriage was overtaken as it was entering the city and the President's permission was revoked.[14] This was one of the few times when Lincoln's political sagacity forsook him. What an explosion of wrath would have occurred in the North had the legislature been permitted to convene may be estimated from the storm of anger which swept the country when the terms of surrender which Sherman gave to General Joseph E. Johnston were made known.

Within another hour on this eventful night Lincoln had an extraordinary interview with a shabby-looking man dressed in gray homespun and carrying a long and heavy staff. When he first appeared at the landing and asked permission to go on board, the officer at the landing told him no one could go on board unless he had important business. "I am Duff Green," the man said. "I want to see Abraham Lincoln, and my business concerns me alone. You tell Abraham Lincoln Duff Green wants

[14] This incident is related by Porter both in his *Incidents and Anecdotes of the Civil War* and his *Naval History of the Civil War*. Nicolay and Hay in their *Abraham Lincoln, A History*, X, 228, dismiss Porter's account as "evidently written from memory" and "wholly inaccurate." There is no question, however, as to the main facts related by Porter; namely that Lincoln gave Judge Campbell what he took to be permission to assemble the Virginia legislature, and then withdrew the permission.

to see him." When this message was brought to the cabin, Porter arose and said, "I will go up and send him away." But the President said: "Let him come on board. Duff is an old friend of mine, and I would like to talk with him." When Green was brought on board and, at Porter's command, had thrown away his staff, he was conducted to the cabin. As Lincoln rose and extended his hand in greeting, Green said: "No; it is red with blood; I can't touch it. When I knew it, it was an honest hand. It has cut the throats of thousands of my people, and their blood which now lies soaking in the ground cries aloud to heaven for vengeance."

The smile with which Lincoln had greeted his old friend of Kentucky days vanished from his face. In one of his rare moments of great anger, Lincoln, shaking his finger in Green's face, said: "Stop, you political tramp; you, the aider and abettor of those who have brought all this ruin upon your country, a man who had no principles in the North, and took none South with him. A political hyena who robbed the graves of the dead, and adopted their language as his own. Miserable impostor, vile intruder! Go, before I forget myself and the high position I hold! Go, I tell you, and don't desecrate this vessel another minute!" [15]

On the way down the river the *Malvern* passed one of the transports loaded with Confederate prisoners. One of the prisoners called out, "Three cheers for Old Abe!" Another shouted: "Haloo, Abe; your bread and butter and meat's better than popcorn." Looking at them from the deck of the *Malvern* and hearing them call to him, Lincoln said: "They will never shoulder a musket again in anger; and if Grant is wise he will leave them their guns to shoot crows with, and their horses to plow with; it would do no harm."

[15] Duff Green was a Kentuckian, connected through his wife with the Edwards family to which Lincoln's wife was related. He had edited papers in St. Louis, Washington and New York and was for a time printer to Congress. After the election of Lincoln, President Buchanan sent Green to sound out the President-elect on his attitude toward secession.

After Lee's surrender at Appomattox, and also because he had received word of the serious injury Secretary of State Seward had suffered in a runaway, Lincoln decided to return to Washington. Porter was glad to have him go, for he had a "feeling that something would happen to him if he remained longer at City Point." Nor did Porter's anxiety subside when the President started on his homeward journey on the *River Queen.* With Lincoln's permission, he assigned Lieutenant Commander John Barnes, commanding officer of the *Bat,* to accompany the President on the *River Queen* and never leave his side. The *Bat,* a very fast ship, was directed to keep close to the *River Queen* all the way to Washington. Barnes was instructed to be armed at all times and to keep watch over the President until he was safe at the White House. After Commander Barnes had carried out his mission and returned to City Point, Porter still felt uneasy, and started for Washington himself, determined to see that Lincoln was not exposed to danger from assassination. On a fast steamer, the *Tristram Shandy,* he set out for Baltimore, thinking to make better time by landing there and proceeding thence by train. When the *Tristram Shandy* reached Baltimore, Porter sent the mate ashore for a cab to convey him to the depot. When the mate returned, Porter read in his "ghastly face" the tidings of the tragedy of the night of April 14th. The mate was trembling and unable to speak. "Be a man and tell me," ordered Porter. "Is the President dead?" The mate then stammered out, "Assassinated!" "Then I knew," said Porter, "that I had come too late. I might perhaps have saved his life with my persistent precautions, which he did not at all object to. I should have been about him until all excitement was over, and would have impressed the Cabinet with the necessity of guarding his person." When one reads of the extraordinarily loose measures taken to guard the President on the night of the fatal 14th of April, one feels it might have been different if Admiral Porter had accompanied him to Ford's Theatre. Yet Porter, despite his great grief, for he says he was "completely unmanned" by the tidings, took the long and true view of the President's taking off, for he wrote: "Perhaps it was better for Lincoln's happiness that he died when he did. Had he lived, he would likely have been involved in bitter political feuds, owing to his liberal opinions in regard to the reconstruction of the States. He was of too sensitive a nature not to feel the shafts that would have been hurled at him by those whom he thought to be his friends, and he would not likely have been permitted to carry out his ideas." [16]

Porter, regarded by not a few as the ablest naval officer of the Civil War, is an engaging character study. He was consistently inconsistent. When he first learned that Lincoln wished him to cooperate with General McClernand in the campaign against Vicksburg, he expressed delight that he was to be associated with a civilian general rather than a West Pointer; yet when he assumed command of the Mississippi squadron he was rude and scornful in his attitude toward McClernand, but full of enthusiasm for Sherman and Grant. When war was imminent and naval officers, Northern and Southern alike, were leaving no doubt as to their stand for the Union or for the Confederacy, he sought an appointment in the Coast Survey in California with the intention of taking command of a commercial vessel when the opportunity presented itself. Yet, in the end none surpassed him in zeal and courage for the maintenance of the Union.

He was boastful of his own achievements and had a tendency to disparage those of others. Even Farragut, for whose appointment he was chiefly responsible, did not escape his censure. Writing to the Assistant Secretary of the Navy when Farragut made his first effort against Vicksburg, Porter said: "I never expect to hear of Farragut again. I have an idea he will

---

[16] In an arresting comment on Lincoln's assassination, Porter said: "I do not think the prime instigator was ever suspected, though I have my own opinion on the subject." He intimates also that Senator James W. Nye, of Nevada, held the same opinion. Porter, *Incidents and Anecdotes of the Civil War*, 319.

ground on the bars of the Mississippi, and remain there for the rest of the Mississippi season. He went up without good pilots in those large ships, where gunboats was all he wanted. He went up at a high stage of the river, and if the water falls he is done for, and you may make up your mind to fit out a new squadron. . . . If you can get one up without having an old fogy in it, what a blessing it will be to the country." A displeased captain, writing to Admiral Du Pont, had this to say of Porter: "Porter would assassinate the reputation of any one in his way, without compunction of conscience, I think." [17]

One of Porter's chief faults was a recklessness in speech and in writing. After praising Porter for his courage and genius and ranking him with Lord Nelson as a great naval commander, General Grant said of him, "It would have been a great thing for Porter if he had never been able to read or write." The supreme example of Porter's recklessness with tongue and pen is the letter he wrote to the Secretary of the Navy about Grant after the capture of Fort Fisher in January, 1865. In this amazing letter, Porter, still angry over the failure of the first attack on the fort, said:

To General Grant who is always ready to take the credit when anything is done, and equally ready to lay the blame of the failure on the navy, when a failure takes place, I feel under no obligation, for receiving and allowing a report to be spread from his headquarters that there were three days when the navy might have operated and did not. . . . I served with the General before, where I never worked so hard in my life to make a man succeed as I did for him. . . . You will scarcely notice in his reports that the navy did him any service, when without the help of it given him all through the war he never would have been Lieutenant General. He wants magnanimity, like most officers of the army, and is so avaricious as regards fame that he will never, if he can help it, do justice to our department. . . . I do not

[17] Letter to Du Pont, April 20th, 1865, by J. S. Missroon, an officer with the fleet at Charleston, S.C. Du Pont Collections, Longwood Library, Kennett Square, Pa.

feel at all kindly towards General Grant for the indifference he displayed in the matter until he found his own reputation at stake; then he was willing to throw the elephant[18] overboard that had weighed him down so heavily. In a conversation with Grant I expressly told him that I would have nothing to do with General Butler, and he promised me faithfully that he would have nothing to do with the expedition. His course proves to me that he would sacrifice his best friend rather than let any odium fall on Lieutenant General Grant. He will take to himself all the credit of this [the capture of Fort Fisher] all the more that it has succeeded, when he deserves all the blame for the first failure to take the place. All this is now saddled on General Butler, and history will tell nothing of General Grant's share in it.

Five years later this extraordinary letter arose to plague Porter. Grant was President and his administration was under fire by his political enemies, both Democrats and Republicans; but nothing more derogatory was ever written about him than this letter by Porter. When Admiral Farragut died in August, 1870, Grant at once named Porter Admiral of the Navy to succeed him. When the matter came before the Senate for confirmation, Porter's enemies, of whom there were not a few, General Butler chief of them, fought against his promotion.

There was no little stir in army and navy circles and among the politicians when a copy of the letter appeared in the New York *World* and the New York *Sun* December 2nd, 1870. The letter had not been released by the authority of Welles, who was then out of the cabinet and had become a severe critic of Grant and his administration; but some of Porter's foes searched the files of the Navy Department. When they came upon the letter he had written to Welles, they might have repeated among themselves, and with no little glee, Job's exclamation, "Oh that mine adversary had written a book!"

Porter, greatly embarrassed, and fearful that the publication of this letter would cost him his promotion, did what he could to take the sting out of it. He told Grant that he had written

[18] General Butler, whom Grant dismissed after the failure of the first attempt to take Fort Fisher.

impulsively and when under a false impression, and asked the President not to judge him by one indiscreet letter, but by his friendship and good opinion in the past. In his bitter letter to Welles Porter said of Grant, "He wants magnanimity, like most officers of the army." But there Porter was mistaken. Whatever Grant lacked, it was not magnanimity. He refused to withdraw the appointment, and Porter was confirmed as Admiral of the Navy.

Over and against these blemishes and faults in Porter's character is his record of organizing power, initiative, daring, buoyancy of spirit, resourcefulness in desperate situations, and flaming courage. After his disappointment over Du Pont's repulse at Charleston in April, 1863, the Assistant Secretary of the Navy wrote to Porter: "We can have no friends in this business however great their names who look back in the great work of crushing out the rebellion. Our ironclads at Charleston were only dented; yours have been perforated through and through in every engagement, yet we get no dispatches from you that they are failures, and that nothing can be done."

Undismayed even under the most adverse circumstances, Porter did not belong to that class of officers described by Assistant Secretary Fox as men who "looked back" on the great work of the army and navy in overthrowing the Confederacy and maintaining the Union. Du Pont and Dahlgren got their ships "dented," and then withdrew. Not so Porter; always a fighter, he was ever ready to have his ships not only "dented," but also "perforated," for the sake of the cause.

BIBLIOGRAPHY

THE CHAPTERS of this book are based upon primary sources. These sources are threefold. First, the great compilation of orders, reports, and correspondence of the officers of the armies and navies, Union and Confederate, known as *The Official Records of the War of the Rebellion*. One hundred and twenty-eight of these volumes deal with the armies and twenty-seven of them with the navies. Second in the list of primary sources are the personal letters and papers of those who served in the war: officers, privates, and seamen. Among the more important collections which have been examined are the following: the papers of Admirals Dahlgren, Foote, and Porter in the manuscript division of the Library of Congress; the great collection of Du Pont letters in the vaults of the Longwood Library at Kennett Square, Pennsylvania; the correspondence of Gustavus V. Fox, the Assistant Secretary of the Navy, in the New-York Historical Society (nearly all the prominent naval officers wrote freely and confidentially to Fox during the war; a portion of these letters was published in 1920 by the Naval History Society under the title, *Confidential Correspondence of Gustavus Vasa Fox*); Captain Percival Drayton's papers in the New York Public Library (Drayton served under Du Pont at Port Royal and was Farragut's fleet-captain and captain of the *Hartford* in the battle of Mobile Bay); certain Winslow papers in the New-York Historical Society; and the Worden papers in the Lincoln Museum of the Lincoln Memorial University, at Harrogate, Tennessee.

In connection with Admiral Farragut, one of the most valuable and interesting documents is a manuscript, *Recollections of the War Cruise of the U.S.S. Hartford, January to December, 1862-1864*. This manuscript was written by Bartholomew Diggins, a gunner on Farragut's flagship. Diggins' name appears twice in the *Official Records;* and Farragut commended him to the Navy Department as one of those who "were conspicuous for gallantry" in the battle at Mobile Bay. Diggins had the honor of raising the admiral's flag on a mast planted near the pedestal when Farragut's statue was unveiled at Washington in March, 1881.

In contrast with the commanders of the armies, many of whom wrote and published memoirs and personal recollections—such as those of Grant, Sherman, Sheridan, Joseph E. Johnston, Hood, and others—comparatively few of the chief naval commanders left behind them memoirs, formal histories, or autobiographies. Foote died during the war, and Du Pont two months after it ended. Of the others, Farragut kept a journal and wrote numerous family letters. The most important of these are found in the biography written by his son, Loyall Farragut. Admiral Porter wrote *The Naval History of the Civil War*, and also an interesting, and ofttimes amusing, book of personal recollections entitled *Incidents and Anecdotes of the Civil War*. Porter wrote as he talked, impulsively and, on occasion, with considerable exaggeration; but what he says is always full of interest, and here and there facts otherwise unknown are recorded.

In his *Memoirs of Service Afloat*, Raphael Semmes tells his story of the battle between the *Kearsarge* and the *Alabama*. Captain Henry Walke, who claimed to have seen more fighting than any other officer in the navy, wrote an important and most interesting book, *Naval Scenes and Reminiscences of the Civil War*. Walke was gifted also as an artist, and the sketches with which he illustrated his book give one a clear picture of the river gunboats in action.

The most notable collection of battle stories is found in the four volumes, *Battles and Leaders of the Civil War*. These articles, written by various participants, appeared first, and in complete text, in *The Century* Magazine.

Daniel Ammen, who saw much fighting in the Atlantic, wrote a worthwhile history of the naval war in the east under the title, *The Atlantic Coast*. Both George Dewey and Winfield Scott Schley, who later won high distinction in the Spanish War, served under Farragut and wrote interesting accounts of him and his battles, Dewey in his *Autobiography* and Schley in his *Forty-five Years Under the Flag*.

Nothing can surpass the *Diary* of Gideon Welles, Lincoln's Secretary of the Navy, as a study of the character and personalities of the chief officers of the Civil War navy. Welles had his failings, and his characterizations are sometimes unkind and occasionally unjust; nevertheless his daily entries during the war years bring to life the noted officers of the navy as does no other contemporary record.

In addition to many years of study and research in the history of the Civil War, visits to Hampton Roads, Charleston, Fort Sumter, Cherbourg, Fort Donelson, Vicksburg, and New Orleans, have helped me to picture the battles fought in these waters. Very early in life I had the opportunity of hearing a never-forgotten account of the fight between the *Monitor* and *Merrimac* by one who was on the *Monitor* on that memorable 9th of March, 1862.

Rather than list long columns and many pages of references, I have selected those which I feel will be useful to students who may wish to pursue studies of their own in the naval history of the war. For the sake of convenience, I have grouped the references around each of the officers discussed. Page references are made where I felt the reader might find items of especial interest.

GIDEON WELLES and GUSTAVUS VASA FOX

Du Pont, Samuel F. Letter to Charles H. Davis, May 2, 1863. Du Pont Collection, Longwood Library, Kennett Square, Pa.

Fox, Gustavus V. Letter to Samuel F. Du Pont, November 16, 1861. Du Pont Collection, Longwood Library, Kennett Square, Pa.

Frank Leslie's Illustrated Newspaper, June 5, 1862

Official Records (Navy) Series 1, VOL. IV, 247; VOL. VI, 251-257; VOL. XII, 421-423

Porter, David D., *Naval History of the Civil War*, 383

Weed, Thurlow, *Autobiography*, 611

Welles, Gideon, *Diary*, VOL. I, 213-214

DAVID GLASGOW FARRAGUT

Bartlett, John R., "The *Brooklyn* at the Passage of the Forts," *Battles and Leaders of the Civil War*, VOL. II, 65

Beacon, Dr. Thomas C., "The Fight at Port Hudson," *Independent*, VOL. LIII, 589-98 (March, 1901)

Cable, George W., "New Orleans before the Capture," *Battles and Leaders of the Civil War*, VOL. II, 14-21

Chief of Naval Operations, Navy Department. Letter to the author, 1955

Dewey, George, *Autobiography of George Dewey*

Diggins, Bartholomew, *Recollections of the War Cruise of the U.S.S. Hartford from January 1862 to December 24, 1864.* (Manuscript in New York Public Library)

Drayton, Percival. Letter to A. Hamilton. New York Public Library

Farragut Journal and Letters (in *Life and Letters of David Glasgow Farragut* by Loyall Farragut)

Fox, Gustavus V., *Confidential Correspondence*, VOL. I, 297-353

Heitman, F. B., *Army Register*, VOL. II, 180-184

Johnston, James D., Commander of the *Tennessee*, "The Ram *Tennessee* at Mobile Bay," *Battles and Leaders of the Civil War*, VOL. IV, 401-406

Kinney, J. C., "An August Morning with Farragut," *Century*, May 1881

Knoxville *Journal*, May 15, 1900

Mahan, A. T., *The Gulf and Inland Waters;* also, *Admiral Farragut*

Missroon, John S. Letter to Admiral Du Pont, April 20, 1865. Du Pont Papers, Longwood Library, Kennett Square, Pa. (On Jouett's exchange with Alden.)

National Republican, August 5, 1865, "Percival Drayton"

Official Records (Navy), Series I, VOLS. I-XXVII; Series II, VOLS. I, II

Parker, Foxhall A., *Battle of Mobile Bay*

Porter, David D., *Naval History of the Civil War*, 175-254
Renshaw, W. B. Letter to David D. Porter. Porter Papers, Library of Congress
Schley, Winfield Scott, *Forty-five Years Under the Flag*, 45-46
U. S. Naval Institute Proceedings, VOL. XLIX (1923) 1961-86
Watson, J. Crittenden, "The Lashing of Admiral Farragut to the Rigging," *Battles and Leaders of the Civil War*, VOL. IV, 406
Welles, Gideon, *Diary*, VOL. I, 72, 79, 88, 145, 190, 191, 218, 230, 237, 249, 274, 314, 396, 440, 477; VOL. II, 100, 105, 119, 124, 133, 145, 146, 159, 223, 230-233, 396, 562; VOL. III, 101, 164, 469, 582
——— "Admiral Farragut and New Orleans," *Galaxy* Magazine, November and December, 1871
Winslow, John A. Papers in New-York Historical Library

ANDREW HULL FOOTE

Davis, Charles H., *Life of Rear Admiral Charles Henry Davis*
Eads, James B., "Recollections of Foote and the Gunboats," *Battles and Leaders of the Civil War*, VOL. I, 338, 346
Foote, John A., "Notes on the Life of Admiral Foote," *Battles and Leaders of the Civil War*, VOL. I, 347
Foote Papers. Library of Congress
Fox, Gustavus V., *Confidential Correspondence*, 5-55
Grant, Ulysses S., *Personal Memoirs*, VOL. I, 282-315, 330-352
Headley, J. T., *Farragut and our Naval Commanders*
Hoppin, T. M., *Life of Admiral Foote*
Official Records (*Navy*), Series I, VOLS. I-IX, XII-XIV, XVIII-XX, XXII-XXV
Scharf, J. Thomas, *History of the Confederate States Navy*, 242
Walke, Henry, *Naval Scenes and Reminiscences of the Civil War*, (Chapters on Fort Henry, Fort Donelson and Island No. 10)
Welles, Gideon, *Diary*, VOL. I, 74, 75, 92, 93, 120, 167, 191, 217, 256, 260, 311, 314, 318, 325, 326, 334-347; VOL. II, 135

FRANCIS SAMUEL DU PONT

Ammen, Daniel, "Du Pont and the Port Royal Expedition," *Battles and Leaders of the Civil War*, VOL. I, 671-691
——— *The Atlantic Coast*
Bennett, Frank M., *The Steam Navy of the United States*, 149
Du Pont, Henry A., *Rear Admiral Samuel Francis Du Pont*
Du Pont, Samuel F. Letters and Papers. Longwood Library, Kennett Square, Pa.
Dutton, W. S., *Du Pont, One Hundred and Forty Years*
Fox, Gustavus V., *Confidential Correspondence*, VOL. I, 47-197
Headley, J. T., *Farragut and our Naval Commanders*, 123-150

Johnson, John, "The Confederate Defense of Fort Sumter," *Battles and Leaders of the Civil War*, VOL. IV, 23-26

Letters and State Papers of Abraham Lincoln, VOL. II, 323-324

Nicolay, J. G., and Hay, John, *Abraham Lincoln*, VOL. V, 14-16; VOL. VII, 61-85

Official Records (Navy), Series I, VOLS. I-IX, XII-XVI, XX-XXVII; Series II, VOLS. I-III

Rodgers, C. R. P., "Du Pont's Attack at Charleston," *Battles and Leaders of the Civil War*, VOL. I, 671-691

Welles, Gideon, *Diary*, VOL. I, 72, 158, 160, 216-222, 234, 236, 247-249, 262-269, 273-277, 288, 295-344, 440; VOL. II, 30, 117, 118, 173, 320, 321; VOL. III, 217

JOHN AUGUSTUS BERNARD DAHLGREN

Beauregard, P. G. T., "Torpedo Service in the Harbor and Water Defences of Charleston," *Southern Historical Papers*, VOL. V, No. 4, 145

Bennett, F. M., *The Monitor and the Navy under Steam*, 177

Dahlgren, Madeleine V., *Memoir of John A. Dahlgren* (Made up largely of excerpts from the journal kept by Admiral Dahlgren)
———— *Memoir of Ulric Dahlgren* (Edited from the writings of Admiral Dahlgren)

Dahlgren Report to the Committee on the Conduct of the War, 1865, VOL. III

Davis, Jefferson, *Rise and Fall of the Confederate Government*, VOL. II, 507

Doubleday, Abner, *Chancellorsville and Gettysburg*, 179

Gillmore, Quincy A., "The Army before Charleston in 1863," *Battles and Leaders of the Civil War*, VOL. IV, 52-71

Headley, J. T., *Farragut and our Naval Commanders*, 456-495

Meade, George, *Life and Letters of General George Gordon Meade*, VOL. II, 190

Official Records (Army), Series I, VOL. XXXIII, 218, 222

Official Records (Navy), Series I, VOLS. VII-XIV, XVII-XXVII; Series II, VOL. II

Pollard, E. A., *Third Year of the War*, 243

Roman, Alfred, *Military Operations of General Beauregard*, VOL. II, 181, 187

Siviter, Anne P., *Recollections of War and Peace*, 276-283

Stevens, Thomas H., "The Boat Attack on Sumter," *Battles and Leaders of the Civil War*, VOL. IV, 47-51

Welles, Gideon, *Diary*, VOL. I, 62-66, 158, 163, 164, 179, 239, 311-15, 338, 342, 372, 382, 401, 406, 434, 449, 534-544, 547; VOL. II, 7, 128, 134, 147, 173, 200, 202, 311-313, 320, 331, 484, 604; VOL. III, 27, 69, 70, 484, 562

Willis, N. P., *Home Journal* (Philadelphia), June 29, 1861

JOHN LORIMER WORDEN

Army and Navy Journal, Oct. 23, 1897
Bennett, F. M., *The Steam Navy of the United States*, 230-242
Church, W. C., *The Life of John Ericsson* (Contains full information about the building of the *Monitor*)
Greene, S. Dana, *In the Monitor's Turret* (The best account of the battle with the *Merrimac* from the Union side)
———— (Second in command on the *Monitor*), United Service (Phila., Pa.) VOL. X, 350
Lewis, Charles L., *Admiral Franklin Buchanan: Fearless Man of Action*
Littlepage, Lt., *"Merrimac vs. Monitor*, A Midshipman's Account of the Battle with the 'Cheese Box'," in *Camp Fire Sketches and Battlefield Echoes*
Official Records (Navy), Series I, VOLS. I-IV, VI-VIII, XII-XIV, XVI, XXII
Samuel, Lewis, alias Peter Truskitt, *Life on the Monitor;* A Seaman's Story of the Fight with the *Merrimac*
Schley, Winfield Scott, *Forty-five Years Under the Flag*
Seward, Frederick, *Seward at Washington*, VOL. III, 73
Welles, Gideon, *Diary*, VOL. I, 30, 31; VOL. II, 7; VOL. III, 357
Wood, John T. (Lieutenant on the *Merrimac*), *The First Fight of Iron-Clads* (Perhaps the best account of the battle between the *Monitor* and the *Merrimac* by a Confederate participant.)
Worden Papers and Scrap Book. Lincoln Museum, Lincoln University, Harrogate, Tenn.

WILLIAM BARKER CUSHING

Ammen, Daniel, *The Atlantic Coast*, 194-198, 211, 236
Cushing, W. B., Narrative of the destruction of the *Albemarle*, *Battles and Leaders of the Civil War*, VOL. IV, 636
Edwards, M. H., *William Barker Cushing of the U. S. Navy*
Elliot, Gilbert, "The First Battle of the Confederate Ram *Albemarle*," *Battles and Leaders of the Civil War*, VOL. IV, 625
Haight, Theron W., Wisconsin History Commission, *Three Wisconsin Cushings*
Hamersley, L. R., *Records of Living Officers in the U. S. Navy and Marine Corps, 1870*
Memoirs of Ensign Joseph E. Jones: *Prince and Boatswain, Sea Tales from Recollection of Rear Admiral Charles E. Clark.* (James Morgan and John P. Marquand)
Nicolay and Hay, *Abraham Lincoln*, VOL. X, 45-51
Official Records (Navy), Series I, VOLS. III-XII; Series II, VOL. I

Porter, David, *Naval History of the Civil War*, 401, 403, 417, 422, 428, 473, 478, 684, 689
Soley, J. R., *The Blockade and the Cruisers*, 95-97
Stuart, Charles W., "William Barker Cushing," *U. S. Naval Institute Proceedings*, VOL. XXXVIII, Nos. II, III
Welles, Gideon, *Diary*, VOL. II, 245

JOHN ANCRUM WINSLOW

Adams, Charles F., *Memorial Address on William E. Seward*, 32
Bennett, Frank M., *The Steam Navy of the United States*, 435
Browne, John M., (Surgeon on the *Kearsarge*), "The Duel Between the *Alabama* and the *Kearsarge*," *Battles and Leaders of the Civil War*, VOL. IV, 615-625
Bulloch, J. D., *The Secret Service of the Confederate States in Europe*, VOL. II, 283, 288
Ellicott, J. M., *Life of John Ancrum Winslow*
Gorham, G. C., *Life and Public Services of Edwin M. Stanton*, VOL. I, 222-223
Hoppin, J. M., *Life of Admiral Foote*
Kell, John M., "Cruise and Combats of the *Alabama*," *Battles and Leaders of the Civil War*, VOL. IV, 600-614
Official Records (Navy), Series I, VOLS. I-III, XXI-XXIII; Series II, VOLS. I, II
Robinson, W. M., "The *Alabama-Kearsarge* Battle," *Essex Institute Historical Collection*, VOL. IX
Schley, Winfield S., *Forty-Five Years Under the Flag*, 35-36
Soley, J. R., *The Blockade and the Cruisers*, 210
Semmes, Raphael, *Memoirs of Service Afloat During the War Between the States*
Sinclair, Arthur, *Two Years on the Alabama*
Welles, Gideon, *Diary*, VOL. II, 65, 67
Winslow, John A. Papers. New-York Historical Society

NAPOLEON COLLINS

Army & Navy Journal, August 28, September 11, 1875, June 17, 1876
Davis, Jefferson, *Rise and Fall of the Confederate Government*, VOL. II, 213, 266, 461, 462
Hale, Edgar E., *William H. Seward*, 314, 318, 321
Hamersley, L. R., *Records of Living Officers in the U. S. Navy and Marine Corps, 1870*
Hudson Lowe Papers in The British Museum
Macartney, C. E., and Dorrance, Gordon, *The Bonapartes in America*
Nicolay and Hay, *Abraham Lincoln, A History*, VOL. IX, 129-133
Official Records (Navy), Series I, VOL. I, 265, 384; VOL. III, 23, 458

Porter, David, *Naval History of the Civil War*, 55, 83, 627, 813, 815, 816

Richardson, James D., *Messages and Papers of the Confederacy*, VOL. II, 681, 683, 689

Semmes, Raphael, *Memoirs of Service Afloat*

Welles, Gideon, *Diary*, VOL. I, 140, 141, 417, 421, 423, 434; VOL. II, 39, 184, 186, 197, 275; VOL. III, 120, 554

DAVID DIXON PORTER

Ammen, Daniel, *The Atlantic Coast*

Butler, Benjamin F., *Butler's Book*, 371, 550, 1126, appendix 144

Diggins, Bartholomew, *Recollections of the War Cruise of the U. S. S. Hartford, from January 1862 to December 1864*

Fox, Gustavus V., *Confidential Correspondence*, VOL. II, 73-201

Grant, Ulysses S., *Personal Memoirs of U. S. Grant*, VOL. I, 390, 439-464, 475-478, 537-574, 641; VOL. II, 397, 505

Lamon, Ward, *Recollections of Lincoln*, 74

Lincoln Papers, May 1, 1861

Macartney, Clarence Edward, *Grant and His Generals*, 186, 211-215

Mahan, Alfred T., *The Gulf and Inland Waters*

Official Records (*Navy*), Series I, VOLS. I, III-XIII, XV-XXVII; Series II, VOLS. I, III

Porter, David D., *Incidents and Anecdotes of the Civil War*

——— *Naval History of the Civil War*

——— Papers and Letters. Library of Congress

——— "The Opening of the Lower Mississippi," *Battles and Leaders of the Civil War*, VOL. II, 22-54

Selfridge, Thomas O., "The Navy at Fort Fisher," *Battles and Leaders of the Civil War*, VOL. IV, 655-661

Sherman, William T., *Memoirs of General William T. Sherman*, VOL. I, 309-321, 323-328, 331, 335-338

Soley, J. R., *Admiral Porter*

Thomas, Captain, U. S. Navy, in *Battles and Leaders of the Civil War*, VOL. IV, 660

Welles, Gideon, "Admiral Farragut and New Orleans," *Galaxy*, November-December, 1871

——— *Diary*, VOL. I, 17-38, 87, 88, 157-167, 220, 238-259, 311, 369; VOL. II, 18, 26, 116, 134, 215, 235, 255; VOL. III, 384, 389

Young, John R., *Around the World with General Grant*, VOL. II, 305

CHRONOLOGY

Mar. 4	Inauguration of President Abraham Lincoln
Apr. 12	Fort Sumter fired upon
Apr. 19	Lincoln proclaims blockade of southern states
Apr. 20–21	Norfolk Navy Yard abandoned
Apr. 27	Blockade extended to North Carolina and Virginia
July 21	First Battle of Bull Run; Beauregard defeats McDowell
Aug. 28–29	Federal forces seize Hatteras Inlet, North Carolina
Nov. 7	Du Pont captures forts at Port Royal, South Carolina
Nov. 8	Two Southern envoys seized from British ship *Trent*

1862

Feb. 6	Foote captures Fort Henry, Tennessee
Feb. 14	Foote repulsed at Fort Donelson, Tennessee
Feb. 16	Grant captures Fort Donelson
Mar. 8	Ironclad *Merrimac* destroys *Congress* and *Cumberland*
Mar. 9	Duel between *Merrimac* and U.S.S. *Monitor*
Mar. 17	McClellan begins embarkation for Peninsula Campaign
Apr. 4	McClellan begins Peninsula Campaign north from Fort Monroe
Apr. 4	Walke runs Island No. 10 in *Carondelet*
Apr. 6–7	Grant holds against A. S. Johnston at Shiloh, Tennessee
Apr. 24–25	Farragut runs forts below New Orleans
May 11	South abandons Norfolk; *Merrimac* blown up
June 6	Memphis surrenders to Charles H. Davis after naval battle
June 28	Farragut passes batteries at Vicksburg, Mississippi
July 1	Battle of Malverne Hill. End of Peninsula Campaign
July 15	*Arkansas* escapes through Federal fleet in Mississippi
Aug. 6	C.S.S. *Arkansas* destroyed
Aug. 29–30	Second Battle of Bull Run. Lee defeats Pope
Sept. 17	McClellan defeats Lee at Antietam Creek, Maryland
Nov. 2	Grant begins Vicksburg campaign
Dec. 13	Lee defeats Burnside at Fredericksburg, Virginia
Dec. 31	U.S.S. *Monitor* founders off Cape Hatteras

1863

Jan. 16	C.S.S. *Alabama* sinks U.S.S. *Hatteras* off Galveston, Texas
Feb. 24	U.S.S. *Indianola* captured below Vicksburg
Mar. 14	Farragut attacks Port Hudson. Loses U.S.S. *Mississippi*
Apr. 7	Du Pont attacks Charleston, South Carolina
Apr. 16	Porter's transports and warship run past Vicksburg
Apr. 30	Grant crosses to east bank of the Mississippi below Vicksburg
May 2–4	Lee defeats Hooker at Chancellorsville, Virginia
May 22	Grant besieges Vicksburg
June 17	*Weehawken* captures C.S.S. *Atlanta*, Warsaw Sound, Georgia
July 1–3	Meade defeats Lee at Gettysburg, Pennsylvania
July 4	Grant captures Vicksburg
Sept. 8–9	Repulse of naval boat assault on Fort Sumter
Sept. 19-20	Bragg defeats Rosecrans at Chickamauga, Tennessee
Nov. 23–25	Grant defeats Bragg at Chattanooga, Tennessee

1864

Feb. 18	U.S.S. *Housatonic* sunk off Charleston by torpedo vessel
Apr. 19	Two wooden ships engage *Albemarle*, Portsmouth, North Carolina
May 4	*Albemarle* duels eight wooden ships, Albemarle Sound
May 5–6	The Wilderness. Grant begins his Virginia campaign
May 7	Sherman begins his march on Atlanta
May 13	Porter's fleet saved near Alexandria, Louisiana
June 19	Winslow in U.S.S. *Kearsarge* sinks C.S.S. *Alabama*
Aug. 5	Farragut wins at Mobile Bay, Alabama
Sept. 2	Sherman takes Atlanta
Oct. 7	Napoleon Collins seizes C.S.S. *Florida*
Oct. 27	Cushing sinks the *Albemarle*
Dec. 22	Sherman takes Savannah
Dec. 24–25	First assault on Fort Fisher, North Carolina, fails

1865

Jan. 15	Porter, General Alfred Terry succeed at Fort Fisher
Feb. 18	Sherman's army takes Charleston
Apr. 2	Lee evacuates Richmond and Petersburg
Apr. 9	Lee surrenders to Grant at Appomattox Court House, Virginia
Apr. 14	Abraham Lincoln assassinated

INDEX